PRO/CON VOLUME 20

RELIGION AND MORALITY

Published 2005 by Grolier,
an imprint of Scholastic Library Publishing
Old Sherman Turnpike
Danbury, Connecticut 06816

Library of Congress Cataloging-in-Publication Data

Pro/con
   p. cm
  Includes bibliographical references and index.
  Contents: v. 19. World Politics – v. 20 Religion and Morality – v. 21. U.S.
Judiciary – v. 22. International Law – v. 23. Poverty and Wealth – v. 24. Work and
the Workplace.
   ISBN 0-7172-5950-1 (set : alk. paper) – ISBN 0-7172-5951–X (vol. 19 : alk. paper) –
ISBN 0-7172-5952-8 (vol. 20 : alk. paper) – ISBN 0-7172-5953-6 (vol. 21 : alk. paper)
 – ISBN 0-7172-5954-4 (vol. 22 : alk. paper) – ISBN 0-7172-5955-2 (vol. 23 : alk.
paper) – ISBN 0-7172-5956-0 (vol. 24 : alk. paper)
  1. Social problems. I. Scholastic Publishing Ltd Grolier (Firm)

HN17.5 P756 2002
361.1–dc22

                                                                   2001053234

Printed and bound in Singapore

SET ISBN 0-7172-5950-1
VOLUME ISBN 0-7172-5952-8

For The Brown Reference Group plc
Project Editors: Aruna Vasudevan, Claire Chandler
Editors: Fiona Plowman, Chris Marshall
Consultant Editor: Tim Murphy, Assistant Professor, Department of
Religious Studies, University of Alabama, Tuscaloosa, AL
Designer: Sarah Williams
Picture Research and Permissions: Clare Newman, Susy Forbes
Set Index: Kay Ollerenshaw

Senior Managing Editor: Tim Cooke
Art Director: Dave Goodman
Production Manager: Alastair Gourlay

GENERAL PREFACE

*"All that is necessary for evil to
triumph is for good men to
do nothing."*
—Edmund Burke, 18th-century
English political philosopher

Decisions

Life is full of choices and decisions.
Some are more important than others.
Some affect only your daily life—the
route you take to school, for example,
or what you prefer to eat for supper—
while others are more abstract and
concern questions of right and wrong
rather than practicality. That does not
mean that your choice of presidential
candidate or your views on abortion
are necessarily more important than
your answers to purely personal
questions. But it is likely that those
wider questions are more complex
and subtle and that you therefore will
need to know more information about
the subject before you can try to
answer them. They are also likely to be
questions about which you might have
to justify your views to other people. In
order to do that, you need to be able to
make informed decisions, be able to
analyze every fact at your disposal, and
evaluate them in an unbiased manner.

What Is *Pro/Con*?

Pro/Con is a collection of debates that
presents conflicting views on some of
the more complex and general issues
facing Americans today. By bringing
together extracts from a wide range of
sources—mainstream newspapers and
magazines, books, famous speeches,
legal judgments, religious tracts,
government surveys—the set reflects
current informed attitudes toward
dilemmas that range from the best way

to feed the world's growing population
to gay rights, from the connection
between political freedom and
capitalism to the fate of Napster.

The people whose arguments make
up the set are for the most part
acknowledged experts in their fields,
making the vast differences in their
points of view even more remarkable.
The arguments are presented in the
form of debates for and against various
propositions, such as "Do extradition
treaties violate human rights?" or
"Should companies be allowed to
relocate abroad?" This question format
reflects the way in which ideas often
occur in daily life: in the classroom, on
TV shows, in business meetings, or even
in state or federal politics.

The contents

The subjects of the six volumes of
*Pro/Con 4—World Politics, Religion
and Morality, U.S. Judiciary,
International Law, Poverty and
Wealth,* and *Work and the Workplace*—
are issues on which it is preferable
that people's opinions be based on
information rather than personal bias.

Special boxes throughout *Pro/Con*
comment on the debates as you
are reading them, pointing out
facts, explaining terms, or analyzing
arguments to help you think about
what is being said.

Introductions and summaries also
provide background information that
might help you reach your own
conclusions. There are also tips about
how to structure an argument that
you can apply on an everyday basis to
any debate or conversation, learning
how to present your point of view as
effectively and persuasively as possible.

VOLUME PREFACE
Religion and Morality

Morality is a code of conduct based on the notions of what is right and wrong. Many notable philosophers, such as Aristotle, David Hume, and Immanuel Kant, have argued about where morality comes from. Some experts believe that morality is based on rationality, others that an innate sense of duty produces morality, or that morality springs from feelings. In contrast, there are also many people whose morality is based in religion, such as the Five Pillars of Islam or the Ten Commandments.

A religious matter?

One of the most debated issues is how far, if at all, religion and morality are linked. Some people believe that religions are too judgmental and do not deal in the real world. They claim that formal religions stifle free thought and often lead to the repression of groups who do not behave in ways that are acceptable. Contraception and abortion are thought to be basic reproductive rights by human and women's rights groups, among others, but the Catholic Church, for example, states that both are wrong. How do people decide what is right or wrong in these cases? Making informed and rational decisions is the only way to do this, and critical thinking skills help.

Understanding conflict

The 20th century saw a rise in religion-based politics and conflict. In order to try to understand what is going on in many regions of the world, an understanding of the ins and outs of different religions is essential. Recent conflicts in Bosnia, Northern Ireland, and the Middle East have all arguably been founded on basic conflicts between people of different religious faiths and beliefs.

Since the terrorist attacks of September 11, 2001, there has been distrust from some commentators of Islam, which they claim is an aggressive religion that encourages "holy war." However, many scholars counter that Islam is a peaceful religion, and that just as a Christian fundamentalists are not reflective of all Christians, the same can be said of Islamic fundamentalists.

The majority of Americans are Christian, and yet Christianity is not the nation's official religion: The First Amendment states that "Congress shall make no law respecting an establishment of religion." Many people believe that by separating the church from the state, the nation has suffered a moral decline, while numerous other commentators fear that the rights of minority groups, such as gays, would be affected if Christian fundamentalists were allowed to impose their beliefs. Some critics are even convinced that the influence of the religious right in America has grown too powerful, and that the U.S. decision to invade Iraq in 2003 was based on a foreign policy with a theological basis.

Pro/Con

Religion and Morality looks at 16 key debates in these areas. By reprinting existing articles from credible sources, the book enables readers to make up their own minds on key issues affecting the 21st-century world, including whether religion and war are related.

HOW TO USE THIS BOOK

Each volume of *Pro/Con* is divided into sections, each of which has an introduction that examines its theme. Within each section are a series of debates that present arguments for and against a proposition, such as whether or not the death penalty should be abolished. An introduction to each debate puts it into its wider context, and a summary and key map (see below) highlight the main points of the debate clearly and concisely. Each debate has marginal boxes that focus on particular points, give tips on how to present an argument, or help question the writer's case. The summary page to the debates contains supplementary material to help you do further research.

Boxes and other materials provide additional background information. There are also special spreads on how to improve your debating and writing skills. At the end of each book is a glossary and an index. The glossary provides explanations of key words in the volume. The index covers all 24 books; it will help you find topics throughout this set and previous ones.

background information
Frequent text boxes provide background information on important concepts and key individuals or events.

summary boxes
Summary boxes are useful reminders of both sides of the argument.

further information
Further Reading lists for each debate direct you to related books, articles, and websites so you can do your own research.

other articles in the *Pro/Con* series
This box lists related debates throughout the *Pro/Con* series.

marginal boxes
Margin boxes highlight key points of the argument, give extra information, or help you question the author's meaning.

key map
Key maps provide a graphic representation of the central points of the debate.

CONTENTS

ISSUES IN RELIGION

INTRODUCTION

Religions are organized codes of belief or philosophy that provide their followers with spiritual and moral guidance, and often give their own answer to profound questions about the nature and purpose of existence. As such, they provide spiritual comfort to billions of people around the world. They play an important part in shaping not only individual actions but also the values of whole societies. Governments are often highly influenced by religious principles, from the Catholic government of colonial Spain that wanted to spread Christianity to the Americas to Islamic states such as Saudi Arabia and Algeria.

Faith or reason

At the heart of nearly all religions is a belief in the existence of a god or gods. Such a belief is a question of faith rather than reason: Although the presence of a divine being might be inferred from the universe itself, it can never be rationally proven, critics believe. In the ultimate reckoning religious adherents take the existence of their god or gods on trust.

The dieties are often credited with having created the world and with laying down rules for human behavior. Even religions that do not depend on belief in a supernatural power— examples include Buddhism and Confucianism—place a duty on their followers to adhere to codes of behavior and to follow set rituals or worship of religious celebration.

Many religions have evolved more or less complex rites, ranging from the maintenance of small home shrines among Hindus to the lavish celebrations of the Mass in medieval Catholic cathedrals in Europe. Most religions have priests of one type or another, whose job is to officiate at rituals and to guide worshipers in their interpretation of holy law. Most also have written scriptures, which either claim to record the word of God—the Koran in Islam or the Bible in Judaism and Christianity, for example—or to embody accepted traditions of religious custom and interpretation.

Polytheism and monotheism

The earliest religions of which we are aware tended to be pantheistic, meaning that they detected the presence of divinity everywhere. Often the religions of, for example, ancient Babylonia, Assyria, Egypt, Greece, or Rome were also polytheistic: They had many gods and goddesses, each of whom was responsible for a particular aspect of creation such as crops, thunder, or the oceans. The gods were sometimes viewed as a family or group who acted much like humans: They quarreled, sulked, and fell in love. The most important polytheistic religion today is Hinduism, which has some 840 million believers, most of whom are concentrated in South Asia. Hinduism has many gods, but the most important is Brahman, the chief spirit, along with a group of three other gods, Brahma, Vishnu, and Siva. Hindu gods such as Siva are both creators and destroyers: Their nature is not as fixed as that of the god in the great religions that are described as monotheistic.

Monotheistic religions worship only one supreme being. They include Christianity, Judaism, and Islam, whose divinities are respectively known as God, Yaweh, and Allah. God may have prophets and other messengers, such as Abraham in all three faiths, Jesus in

around the world. While people may acknowledge the distinction, those without religious beliefs or those who follow a faith that is not dualistic doubt the existence of evil as a quality that is distinct from individual actions or their consequences. They argue that morals and values are comparative, and that evil as a concept does not exist. This issue is examined in Topic 1.

Make love not war?

In many societies around the world religious faith is in fact declining as organized religions are coming under increasing pressure for being outdated

---

"Religion is the dream of the human mind. But even in dreams we do not find ourselves in emptiness or in heaven, but on earth, in the realm of reality."

—LUDWIG FEUERBACH (1804–1872), GERMAN PHILOSOPHER

Christianity, and Muhammad in Islam. Some faiths place great emphasis on the individual worshiper's experience of God; others emphasize the importance of priests and rituals in interpreting the religious experience for the worshiper.

Good and evil

A religion such as Christianity is essentially dualistic: It sees the universe as comprising two contradictory qualities, good and evil. Good defines everything that obeys the laws of God; that which does not obey such laws is evil. The distinction between good and bad—also sometimes viewed as the permitted and the forbidden—is the basis of all social and legal codes

and failing to answer the needs of their congregations. One criticism that has long been leveled at religions is that while they promote tolerance and love, they are also often used as a justification for war. Some people believe that if religions did not exist, there would be far fewer wars. Topic 2 looks at this question.

Another criticism directed at religion is that it stifles free thought: Topic 3 examines this issue further. The last topic in this section, Topic 4, focuses on a much debated issue—the relationship between religion and government. Governments are sometimes suspicious of religions and may ban them, but is this right?

Topic 1
DOES EVIL EXIST?

YES
FROM "WHY DOES EVIL EXIST?"
THE GOOD NEWS MAGAZINE (UNITED CHURCH OF GOD), JANUARY/FEBRUARY 2002
BILL BRADFORD

NO
"DOES EVIL EXIST?"
HTTP://WWW.APOCRYPHILE.NET/JRM/ARTICLES/EVIL.HTML
JOHN R. MABRY

INTRODUCTION

The word "evil" is common in modern society. It is often applied to people such as murderers or tyrants, to actions, or even to nations. In 2002, responding to the September 11, 2001, terrorist attacks on Manhattan and Washington, D.C., President George W. Bush (2001–) described some states—Iran, Iraq, and North Korea—as "axis of evil" nations. An exact definition of evil, however, is difficult to reach, and some critics have questioned whether the nations that Bush named have acted in ways that everyone would consider evil, or whether they simply do not believe in the values of the United States.

For many people evil is a relative concept: It implies a degree that is worse and more harmful than "good" or even simply "bad." It tends to denote behavior that is not just forbidden, but that has an inherent negative quality. Parking violations, for example, are legally wrong, but few people would argue that they are evil; abortion, on the other hand, is legal in many places, but its opponents describe it as evil.

The idea of evil features heavily in a number of major world religions, including Christianity. Such religions are defined as dualistic: Their world view sets up two qualities—good and evil—in absolute opposition to one another. If something is one, then it cannot become the other. The opposition between the two is often personified as a struggle between different deities, such as between God and Satan in Christian thought and culture. Lucifer and his band of evil angels tried to overthrow God and the good angels; good triumphed, and Lucifer—who became known as Satan—and his followers were banished to Hell, a place of eternal suffering diametrically opposed to the bliss of Heaven.

In the Christian tradition evil exists as an absolute value, and the struggle between good and evil is ongoing and constant. That is one reason why Christian teaching places such value on qualities like sobriety, chastity, and resisting temptation. The opposites—drunkenness, promiscuity, and indulgence—belong to the evil forces that constantly threaten to overthrow good and so must be defeated. In such a view evil is a perpetual presence in the world.

The idea of evil has posed a problem for Christian thinkers. It is difficult to reconcile its existence with the idea of an all-powerful, benevolent God. The church fathers, such as Saint Augustine (354–430) and Saint Thomas Aquinas (about 1225–1274), concluded that God did not actually create evil but instead gave humanity free will; it was individuals who chose to do evil deeds.

"With or without religion, you would have good people doing good things and evil people doing evil things. But for good people to do evil things, that takes religion."

—STEVEN WEINBERG (1933–),

PHYSICIST

For many people brought up in a dualistic faith it is clear that some acts are inherently evil, and that therefore evil does indeed exist. Not all religions divide the universe in such a clear-cut way, however. Nondualistic faiths acknowledge a world in which qualities such as good and evil are graduated rather than categorically opposed. In Hinduism, for example, there are many gods who have qualities that appear to be conflicting. One of the major gods is Siva, a highly complex figure. He is the destroyer–creator. He is often portrayed holding a skull, which signifies the concept of "samsara," the cycle of life, death, and rebirth. As Makhala, Lord of Time, Siva represents all these things, destroying and creating at the same time. It is therefore impossible to say whether he is good or evil.

A major consideration in the arguments of those who believe that there is no such quality or force as evil that exists separately from individual actions or motives or viewpoints is that it it often impossible to say where evil starts. Is all murder equally evil, for example? Is a starving person who kills another for food evil or desperate? Is someone who has killed one person as evil as someone like the Nazi dictator Adolf Hitler (1889–1945)? The family of the victim would probably think so, but others may disagree strongly, blaming Hitler for inspiring many atrocities during World War II. In the same way, Jewish Israelis condemn as evil Palestinian suicide bombers who blow up themselves and Israeli citizens as part of their protest against what they see as Jewish occupation of Arab lands; to the Palestinians, however, such people are heroes of the Islamic faith. The 18th-century German philosopher Immanuel Kant (1724–1804) explained such opposing views by arguing that neither good nor evil exists on its own; both exist only in relation to the other.

Dualist religions, however, are based on the understanding that good and evil are absolute terms, and that there is a clear dividing line between them. Followers of such religions turn to scripture or religious teaching to help establish that line. Even though there may be debate about which side of the line some things fall, the line still exists.

The articles discuss this topic further.

WHY DOES EVIL EXIST?
Bill Bradford

Bill Bradford wrote this article in 2002 for Good News, the online magazine of the United Church of God.

YES

The Bible consistently explains evil as rebellion against God and His way of selfless, outflowing love for others—His way of giving. Evil is self-absorbed and uncaring of others, the way of getting and taking.

God's way of life is expressed in His law of love, and evil is the violation of that law. Thus evil is synonymous with sin (1 John 3:4), which is contrary to God. Any calamity that He allows or brings is actually done out of love.

But, some might argue, isn't all evil God's fault? The reasoning goes like this: Since God created everything, and evil exists, then God must be the author of evil.

Yet the Bible paints a picture in which God, in the beginning, created perfect surroundings for the first man and woman to live in. "Then God saw everything that He had made, and indeed it was very good" (Genesis 1:31). That included man. How, then, did evil come into the picture?

The story tells us that a cunning "serpent" introduced evil into God's perfect creation. But Genesis 3:1 seems to say that God created the serpent, too, so that doesn't really answer the question. Maybe there is some force equal to or greater than God that is beyond His control. Or maybe God isn't good after all.

There is a better answer, a biblical one. We have seen that God made everything good, without the presence of evil. Yet, in doing so, He created man with moral freedom—with the ability to choose between good and evil. God did not create evil. He created us with free will. That is the framework for the existence of evil.

Free moral choice

But, since God is good, why didn't He create man unalterably good?… God's overall plan was to create something special. His long-term purpose was to create additional members of His divine family, of which the Genesis creation was only the first step. To eventually achieve this creation, the development of divine character was essential to His plan. Hence the need to create human beings as free moral agents.

His choice, then, was to create beings with freedom. Without freedom they would never sin. But without freedom

Do you accept the belief that suffering in the world happens because of God's love for us?

The word "serpent" is often used in a mythical context to distinguish it from the snake. Although today the serpent is associated with evil, in prebiblical societies it was seen as a symbol of wisdom and regeneration.

"Free will" is the philosophical doctrine that refers to the freedom of humans to make choices unconstrained by outside agencies.

they would never have the opportunity to choose their own future; they could not have imagination, and they could not love others or appreciate love….

The highest of God's creation would then be as robots, which do not choose right or wrong, love or hate. God created us with the ability to choose love, hate or any feeling or attitude in between. It is only with free choice that we can attain to the love that God Himself possesses, the most important of all divine character traits. God is love!

When God created man, He began the process of bringing forth children in His image (Genesis 1:26; compare 5:1-3). We cannot force our own children to love us or do what is right. We can teach them these virtues and hope they will choose to follow them in spite of the negative evil influences they encounter. We can also enjoy a trusting and close relationship with our children, and we want that to continue long after they are grown.

When God embarked on His ambitious plan to create children for Himself who would have to choose to return His love, He also knew the risks. He was aware that they could choose an alternative way of life. He knew that there was a choice that existed between good and evil.

Yet man was not the first created entity to whom God gave such a choice.

When only God (the Father and the Word, John 1:1) existed, there was no evil. Yet long before the time of Adam and even before God created the heavens and earth, God created millions of spirit beings with free moral choice—the angels. His intention was to produce beings who would accept His way and live like Him forever.

But one of the most powerful spirit beings would disappoint Him.

Origin of evil

Ezekiel 28 begins with God addressing the "prince of Tyre," a human ruler of that ancient city-state along the Lebanese coast. But, starting in verse 11, the message shifts to the "king of Tyre," and it quickly becomes apparent that no human being is meant. Rather, the subject becomes the spiritual power behind the throne, the primary influence on the earthly ruler, for this power is specifically called a cherub, an angelic being (verse 14).

God tells him, "You were perfect in your ways from the day you were created, till iniquity was found in you" (verse 15). This angel, then, was part of God's perfect creation. Yet, because he had freedom to choose, he had the capacity to

The belief that evil is essential to human growth is central to the issue of the existence of evil for Christians. Freedom is a double-edged sword for humanity—it brings with it the opportunity for both good and evil.

In Christian theology angels represent God in a more worldly form. They embody God's greatest qualities— love, compassion, understanding— and bring these qualities down to earth. The symbol of the angel has come to represent the idea of service to others.

Tyre was a city-state in Phoenicia, in the eastern Mediterranean. Such city-states were among the first examples of democracy in history.

A "cherub" belongs to a certain order of angels. They are usually represented in sculpture and painting as a winged child.

Babylon was the chief city of the ancient kingdom of Babylonia in Mesopotamia. The Bible depicts it as a city devoted to materialism and sensual pleasure.

choose evil. We read here that "iniquity," or lawlessness, was, at some point, found in him. This was the first recorded instance of evil.

Isaiah 14 includes a similar description when God addresses the "king of Babylon." But this message, too, switches to the spiritual power behind the throne. Starting in verse 12, this entity is called Heylel (Lucifer in Latin), meaning "Light-Bringer"—for at first he was a vessel of the light of God's truth. Yet, as verse 13 shows, he began to imagine evil in his heart.

The emergence of Satan

Moral relativism is the philosophical belief that moral standards are not absolute but instead originate from social traditions and other sources.

No one knows how long it took for this being to develop the way of evil in his heart. In any case, the philosophy he developed was all about self and what he could get. In essence, he was the first moral relativist. He denied absolute good and evil as defined by God and chose to define good and evil for himself. Eventually, he considered how he could be exalted above everyone else and acquire everything in existence, replacing God as ruler of all creation. Thus God changed his name to Satan, meaning "Adversary."

God did not create Satan. Rather, God created this angelic being as the "seal of perfection, full of wisdom and perfect in beauty" (Ezekiel 28:12). But he developed pride in his beauty (verse 17). He corrupted his wisdom by getting caught up in his own self-importance. This was his choice. So he turned himself into Satan.

Verse 16 says that he became filled with violence within. He ascended into heaven to exalt his throne (Isaiah 14:13). Revelation 12:2-3 speaks of this fallen angel as a dragon who draws a third of the [angels] (Revelation 1:20) with him. Satan induced one third of the created angelic beings to turn against God....

The third of the angels who followed Satan chose to oppose God and adopt the devil's philosophy.... In doing so they became demons, evil spirits....

God cast Satan and his demons out of heaven. They fell to earth like lightning (Luke 10:18). The next we see of Satan is his appearance to Eve in the Garden of Eden as the serpent.

Are you convinced that the suffering in the world today is because of the choice Adam and Eve made? If not, what do you think causes suffering?

Man embraces evil

… The choice our first parents made is why we see so much suffering, violence and killing in the world. When Lucifer chose to follow the alternative way of taking, the end was inevitably violence toward God. Once Adam and Eve chose to reject the way of life God revealed to them and to determine right and wrong on their own, the world was set on the path of serving the self at the expense of other people. This would mean suffering for all humanity down through the ages.

An immediate example of the consequence of Adam's and Eve's decision was that their son Cain murdered his brother Abel, setting a course mankind would follow from that point forward. Our civilizations have been wracked by war because someone wanted to have something or be someone greater than he was. The inflicting of harm has never abated.

But why would God allow such suffering? God's intent is for His children to choose His way of love forever and never consider turning against Him. To ensure this, they must experience the consequences of choosing wrongly. The ultimate consequence is eternal death, because God will not permit evil to persist in a universe He rules (Romans 6:23). Thankfully, Jesus' death redeems us from that fate if we repent of the devil's way of life.

However, we must understand that there are consequences to sin. Sin means a lot of misery along life's way. God created us so we can experience pain temporarily for a good purpose. We learn through pain that what we do is not good for us. A little suffering because we do something minor saves us grief and anguish later if we learn the lesson and have the sense to avoid doing something major....

Dealing with the cause

Ultimately God will remove evil altogether. None will be allowed in the new heavens and new earth described in Revelation 21 and 22. But this requires that every being of free choice either decide ultimately never to sin again or be taken out of the picture forever.

What is to guarantee no future rebellion beyond that? The first answer is pain. Yes, suffering.... The second answer is that all people one day will face the goodness of God that He demonstrated through Jesus Christ....

We cannot ever find this level of goodness in other human beings (Romans 5:6-8). To be convicted of our own sin, we must come face to face with the sacrifices God and Christ made for others who are so obviously undeserving of them. It is this compelling example of undeserved love from our Creator that brings us to the point that we never want to perpetrate any kind of evil on others.

In the end, those in God's family will nevermore consider evil as an option, and pain and sorrow will be no more (Revelation 21:4). God in His wisdom permits evil in our time to accomplish this grand purpose.

Cain was the eldest son of Adam and Eve and the first man born in creation according to the Genesis stories common to Judaism, Christianity, and Islam. Cain killed his brother out of jealousy and was exiled by God from Eden.

If this argument is correct, would it mean that people who live perfectly Christian lives would never suffer pain? What lessons would they have to learn through suffering?

Revelation is a book based on apocalyptic writing addressed to the early Christians of Asia Minor and included in the New Testament. The biblical meaning of "revelation" is a bringing to light of that which had been previously hidden or obscured.

DOES EVIL EXIST?
John R. Mabry

NO

John R. Mabry is a lay preacher who writes about philosophy, theology, and religion.

X Good versus evil

Humans like to categorize; we especially like to polarize ("He's a nice man"/He's a bad man," "That was a great meal"/"Dinner really sucked!" etc.).

Things are seldom considered unless we tack on a moral or evaluative judgement, often unconsciously. This is especially true when we consider one another, and one another's traits. We appreciate the "good" and condemn the "evil". Evil, as defined by Webster, is "1. Morally bad or wrong; wicked; malevolent; sinful. 2. Causing an undesirable condition, as ruin, injury or pain."

The author uses the debating technique of raising questions that he then proceeds to systematically answer.

But is the concept of evil in man valid? Do we have an evil streak? Are there such things as "wholly evil" persons?

Does evil exist in nature?

Let us first question whether evil exists outside the human race, in nature. The word "nature" these days is almost synonymous with "wholesome" and "good". We understand that animals do violent things, injurous things, painful things. Like fighting and killing for legitimate purposes: Dominance and Survival. These traits are not learned, they are instincts; as much a part of the animal as it's teeth or fur. Is man any different—or are the motivations found in nature (dominance & survival) also found in us?

The idea that the animals most adapted to their environment are the ones most likely to survive was developed by Charles Darwin (1809–1882) in his theory of evolution. It is often expressed by the term "survival of the fittest."

Animals fight to survive. Once flight proves impossible, fangs are bared and claws wielded, often unto death. They hunt, and kill for food. In some instances, larger predators kill for sport, leaving the carcasses for other animals to dispose of. They also kill to protect their families and territories. Is this wrong? The animals, so far as we know, have no moral dilemmas. They do what they must to survive, and often it involves "ruin, injury and pain".

Do you agree that people will do what they need to in order to survive? Should society punish someone who is so poor that he or she has to steal food? If so, who would compensate the victim of the theft?

Man is a meat eater (for the most part), and few people have qualms about the animal who suffered death to fill their digestive cavities. How about killing another human, though? Self-defense is certainly legitimate. A man may steal because he must eat. This, too, is survival. Many animals are natural thieves (crows for example), indicating that perhaps thievery is a valid occupation in the natural

This 18th-century engraving by J. Huyot, after Gustave Dore, shows the angel Abdiel leading the good angels into a fight against Satan.

COMMENTARY: Satan in literature and film

Satan has been characterized in numerous ways in literature and film throughout history. Satan—also commonly known as the Devil, the "Prince of Darkness," Beelzebub, and Lucifer—made his first literary appearance in the Hebrew and Christian Bibles. In the Hebrew Bible Satan is an angel or messenger who is sent by God to test humankind. In the New Testament he is an evil demon who is the enemy of God and humankind.

Milton's Satan

One of the most famous interpretations of Satan in literature is in *Paradise Lost*, the epic poem by English writer John Milton (1608–1674), which tells the biblical story of Adam and Eve's fall from grace. Some critics argue that Satan is actually the true hero of *Paradise Lost* because of his courage, rebelliousness, and heroic willingness to fight God. One writer states that "Milton's Satan is far more charismatic than the squeaky clean God."

The German writer Johann Wolfgang von Goethe (1749–1832) characterizes Satan as Mephistopheles, an alternative form of Satan, in his rendition of the Faust myth. According to the story, Faust, a righteous elderly man, sells his soul to the Devil in return for eternal youth. By representing Mephistopheles as a completely independent character, Goethe is suggesting that evil is internal and lurks within us all.

Satan on screen

On screen Satan has tended to feature mainly in the horror and supernatural genres. In *The Exorcist* (1973) the age-old struggle between good and evil centers on a possessed 12-year-old girl, Regan. The film is based on William Peter Blatty's novel, which in turn draws inspiration from an actual recorded case of possession. The signs of Regan's demonic possession include foul language, head spinning, and projectile vomiting.

By contrast, in *Angel Heart* (1987) Satan takes on a human form in Louis Cyphre, a dark, mysterious figure with long pointed fingernails—a role chillingly performed by the actor Robert De Niro.

Satan does not appear in *The Sixth Sense* (1999), but there is a heavy overtone of supernatural evil represented by the color red. The movie focuses on the relationship between a psychiatrist and a disturbed boy tormented by his ability to see the spirits of people who have died violently.

The Witches of Eastwick (1987), based on John Updike's novel of the same name, features Satan as the hedonistic character Darrel Van Horn. Memorably played by Jack Nicholson, Horn is a vulgar womanizer summoned by three bored women to a provincial New England town.

Satan is often portrayed as a charming, charismatic, and attractive man, but in the movie *Bedazzled* (2000) he appears as a conniving woman. A female characterization of Satan is, however, rare.

order of things. All these are not exclusive to human beings—the instinct to survive is indicative of all creation.

The evil of war

How about wars, then? What about the great holocausts that have been endured for the sake of a tract of land, a difference of opinion or an opposing ideal? is this not a struggle for dominance? Why is one government fighting another for possession of a certain real estate any different than the wolf defending to the death a territory he has carefully designated as his? Why is a man shooting another man who has been caught in adultery with the wife of the first any different than two bucks knocking themselves into oblivion as they butt antlers to decide the prize of a doe? Are not wars a struggle for a basically animal dominance? Holy wars are waged over the dominance of one idea over another.

Do you see a parallel between the examples the author suggests, or are they simply distracting?

Natural need for dominance

Dominance is also a necessary factor for any sort of organized society. There must be leaders (this, too, is natural) and would-be leaders must fight for dominance, whether it be tooth and claw or the political arena.

But, the reader might protest, what about Hitler? Or the Son of Sam? It could be argued that Hitler is guilty of no evil. He believed in the dominance of his race and pursued it. He may have been wrong, but since when "does being wrong make one evil? Here we must also take into account the factor of mental illness. There are simply people who are hostile and irrationally destructive to themselves and society as a result of some internal defect. Are these people evil? Probably, no. Simply ill, for which they can bear no responsibility.

David Berkowitz (1953–), or "Son of Sam," was a notorious serial killer in the late 1970s. He is in jail serving six life sentences and is now a born-again Christian. Go to http://www.forteantimes.com/articles/161_sonofsam.shtml to find out more.

So what of this thing called evil? This malignant force we attribute to the darker nature of man? It is no more existent in us than in our brothers of the lower animal orders. Let us say, rather, that in spite of all of our righteous self-examination, we are, in fact, living up to nature's standards. We may dominate, but we govern ourselves. We may kill, but we survive. We may think, but we are, at our best, still animals.

In the United States the mentally ill can be prosecuted and punished for criminal conduct unless they are deemed insane. There is great debate about what constitutes insanity. Around 5 to 10 percent of death row prisoners are believed to have a mental illness.

Summary

Bill Bradford, the author of the first article, takes the largely orthodox Christian view that evil does indeed exist. He says that the Bible explains evil as rebellion against God, and contends that because God chose to create human beings as free moral agents, people have the capacity to choose between good or evil. Likewise, God also created the angel Lucifer, but Lucifer chose to make himself God's adversary and became Satan. Humankind's suffering is a consequence of transgressing God's holy law. In the end, according to Christian theology, those who choose to join God's family and accept his salvation will no longer endure pain and sorrow.

The author of the second article, John R. Mabry, questions the whole concept of evil. He argues that humans have always liked to polarize issues into "good" and "evil," especially when judging one another. Mabry points out that animals do violent, injurious, and painful things in the natural world for the legitimate purposes of dominance and survival. He argues that wars in the human world are similarly a struggle for basic animal dominance, while dominance is a necessary factor for any sort of organized society. Since humans are, at best, still animals, Mabry concludes we are living up to nature's standards by acting out our natural instincts for violence and dominance.

FURTHER INFORMATION:

Books:

Adams, Marilyn McCord, and Robert M. Adams (eds.), *The Problem of Evil*. Oxford, England: Clarendon Press, 1991.

Lara, Maria Pia (ed.), *Rethinking Evil: Contemporary Perspectives*. Berkeley, CA: University of California Press, 2001.

Peterson, Michael, *God and Evil: An Introduction to the Issues*. Boulder, CO: Westview Press, 1998.

Articles:

Rosenbaum, Ron, "Degrees of Evil: Some Thoughts on Hitler, Bin Laden, and the Hierarchy of Wickedness." *The Atlantic Monthly*, February, 2002.

Useful websites:

http://iaia.essortment.com/
argumentsexist_rzgh.htm
Outline of St. Augustine's and Thomas Aquinas's arguments for the existence of God.
http://www.pytlik.com/observe/deliverus/
Article, "Does Evil Exist or Do Bad Things Just Happen?"

The following debates in the Pro/Con series may also be of interest:

In this volume:
Part 1: Issues in religion, pages 8–9

Topic 2 Would there be fewer wars if religion did not exist?

Topic 3 Does organized religion stifle free thought?

Topic 5 Is morality possible without a religious basis?

Topic 10 Should the Bible be interpreted literally?

DOES EVIL EXIST?

Yes: The fact that evil is so widely recognized and that different cultures' interpretations of it are broadly similar suggests that it must exist as an absolute

Yes: Religion provides a clear definition: evil is that which goes against the laws of God

UNIVERSAL CONCEPT

If all cultures have a concept of evil, does this prove that it must exist?

DEFINITIONS

Is it possible to provide a clear definition of what is evil?

No: Cultural concepts of evil reflect merely the necessity of creating the moral scale on which societies depend for their existence

No: Evil is always a question of degree. Things that some people consider evil are perfectly acceptable for others; definitions depend entirely on the individual

DOES EVIL EXIST? KEY POINTS

Yes: Evil is an absolute value, which means that something is either evil or not

Yes: Without the idea of evil to discourage certain behaviors, people would be far more selfish and antisocial

EVIL VS. GOOD

Are some acts always evil?

SOCIAL STRUCTURE

Is the idea of evil necessary in modern society?

No: Evil is a relative concept; for example, the killing of a brutal dictator or a mass murderer is less likely to be condemned as evil than the murder of a child

No: Most people naturally do good things without thinking about self-advancement; goodness is part of our nature

21

Topic 2
WOULD THERE BE FEWER WARS IF RELIGION DID NOT EXIST?

YES
"MURDER IN THE NAME OF RELIGION"
FREE INQUIRY, SUMMER 1990
JAMES A. HAUGHT

NO
"IF THERE WERE NO SUCH THING AS RELIGION THERE
WOULD BE NO WARS"
ADAMANDEVEIT.NET
SIMON COHEN

INTRODUCTION

Religion has been used for millennia to justify warfare. Wars have been fought between faiths, such as the Christian Crusades launched against the Islamic rulers of the Holy Land from the 11th to the 13th centuries. Many wars have also been fought between different branches of the same faith. The Thirty Years' War in Europe (1618–1648) pitted Catholic forces against Protestant enemies; in the Islamic world, meanwhile, the Sunni Muslims of the Ottoman Empire fought against the Shia Muslims of neighboring Persia in a series of battles in the 16th century.

The connection between religion and warfare is complex. Christianity itself changed from being a relatively minor faith to a state religion through warfare. The Roman emperor Constantine (about 255–337) had a vision in 312 in which he saw a symbol composed of the first two Greek letters in the word Christ, with the words "By this sign you will conquer." Constantine's soldiers subsequently carried the symbol on their shields and defeated a pagan army that far outnumbered them. Constantine therefore made Christianity the official religion of the Roman Empire.

Warfare has also served to spread religions. Victors in war have often imposed their religion on the defeated. Islam, for example, was carried throughout Arabia during the last centuries of the first millennium by armed horsemen. The missionaries who first brought Christianity to the Americas accompanied armed troops on a campaign motivated by conquest.

Religion remains a key cause of conflict today. In the Middle East, for example, Muslim Arabs wage a violent campaign against Israeli Jews; in South Asia predominantly Hindu India and predominantly Muslim Pakistan pursue an armed dispute over the territory of Jammu and Kashmir. While some observers believe that such conflicts are actually related to land and resources, many of the combatants believe themselves to be engaged in a holy war.

Some people regard the idea of a holy war as a contradiction in terms. How, they ask, can religions that generally promote tolerance and peace be used as a justification for violence? In fact, the idea of a holy war is deeply rooted in religions such as Christianity, Islam, and Judaism. In the fifth century, for example, Saint Augustine of Hippo (354-430), one of the fathers of the Christian church, extolled the idea of "just war." He defined it as a means to reestablish violated justice, which extended beyond individuals and peoples to the justice due to God. In such an interpretation the denial of the right worship of God can be the motive for just war. It might also place a duty on religious adherents to protect or spread their faith.

"No enemy can harm one so much as one's own thoughts of craving, hate, and jealousy."

—BUDDHA,

DHAMMAPADA: 42

Although it may seem obvious that religion has been the cause of many wars, a different interpretation of history produces another conclusion. Some historians believe that wars tend to be fought mainly for political or economic, rather than spiritual, reasons: They are caused by the need for land or by competition for resources such as water or wealth. They argue that even the Crusades—fought by European Christians to gain control of holy places such as Jerusalem—had more to do with upheavals in European society than with religion. Launching the Crusades served to reinforce the traditional feudal social structure at a time of great change and underlined the power of the Catholic Church.

Few warriors, in this interpretation, are motivated purely by religious concerns. More often, religion is either an excuse to legitimize wars that have other motivations or is just one of a whole series of differences that exist between warring groups of people. From this point of view it makes as much sense to say that people fight wars because they speak different languages as it does to say that religion is the cause.

People who believe this point of view argue that the disappearance of religion would not, for example, lessen the number of wars fought between people who fundamentally follow the same religion. In such cases both sides believe that their cause is just and that they therefore enjoy God's support. The irony of such a situation was summed up by English humorist J.C. Spence in a poem about World War I (1914-1918):

God heard the embattled nations sing and shout;
"Gott straffe England"—"God save the King"—
"God this"—"God that"—and "God the other thing":
"My God," said God, "I've got my work cut out."

Journalists James A. Haught and Simon Cohen further examine issues in this debate.

MURDER IN THE NAME OF RELIGION
James A. Haught

James A. Haught is a U.S. journalist and editor.

See page 26 for information on Pope Pius V and the Battle of Lepanto.

The name "Inquisition" is derived from the Latin verb inquiro, which means to "inquire into." In 1542 Pope Paul III established the Roman Inquisition or Congregration of the Inquisition to combat the spread of Protestantism, particularly in Italy.

The author lists various saints who have committed horrific acts in the name of religion. Go to http://www.newadvent.org/cathen/—the site of the Catholic Encyclopedia—to find out more information.

YES

When you think of saints, you envision stained-glass pictures of piety. But the truth can be horribly different.

Pope Pius V: Grand Inquisitor

Consider Pope Pius V: When he was Grand Inquisitor, he sent Catholic troops to kill 2,000 Waldensian Protestants in Calabria in southern Italy.

After becoming pope, he sent Catholic troops to kill Huguenot Protestants in France. He ordered the commander to execute every prisoner taken.

Pius also launched the final crusade against the Muslims, sending a Christian naval armada to slaughter thousands in the Battle of Lepanto in 1571.

And he intensified the Roman Inquisition, torturing and burning Catholics whose beliefs varied from official dogma.

After his death, he was canonized a saint. He still is venerated by the church.

It is as if Adolf Hitler were elevated to sainthood.

Saints or torturers

Or consider Saint Dominic, the king of torture. He founded the Dominican order, whose priests were judges of the Inquisition. They presided while screaming victims were twisted and ripped on fiendish pain machines until they confessed to thinking unorthodox thoughts. Then the Dominicans led the broken "heretics" in grand processions to the stake. The priests also tortured thousands of women into confessing they were witches who had sex with Satan, changed themselves into animals, flew through the sky, caused storms, and the like. The "witches" also were burned for their confessions.

Or consider Saint Cyril, whose monks and followers beat to death the great woman scientist, Hypatia, director of the Alexandria Library, for her scientific approach to nature.

Or Saint Pedro Arbries, a Spanish inquisitor who tortured and burned former Jews for harboring their old beliefs. An ex-Jew assassinated him, and he was canonized as a martyr.

Pope Pius V, grand inquisitor, ordered Catholic forces to execute thousands of Protestants.

COMMENTARY: Pius V (1504–1572)

The papacy of Pius V was notable for the church's hostility toward non-Catholics, particularly followers of the new Protestant creeds. Born into a poor family in Bosco, Italy, Antonio Ghislieri (Pius V) worked as a shepherd until the age of 14, when he joined a religious brotherhood. He was ordained in 1528 and then studied and taught theology and philosophy for around 16 years before becoming master of novices and prior to several Dominican monasteries. He was named inquisitor for Como and Bergamo at the behest of the powerful Cardinal Carafa (1476–1559), who later became Pope Paul IV. Ghislieri also became commissary-general to Pope Julius III's Inquisition. When Carafa became pope, Ghislieri accelerated through the ranks to become bishop of Nepi and Sutri in 1556, cardinal in 1557, and grand inquisitor in 1558. He was responsible for protecting the faith from heresy, or nonbelief, but his extreme zeal led to criticism. In January 1566 Chislieri became pope under the name Pius V and set about reforming the papal court. He worked hard to raise its morals and to reform the clergy. He was also concerned about religious struggle, however, against Protestantism on the one hand and Islam on the other. One of his greatest successes was uniting Catholic princes to fight against the Muslim Turks. After Selim II (1524–1574) attacked Cyprus in 1570, Pius formed the Holy League, a military alliance of the Republic of Venice (which controlled Cyprus), Spain, and the Holy See.

Battle of Lepanto

On October 7, 1571, the fleet of the Holy League, commanded by Don John of Austria (1547–1578), half-brother of Philip II of Spain, met the Ottoman fleet in a great naval battle off Lepanto, Greece.

The league's fleet comprised around 200 mainly Spanish, Venetian, and papal galleys, with others from a number of Italian states. It faced the 40 galleys of the Ottoman navy, which it virtually destroyed. Around 15,000 Turks were killed or captured and some 10,000 Christian galley slaves set free. The Holy League fleet lost around 7,000 men. Among the wounded was the Spanish writer Miguel de Cervantes (1547–1616), who lost his arm and became known as "el manco de Lepanto" (Lepanto's one-handed).

The Battle of Lepanto was hugely significant. Christian leaders had been concerned about the apparent invincibility of the Ottoman fleet, and Lepanto was the first major Christian victory over the Turks. Some historians believe that had the Turkish fleet won, the Ottoman Empire could have eventually ruled the entire Mediterranean region. Selim II ordered a new fleet to be built, but the Turks never regained their former naval power.

Many historians and scholars believe that after receiving news of the battle's successful outcome, Pius V felt his defense of Christianity was complete: He died the following year.

Love and compassion?

I was a newspaper church columnist for many years.
Endlessly, I heard ministers proclaim that religion instills
love and compassion in believers. It's a universal message.
Meanwhile, back at the paper, our headlines said:

"Hindus, Muslims, Sikhs Massacre Each Other in India"

*"Protestant Gunmen Kill Catholics in Belfast, and Vice
Versa"*

"Shi'ites in Iran Hang Baha'i Teens Who Won't Convert"

*"Christian Snipers Pin Down Muslim Machine-Gunners
in Beirut"*

*"Hands and Feet Chopped Off Under Islamic Law in
Sudan"*

*Politicians always call religion a mighty force for good.
President Reagan labeled it "the bedrock of moral
order." They say it builds brotherhood.*

A crock of lies?

But Christians killed 3 million Jews during Europe's
centuries of religious persecution, before Hitler secularized
the process.

And the Reformation wars pitted Catholics and Protestants
in a ghastly century of slaughter.

And the Third World today still suffers bloodbaths caused
by religious tribalism.

There's a tinge of the Twilight Zone in the constant
declarations that religion creates love, when opposite results
are everywhere.

Did religion make Saint Pius V loving as he killed
Waldensians, Huguenots, Muslims and nonconforming
Catholics?

Did it make the Ayatollah Khomeini compassionate as he
ordered the hanging of Baha'is and demanded the
assassination of a "blaspheming" British writer?

Did it make the Aztecs affectionate as they sacrificed and
skinned maidens to appease a feathered serpent god?

Did it make brotherhood in Lebanon, where religious tribes
wreak endless warfare?

Religion always is hailed as the cure for the world's evils.
But, too often, it's the problem, not the solution.

*Listing examples
can help back up
your argument.
Choose them
carefully, and
use them
judiciously.*

*Is there any
difference between
the Christian
persecution of Jews
throughout history
and the Holocaust
perpetrated by
Hitler's Nazis during
World War II? Or
might they share
similarities?*

*The British author
referred to here is
Salman Rushdie. On
February 14, 1989,
Khomeini, spiritual
leader of Iran,
issued a death
sentence against
Rushdie for his
novel The Satanic
Verses. Go to
http://books.
guardian.co.uk/
departments/
generalfiction/story/
0,6000,1190413,00.
html for further
information.*

IF THERE WERE NO SUCH THING AS RELIGION THERE WOULD BE NO WARS
Simon Cohen

Simon Cohen is a freelance journalist and director of Tolerance Limited, a company that aims to improve religious tolerance in society. In 2003 he set up www.adamandeveit.net to "engage secular society with issues related to faith and diversity." This article is taken from the site.

Cohen is referring to the violence sometimes associated with soccer, mainly in Europe. Does using this popular comparison strengthen or weaken his case?

Former professional soccer player Bill Shankley was a famous manager of Liverpool Football Club in the 1970s. Shankley was very outspoken on the subject of football.

NO

X

"If there were no such thing as religion there would be no wars."

Many people nod their heads and utter an approving 'True.' Others shrug their shoulders somewhat apathetically. There are also those who disagree with the sweeping statement and point to other 'causes' of war, such as disputes over politics and land.

Universal importance

Now is the time to stand up and be counted. In an environment of terror and imminent war, religion is a matter of universal importance. The taboo subject that bartenders wince at its very mention must now be tackled. Fencesitters take note; indifference and impartiality are no longer options. The tale of hijacked planes crashing into skyscrapers is one of sad fact and not science fiction. The last eighteen months have placed in explicit perspective the need to examine our religious prejudices and finger pointing.

I suggest that the inference that religion causes war is as ridiculous as implicating football for hooliganism.

Hooligans often mask their violent ways by wearing football shirts, to exonerate themselves from direct responsibility and parade the cause for which they are fighting. Osama Bin Laden's mask is one of religion. He immerses his fluent rhetoric in religious sentiment and Koranic verse to endorse brutality. A fanatical anti-football protestor might try to convince us that the sport causes terror in the terraces. He might use Bill Shankley's famous quote as evidence to support his theory:

Some people believe football is a matter of life and death. I'm very disappointed with that attitude. I can assure you it is much, much more important than that.

Consider the real possibility that people who know nothing of the essence of football would be susceptible to the hypothetical protestor's argument that football is more

Tony Blair, prime minister of Britain, London, January 15, 2004. Blair denounced Osama Bin Laden's terrorism, stating that it was not motivated by religious faith.

29

COMMENTARY: Robert Green Ingersoll

One of the great American orators of the 19th century, Robert Green Ingersoll (1833–1899) has been labeled many things, from "heretic" and "skeptic" to "liberal," "rationalist," "infidel," and "atheist." Today he is mainly remembered as the source of many topical and pithy quotations, but during his life he was highly respected as a public speaker.

Background

Born to an impoverished Presbyterian minister in 1833 in Dresden, New York, Ingersoll became disillusioned with religion at a young age. He trained as a lawyer, but it was while he was an officer in the Civil War (1861–1865) that he first came to prominence as a powerful speechmaker. In 1867 he was appointed the first attorney general of Illinois, his first and last public appointment. Although his oratorical skills helped his brother Ebon win a successful congressional campaign, and generally promoted the cause of the Republican Party, he was passed over for the state's Republican gubernatorial nomination after he refused to make fewer speeches on controversial subjects.

Rhetoric

For almost 30 years Ingersoll traveled the length and breadth of the United States lecturing to audiences on a variety of subjects. His most popular lectures were on religion, and on occasion thousands of people gathered to listen to him denounce the Bible. He once said, "Shakespeare is my Bible, [Robert] Burns my hymn book." Ingersoll was bitterly opposed to conservative religion, was a supporter of Charles Darwin and evolutionism, and lectured on science and reason. He supported sensitive civil rights issues, such as the struggle for equal rights between sexes and races. This made him a favorite with reformers, including the women's rights advocate Elizabeth Cady Stanton (see Volume 13, *U.S. History*, page 66). He also counted the writer Mark Twain, captain of industry Andrew Carnegie, and leading figures in the political world among his friends. Today Ingersoll's words are still quoted by writers, scholars, and critics everywhere.

Is violence learned behavior or a genetic trait? Go to http://www.rso. cornell.edu/ scitech/archive/ 96fall/behav.html to see Marcelo Vince's article on behavorial genetics.

important than life and death, thus legitimising violence in its name. Ignorance leaves our hearts and minds open to even the most absurd of suggestions. Mr Shankley's words have obviously been taken out of context. He was alluding to the passion football induces in its supporters, and certainly not condoning violence and death in its name.

Hooligans use football as a means of driving their destructive ways into the heart of something pure. Extremists use religion to do the same. The poison currently being spread about Islam by Abu Hamza, Bin Laden and others is a potentially fatal one. Only the antidote of accurate information will render its effects harmless. When we have this information, the messages about Islam will seem as nonsensical as the protestor's life and death football argument. Know knowledge. No nonsense.

Do we know the affirmations regards Islam drilled into our minds by extremists are not taking the religion out of context, in the same way Mr Shankley's words were above? Most of us could not claim to know about the essence of Islam. The Koran is believed by Muslims to be the actual word of God. The Holy Book warns that killing a single innocent individual is like killing all of humanity. God created humankind for the specific purpose of serving Him (51:56), and so the present life is cherished to the full. The call for Muslims to make martyrs of themselves by sacrificing their lives is fundamentally departed from the true essence of Islam. Knowledge of the spirit of Islam exposes the likes of Osama as laden by hatred and intolerance; the antithesis of the religion they claim to espouse.

Go to page 50 to find out more about Sheikh Abu Hamza al-Masri, the imam (prayer leader) of the Finsbury Park Mosque in London, England.

Tony Blair, in a letter to the Muslim media, said about Bin Laden, "Let nobody believe this is about religious faith, when in the pursuit of his goals he has been willing to murder innocent women and children, including Muslims." The motive for terrorism is destruction and not doctrine, corruption and not creed, hatred and not love.

Robert Green Ingersoll said, "Religion has not civilized man, man has civilized religion" [see box on opposite page]. The essence of religion is pure and unifying. The nine major faiths in Britain have different practices, and religious symbols, as football teams have different strips. However, they are all bound by the morals that every civilized person would claim as their own. Nonviolence, care and compassion, respect, forgiveness, faith and community are common themes underpinning all the religious faiths in Britain. Practices that are contrary to these central values are not attributable to religion.

See the box on page 30 for more information on Ingersoll.

People cause war. Not religion. The responsibility for violence lies with humanity, and not the masks we use to cover our prejudiced ways. Relationships grounded in respect, expressed with understanding, and motivated by the desire to co-exist in peace, will represent the weapons of mass instruction that will ultimately prevail in the war against terror.

The author cleverly plays on words— referring to "weapons of mass instruction" rather than the more popular phrase "weapons of mass destruction." This is a good way to make a point more memorable.

Summary

In the first article James A. Haught, a former church newspaper columnist, argues that there would be fewer wars if religion did not exist. Haught powerfully contrasts the saintly figures depicted in stained-glass church windows with religious figures from history, such as Saint Dominic, who founded the Dominican order that led the Inquisition, torturing nonbelievers in the name of the Catholic Church. Haught lists historical figure after historical figure who killed in the name of religion and were rewarded with canonization by their churches. This religious slaughter continues in modern times, he says, as can be seen by daily news headlines around the world. Haught points out that religion is said to promote love, but that the opposite is evident all around us. Too often, he holds, religion is the cause of the evils of the world rather than the solution.

Simon Cohen is the founder and editor of adamandeveit.net, a website that relates religious faith to society. In the second article Cohen argues that people cause war, not religion, by drawing on an unusual analogy between religious war and soccer hooliganism. He says that religious extremists use religion, just as Europe's soccer hooligans use their sport, as a mask to disguise their prejudiced ways. Religions, he contends, are in general bound by morals supporting nonviolence, compassion, respect, and forgiveness. Extremists, like Osama Bin Laden, are the antithesis of the religion they espouse: "The motive for terrorism is destruction and not doctrine, corruption and not creed, hatred and not love." Cohen concludes that only the "weapons of mass instruction"—respect, understanding, and a desire for peace—will end the war against terror.

FURTHER INFORMATION:

Books:

Palmer-Fernandez, Gabriel, and Iain Maclean (eds.) *An Encyclopedia of Religion and War*. New York: Routledge, 2003.

Useful websites:

http://www.catholic.net/rcc/Periodicals/lgpress/2002-04/opinion2.html
"Does Religion Cause War?" by James Hitchcock.
http://www.holytrinitydoncaster.org.au/questions/conflict.htm
Looks at whether religion causes war.
http://www.nationalreview.com/comment/comment-carroll092601.shtml
"It's Not about Religion" by Vincent Carroll. Guest column in the *National Review*.

The following debates in the Pro/Con series may also be of interest:

In this volume:
Part 1: Issues in religion

Topic 12 Are monotheistic religions more intolerant than other religions?

In *World Politics*:
Topic 7 Can Israel and Palestine ever reach a peace settlement?

WOULD THERE BE FEWER WARS IF RELIGION DID NOT EXIST?

YES: Religion is a factor that underlines differences between groups of people and can lead to suspicion, intolerance, and hatred

YES: Many wars and atrocities in history were rooted in religion. It still causes bloody conflict in the world today.

LOVE OR HATE?
Does religion encourage hatred?

CAUSES OF WAR
Has religion caused most wars in history?

NO: The basic message of most religions is to love each other and turn the other cheek. Religion has been the cause of great good in the world.

NO: Most wars are due to political, not religious, reasons. Wars have also been fought because of greed, class, and race.

WOULD THERE BE FEWER WARS IF RELIGION DID NOT EXIST?

KEY POINTS

YES: There would be no fanatical Muslims, Hindus, Sikhs, and Christians, for example, if there were no religion. The world would then be an altogether more peaceful place.

YES: The military action conducted as part of the War on Terrorism since the attacks of September 11, 2001, for example, is a response to religious extremism

EXTREMISM
Would there be fewer fanatics if religion did not exist?

NO: Humanity is responsible for violence, not religion. Extremists use religion as a mask for their own prejudice and ambition.

NO: Religious extremists are not an authentic expression of their faith. They would use some other medium for their destructive traits if religion did not exist.

Topic 3
DOES ORGANIZED RELIGION STIFLE FREE THOUGHT?

YES
FROM "RELIGION STOPS A THINKING MIND"
HTTP://HOME.EARTHLINK.NET/~JEHDJH/ANTITHOUGHT.HTML
ERIC HARRINGTON

NO
FROM "LIVING THE QUESTION: EVANGELICAL CHRISTIANITY AND CRITICAL THOUGHT"
CROSS CURRENTS, VOL. 40, ISSUE 2, SUMMER 1990
ROBERT WUTHNOW

INTRODUCTION

Organized religions are usually characterized by a set of accepted beliefs, along with fixed rituals and practices, a hierarchical organization of priests, and authoritative religious texts and moral guidelines or laws. Such structures have often evolved over hundreds of years. Their supporters believe not only that they enshrine important spiritual traditions of the faith, but that they also provide the best framework to allow adherents to practice worship today. Some opponents argue, on the other hand, that the organization of religion tends to be conservative in its nature: It is more concerned with maintaining tradition than with adapting to changing circumstances and beliefs.

There have been numerous cases in history in which opponents have accused various organized religions of stifling the kind of free thinking that questions accepted beliefs and practices. One example was the Protestant Reformation in the early 16th century, when the Christian church split into two branches. The Reformation began when the German priest Martin Luther protested against what he perceived as abuses within the Catholic Church, including worldliness and corruption among the clergy. The refusal of the church leadership to reform to counter Luther's objections led him to establish a new branch of Christianity, Protestantism. The new denomination placed less emphasis on the importance of the priestly hierarchy and more on the relationship between individual worshipers and God. The Catholic Church tried to suppress this new form of the faith; Luther himself was excommunicated. Protestantism became established, however, thanks in part to the support of European princes eager to challenge the power of the Catholic Holy Roman emperor.

One interpretation of the Reformation is that the Catholic Church could not accommodate new currents of thought. This is what Luther and many of his contemporaries believed. Other observers, however, point out that many Catholics who agreed with Luther's criticisms of the church sought to find solutions to the problems by working within Catholicism. Some found a revived spiritualism in the creation of new religious orders, such as the Carmelites founded by Saint Teresa of Avila in 1562. Others found spiritual fulfillment in the changes announced by the church leaders after the Council of Trent (1545–1563). The council reinvigorated the church and launched the Counter-Reformation.

"I do not need the idea of God to explain the world I live in"

—SALMAN RUSHDIE (1947–),
BRITISH WRITER

The relationship between religion and science is often cited as evidence of how organized religion impedes free thought. The Catholic Church imprisoned the Italian scientist Galileo Galilei (1564–1642) for theorizing that the earth orbits the sun. He challenged the accepted belief, supported by the church, that Earth was the center of the universe. Galileo can be seen as one of the first thinkers of the Enlightenment, an intellectual movement of the 17th and 18th centuries that emphasized science and rationalism over faith and superstition. In the 19th century many church leaders also dismissed Charles Darwin's theory of evolution as being

contrary to biblical teaching. Some fundamentalist Christians still reject the teaching of evolution in schools. Despite the opposition of the church, however, Darwin's theory has become widely accepted in Christian countries. That fact could be taken as evidence that organized religion is indeed capable of allowing free thought and absorbing its conclusions. So, too, could the advances in astronomy, medicine, and mathematics made by Islamic scholars during the Middle Ages.

Faith has inspired a wide range of works of art, music, and literature over the centuries, but religions have also suppressed creativity. In 1989, for example, Ayatollah Khomeini (1902–1989), the Iranian Islamic leader, issued a death sentence against the British author Salman Rushdie for "insulting Islam" in his novel *The Satanic Verses*.

Opposed to reactionaries like Khomeini, however, are the many religious leaders who have fought for social change. Quakers were among the first people to speak out against slavery in the American colonies. Some 300 years later Protestants were at the forefront of the civil rights movement led by Dr. Martin Luther King, Jr. (1929–1968), a Baptist minister. In 2003 the Episcopal Church in the United States took steps to promote equality for homosexuals by electing an openly gay bishop. Advocates claim that such examples demonstrate that organized religion does not inevitably impose immutable views on its adherents but is capable of embracing change.

The following articles discuss these issues further. Eric Harrington argues that faith prevents people from thinking rationally. Robert Wuthnow explores the relationship between Christianity and critical thought.

RELIGION STOPS A THINKING MIND
Eric Harrington

Eric Harrington is
an ex-Christian. He
writes on a number
of topics, including
history, religion,
philosophy, and
astronomy.

The author is
referring to the
biblical story of
Jonah, who went
to sea to escape
God's command.
He was thrown
overboard during
a storm and
swallowed by a
huge fish.

Does it matter
whether a religion
is logical? Some
people argue that
a defining quality
of faith is that it
cannot be justified
by reason alone.

YES

I have a bumper sticker that makes fun of a common religious bumper sticker. It looks very much like the more famous one, but it says "Religion stops a thinking mind!" Of course, this is only used for shock value. I'm well aware that people who are religious aren't mindless zombies —under most circumstances. However, there are times when their eyes glaze over and the ability to think is tossed overboard faster than they tossed Jonah into the ocean.

In a conversation, most of the time, you can discuss any subject with a religious person, and they will use normal thinking skills, using their ability to rationally approach the subject at hand. They have their opinions on any subject other than religion, and if they learn something that conflicts with what they thought was true, they accept that they were wrong and internalize that fact. I have often been in conversations with deeply religious people who had simple misconceptions about the subject of astronomy, for instance. Those who don't make a hobby of learning about the universe have lots of bad information about it—like the idea (supported by popular songs) that the north star (Polaris) is the brightest star in the sky—which it emphatically is not. Or that there's a "Dark Side" of the Moon, a place of perpetual darkness, which also is not the case. All I have to do is point out the location of Polaris, and several brighter stars to get the first point across. A couple of minutes with a ball and flashlight to demonstrate the other. Once the point is made, there's no need to worry about the truth of the matter.

Rational approach to religion
This process of rational analysis will even continue when they discuss any religion that isn't their own! I know many thoughtful people who have no problem with finding the logical errors with other religions. Some take great pains to find every shred of evidence possible to prove how wrong other religions are. I once was talking with a person who is a very thoughtful Christian. I mentioned to him that I thought the Muslim religion was just as valid as his. Of course, he took exception to this. The interesting thing about his reaction was that he then went into a list of reasons (nearly all of

The movements of stars captured by long-exposure photography. If people can revise misconceptions about astronomy, should they be more willing to recognize logical problems with their beliefs?

them valid) as to why Islam was not worth believing, including problems with the Koran, the less savory items in the life of Muhammad, and reasons why there could be no valid relationship between Islam and Judaism, as the Muslim claim goes. It was all very admirable.

However, any time I talk with this same person about any of the various logical problems with Christian beliefs, and the sparks start to fly. I once mentioned that the first two chapters of Genesis contradict each other on several points, especially concerning the issue of the order in which things "popped" into existence. I was told that two different people will see an auto accident from different perspectives, and that

Some critics claim that the Koran, the holy book of Islam, contains inflammatory statements about Jews made by Muhammad (about 570–632), the founder of the Islamic faith. Others contend that the Koran teaches religious tolerance.

those will agree on major points—in this case, the two accounts agree that God created the world and all living creatures, including humans. This is an ad hoc argument, and a sloppy one at best. At other times, I have asked the same person about who wrote the book of Genesis (as in "who actually put the words on paper?"). Many believers, especially fundamentalist Christians and definitely including my friend, believe it was written by Moses (they point out that the first five books of the Bible are called "Books of Moses" and that Jesus said they were written by Moses), which sort of shoots down the theory of "two observers of the same event" from the discussion I mentioned earlier.

In Judaism the first five books of the Old Testament, called the Pentateuch, are also traditionally ascribed to Moses.

Blind faith

Now, the question becomes, "Why should this shutdown in thinking occur?" In my opinion, it all boils down to the concept of "faith." Faith is presented to all religious people as a virtue, a thing most pleasing to God and impossible to live without. It also just happens to be the one thing that religions can't exist without. For faith is a mindset, an ability to believe in something in the absence of evidence that could support that belief. In many instances, faith also entails the ability to cling to a belief in the presence of evidence that the belief is wrong. Thus, any questions that can be raised, any contrary evidence is all ignored, in favor of following one's faith. In other words, religions order followers to shut off the rational parts of the mind and accept everything about the religion without using any rational mental processing. This is particularly true in the Christian Bible:

Is a refusal to be deflected from one's faith a strength or a weakness?

> *1 Cor 3:18-20—Do not deceive yourselves. If you think that you are wise in this age, you should become fools so that you may become wise. For the wisdom of this world is foolishness with God. For it is written, "He catches the wise in their craftiness," and again, "The Lord knows the thoughts of the wise, that they are futile."*

Do you agree with the author that these verses discourage people from trying to understand the world?

This leads to the comment about religion stopping a thinking mind.

In my opinion, this is a harmful situation. I consider the ability to take a proposition on faith to be at least an abdication of one's duty to oneself. If someone tells you something, presenting it to you as a fact, it is always prudent, if you're not familiar with it, to do some investigating. Going a little further into the faithful mindset, I have seen it become a regular habit with some people. Superstitions, urban legends, all sorts of rumors are accepted as truth, often without questions of any sort. There's nothing harmful about that much of the time, but that's not always the case. The real harm, however, comes when the con artists arrive. Any con artist practices his art by concocting a plausible story that makes the victim want to participate financially. With a habit of believing in things without looking into the evidence, people of a religious mindset can be easily taken in. This isn't to say that religious people are easily fooled because they believe in God—only that with an established habit of believing things simply because they want the things they believe to be true, that habit can lead them to make extremely poor decisions with disastrous consequences.

Do you think that religious people are more easily taken in than others?

"Pie from the sky"

We then come to another problem with the religious mindset—the faith that God loves and protects a person can (and often does) lead a person to think he or she can live life using God as a sort of metaphysical net over which to perform all sorts of dangerous stunts. I have known many people (and I was one of them) who personified the statement, "Give a man a fish, and he eats for a day. Give a man a religion, and he'll starve to death while praying for a fish." My personal experience with the Christian religion leads me to the opinion that it, in particular, is dangerous in this regard, as reading the Bible will lead to finding the many passages where followers are promised all sorts of divine gifts and supernatural protection from worldly disasters. As a matter of fact, I would be far from surprised to find out that one of the more common problems faced by Christian ministers is dealing with this very issue. Luckily, they have an arsenal of Bible quotes that contradict those verses, which I like to call the "pie from the sky" passages.

In the modern United States people often express concern about the dangers of Islam. Do you think that it is appropriate also to consider the dangers of Christianity?

Damaging mindset

In all, though, it's easy to see that religions and the faithful mindset that they all appear to encourage are harmful to the followers in many aspects of everyday life. The times that faith may be helpful are few and far between, and under nearly all circumstances it is useful only to the religious leaders who are well-trained in its uses. Is thinking and rational inquiry harmful? Not for any individual. It is seen as harmful and detrimental by religious leaders who work at their hardest to stamp it out when it appears in their flocks of intelligent sheep....

LIVING THE QUESTION—EVANGELICAL CHRISTIANITY AND CRITICAL THOUGHT
Robert Wuthnow

Robert Wuthnow teaches sociology of religion at Princeton University. This article appeared in CrossCurrents magazine in 1990.

Merton's book was called Science, Technology, and Society in Seventeenth-Century England. *Wuthnow compares it to Max Weber's book* The Protestant Ethic and the Spirit of Capitalism *(1904–1905), which suggested that Protestantism encourages individual enterprise and the accumulation of wealth.*

Is one of the main points of religion that it does offer "higher-order truths," or truths that cannot be justified by observation but by faith and spirituality?

NO

In 1938 Robert Merton ... published an influential book in which he examined the connection between Puritanism and the rise of science in 17th-century England. Merton argued that the Puritans had a special disposition toward scientific achievement because of their emphasis on this life as well as the life to come, their conviction that nature was the handiwork of God, and their commitment to the rational knowledge and mastery of God's creation. It was a clever thesis reminiscent of—indeed, modeled after—Max Weber's argument about the special connection between ascetic Protestantism and acquisitive capitalism....

I take the Merton controversy to be an instructive metaphor in seeking close connections between evangelical Christianity and a particular style of intellectual orientation. Some have argued that evangelical scholars may be inclined to accept rigorous empirical generalizations because of their belief that truth can be codified in simple propositions. Translated: Christians make better engineers than artists, or in the case of social scientists, better number-crunchers than theorists. Some have maintained on the same grounds that evangelical Christians may be less able than other scholars to appreciate paradox, subtle interpretation, and nuance.... My journey among my various Christian acquaintances ... confirms none of these views.

Diversity in Christian thought

The truth of the matter is that Christian thought, even evangelical Christian thought, is sufficiently diverse that no straightforward influence on the nature of intellectual work is readily found. Christians do not operate from some set of higher-order truths ... from which they derive notions about the sort of work to do and the best way of approaching it. They may make certain assumptions; we all do. But it has not been my experience that Christian scholars are any more likely than any others to take, say, an authoritarian stance toward certain deeply held beliefs, or to argue from first principles in the face of empirical evidence ...

I have borrowed the much-used phrase "living the question" because it seems to me that Christianity does not so much supply the learned person with answers as it does raise questions. It has been said of Marxists that even apostates spend their lives struggling with the questions Marx addressed. The same can probably be said of Christianity. It leaves people with a set of questions they cannot escape, especially when these questions face them from their earliest years.…

An apostate is someone who abandons his or her faith or beliefs.

What Christian stories teach us

[T]ake the story of Adam and Eve. To be sure, one can derive theological propositions from this story. But the most memorable aspects of the story itself are probably the questions it raises—questions about gender roles of course … but more importantly questions about the nature and limits of human knowledge.…

Do you agree that biblical stories are memorable for the questions that they raise?

Or consider the parable of the Good Samaritan. Like virtually all of Jesus' parables, it ends with a question: which of these was neighbor to the man? In the story the answer may be obvious. But a parable is also a mirror in which to observe real life, and in real life it is still the question of neighbor that animates much discussion, not only in theological circles, but in wider scholarly settings such as the social sciences. A Christian sociologist might argue that it is "neighbor" to the countries in Latin America to send financial aid; another might argue that it is "neighbor" to promote economic self-sufficiency. It is on the importance of the question that they agree.…

I am not suggesting that people actually have the questions they learned as children from Bible stories buzzing around in their heads, consciously or subconsciously telling them what is important about the world. It used to be popular to think of motives that way—to imagine that people might embark on a study of social justice in South Africa because the story of Moses and Pharaoh had always made a troubling impression on them. But motives are more complex than that.… They speak to us with many voices. And they do not often, it seems, speak to us in clear, rational voices. Rather, they come to us piecemeal, as the bits and pieces from which a story about why we do what we do can be constructed.…

What does it mean, then, to say "living the question"? It means pursuing the intellectual life because the questions are inherently important, not because one hopes primarily to advance a career or even because one necessarily expects to discover a definitive answer.… What Christianity does is add

Most religions concern the same "important" questions. But just because faiths encourage their followers to consider such questions, does it necessarily mean that they can answer them in any way they want?

seriousness to the enterprise: it says, in effect, these are serious questions that people have raised in one way or another from the beginning of time; do your part to keep them alive....

Putting it differently, we might say that Christianity sacralizes—makes sacred—the intellectual life. It gives the questions we struggle with in our work and in our lives a larger significance. Living the question becomes possible because our questions are animated.... Any religion, any worldview does this, and does it not just to our intellectual questions but to the questions and tasks that confront us in every part of life....

This is one way of saying what it means to live the question, one way of saying how Christian faith and the intellectual life intertwine.... And yet there is surely more to it than that....

Dirty little secrets

There are in fact two dirty little secrets that American higher education, for all its commitment to truth and fair-mindedness, continues to harbor. The first is its disdain for evangelical Christians....

[N]obody in the academy itself dares admit having any affinity with this shameful segment of American society. Universities that might bend over backwards to start programs in women's literature, in African-American or Hispanic culture, or in Jewish studies would never consider a comparable program in evangelical studies. And so, Christian scholars may hide out in hotel rooms or hold forth publicly under the rubric of American religious history, but few are able to appropriate a legitimate past for themselves or to adopt a public identity. This, then, is the tragedy of being a people without a legitimate history, for it is ... the ability to construct a meaningful account of oneself, a story that makes sense of one's activities, that amplifies meaning and augments motivation.

Should evangelical studies be part of the U.S. education system?

The other dirty little secret scholars and intellectuals in American higher education have never been quite willing to confront is the continuing existence of the effects of social class within the academic community....

Anyone who still retains an identity as a Christian, or simply hales from evangelical stock is subjected to a double stigma: first, the stigma of a shameful religious past; and second, the lingering effects of having been reared— as a disproportionate majority of evangelicals were—in disadvantaged ranks of the stratification system....

Do you think religious belief and social class are still important considerations in academic life? What about in other careers?

All of this is often an enormous disadvantage in pursuing the intellectual life, a disadvantage deepened by the fact of its denial. Indeed, it is more the denial of this background than the background itself that troubles me. Quite a few Christians have, as I have said, through hard work and native intelligence joined the ranks of the intelligentsia despite class disadvantages. But to enter a world in which the lessons of disadvantage are no longer valued is to live in a world of denial.

And yet, there are, as we know, certain gains associated with disadvantage and denial, particularly the freedom that comes with exclusion, the creativity that comes with marginality. Exclusion and marginality often facilitate critical thought. Alienation and ambivalence catalyze it subjectively; dispensation from established class roles enhances it objectively. We should no more lose sight of these goods than we should pretend that the problems do not exist.

> What evidence might suggest that poor or disadvantaged artists, writers, or musicians are somehow "better" than wealthy or privileged ones?

Continuing intellectual role

American culture shows few indications as it moves into the 21st century of becoming any less dominated by the rich and powerful, by elite institutions of higher learning, by big government and big industry, or by the competitive materialism to which we desperately cling in hopes of saving our place in the global economy. I am Calvinist enough to believe in that, but I am also Calvinist enough to believe that such experiences as my encounter with the death of [my childhood friend] Harry Charles Kitchen have a permanent impact on one's life, whether we later reinterpret them with more sophisticated theological understanding or not. And thus, there is in my view a continuing role to be played by Christians in the intellectual realm. In living the question, in being true to the realities of their own existence, persons of faith can respond to the challenge of thinking critically about what is going on in the wider world as well.

> Calvinism is a Protestant Christian theology advanced by John Calvin (1509–1564) and his followers.

> Wuthnow refers to Karl Marx's quote that religion is the "opium of the people." Go to http://atheism. about.com/library/ FAQs/religion/blrel_ marx_opium.htm for an explanation of what Marx (1818–1883) meant.

Karl Marx thought Christianity a form of false consciousness that prevented people from seeing reality as it really is. But he was more right when he referred to it as the heart of a heartless world. Lived as a question rather than a set of absolute answers, Christianity can stimulate critical thought. And in so doing, it is likely to continue bearing the burden of misunderstanding and prejudice. But that response should only galvanize its courage to tell a different story. For a story of disinheritance and struggle can also be the story of a legitimate past.

> Do all religions have to bear "the burden of misunderstanding and prejudice"?

Summary

The writers of the two articles have different views on the relationship between free thought and religion. Eric Harrington, the author of the first piece, believes that "religion stops a thinking mind"—a quote from his bumper sticker. He says that religious people often appear rational when discussing everyday matters, science, or religions other than their own. Yet when they are questioned about their own religious beliefs, Harrington argues, their thinking simply shuts down. He blames this reaction on the concept of faith, which he describes as a mindset that enables religious conviction with no evidence or notice of contradictory facts. In Harrington's opinion this mindset is useful only to religious leaders as an aid to controlling their "flocks of intelligent sheep."

In the second article Robert Wuthnow examines the connection between evangelical Christianity and critical thought. While he argues that it is impossible to generalize about Christian scholars, he contends that Christian faith informs academics by encouraging them to think about the questions they struggle with both in work and in daily life—what he calls "living the question." Posing such questions, he believes, is ultimately more important than answering them. Wuthnow also discusses the prejudices that Christian scholars face from higher education institutions—the "double stigma" of having an evangelical background and coming from "disadvantaged ranks of the stratification system." However, these drawbacks can also bring benefits, he argues, because people who are marginalized are more creative and are stimulated to think critically. For this reason Wuthnow believes that Christians make a valid contribution to the academic community.

FURTHER INFORMATION:

Books:

Battin, Margaret Pabst, *Ethics in the Sanctuary: Examining the Practices of Organized Religion*. New Haven, CT: Yale University Press, 1990.

Rauch, Jonathan, *Kindly Inquisitors: The New Attacks on Free Thought*. Chicago: University of Chicago Press, 1993.

Weber, Max, *The Protestant Ethic and the Spirit of Capitalism*. New York: Routledge, 2001.

Useful websites:

http://boundless.org/departments/the_podium/a0000873.html

"Does organized religion hold answers to the problems of the 21st century" by Alan Dershowitz.

www.religion-online.org

Provides full texts of previously published articles.

The following debates in the Pro/Con series may also be of interest:

In this volume:

Topic 10 Should the Bible be interpreted literally?

Topic 12 Are monotheistic religions more intolerant than other religions?

In *Education*:

Topic 11 Should public schools teach creationist theory?

DOES ORGANIZED RELIGION
STIFLE FREE THOUGHT?

YES: Religion draws on established tradition and fixed interpretations of texts; it finds it difficult to react to social change

YES: Many of the texts that form the basis of religious teachings are sexist, racist, or homophobic

CONSERVATIVE
Is religion naturally conservative?

WORLDVIEW
Do the views encouraged by organized religion lag behind changes in society?

NO: Although the basic beliefs and practices of religion are often long established, religious leaders have been instrumental in bringing about social change, such as in the civil rights movement in the United States

NO: Most organized religions move with the times. Certain Christian churches, for example, have church leaders who are women, are from different ethnic groups, or who are openly gay

DOES ORGANIZED RELIGION STIFLE FREE THOUGHT?
KEY POINTS

YES: Many scientists view religious faith as incompatible with a logical and rigorous mindset based on the principle of evidence

YES: Because religion is based on faith rather than scientific proof, it can be presented as being less justifiable in an age when facts and figures are so dominant

IMAGINATION
Does organized religion impede imagination and creativity?

THREAT
Does religion still have anything to fear from science, reason, or secular society?

NO: Religion has inspired many writers, artists, and musicians throughout history

NO: Religions have survived many challenges from science and have proved highly skilled at adapting their teachings to take notice of such challenges

SHOULD GOVERNMENTS HAVE THE RIGHT TO OUTLAW RELIGIONS?

YES
"BAN ISLAM!"
THE SENIOR CONSERVATIVE
DICK O'CONNOR

NO
"THE WRONG CHURCHES IN CHINA"
CHRISTIAN SCIENCE MONITOR, DECEMBER 21, 1999
KEVIN PLATT

INTRODUCTION

Article 18 of the United Nations Declaration of Human Rights (UNDHR), to which the vast majority of the world's nations have signed up, states that "Everyone has the right to freedom of thought, conscience, and religion." In other words, governments or other organizations should not be able to prohibit individuals from practicing whatever religion—or lack of religion—they choose. The First Amendment to the Constitution gives Americans freedom of conscience and prohibits the government from establishing an official religion. Despite such principled commitment to freedom of religion, however, governments around the world continue to ban or suppress various religions. In China, for example, the government has banned the movement Falun Gong; in Japan the activities of a sect known as Aum Shinrikyo are circumscribed; while in the past the United States has taken action against various Christian cults.

In such cases governments and their supporters often argue that it is usually not the tenets of the religion that they are questioning but the actions that they inspire, which can take the form or violence or terrorism in the service of the religion. Such violence threatens the principles of the state itself. The Chinese say that Fulan Gong is "evil" and has claimed the lives of 4,000 people. In Japan leaders of Aum Shinrikyo were tried and convicted for organizing terror attacks on the Tokyo subway in March 1995 that killed a dozen commuters. In the United States government agencies argue that radical Christian sects are often agents of hate speech against other races or faiths. They also have other concerns about sects linked to potential violence. In 1993, for example, the FBI used CS gas to try to end a siege at a compound in Waco, Texas, belonging to a sect known as the Branch Davidians. Sect members had stockpiled illegal weapons and had been accused of child sex abuse. Fires broke out in the compound during the FBI operation—probably started by cult members themselves—and 80 cult members died, including 25 children.

Opponents of such suppression argue that it often uses religion as an excuse. More often, governments are concerned with maintaining political rather than religious power. Bans silence religious groups that are often a powerful focus for political dissent. In the former Soviet Union, for example, most organized religion was forbidden by the ruling Communist Party, which wanted to create a secular state with absolute loyalty to the political leaders. In the same way, Adolf Hitler (1889-1945) discouraged religion in Nazi Germany in the years before and during World War II (1939-1945), although he was prepared to make deals with the Roman Catholic Church to ensure its support for his Nazi Party.

> *"A cult is a religion with no political power."*
> —TOM WOLFE (1931–), WRITER

A question related to whether governments should be able to ban religions—many can, because declarations such as the UNDHR are not binding—is whether banning religion ever actually works. Examples from history suggest that religion has a great ability to survive even when its formal expressions—such as church services and a clergy—are not permitted. For much of English history since the Reformation of the 16th century Catholics were persecuted when

Protestants were in political power; in the shorter periods of Catholic political dominance Protestants were similarly victimized. Neither faith was successfully stamped out; today, both flourish in the United Kingdom. Similarly, after the collapse of the Soviet Union in 1989 the Eastern Orthodox Church—a branch of Christianity— once again became prominent in societies in which it had been largely driven underground for around 70 years. Some commentators argue that, while it may be possible to forbid the outward display and ritual of religion, it is impossible for legislation to control what individuals actually believe in their hearts and minds.

Effective or not, much government action against religious groups has been directed against minor cults. Among the world's major religions Islam has recently suffered much criticism after numerous terrorist actions by Islamic extremists, such as the September 11, 2001, attacks on the World Trade Center and the Pentagon, the 2002 Bali bombing, and the ongoing suicide attacks on civilian targets in Israel. Some commentators argue that Islam is violent by nature and should be banned in America. Opponents counter that while those who incite religion-based violence and hatred should be punished, a ban would punish an inherently peaceful religion for the crimes of a few extremists. They argue that Christianity has absolutist principles similar to Islam—there is only one god and one true faith—that were used in the past to justify violence, forced conversion, and the overthrow of non-Christian rulers.

In the following extracts Dick O'Connor and Kevin Platt examine the debate further.

BAN ISLAM!
Dick O'Connor

Conservative writer Dick O'Connor died in 2002 at the age of 76.

For an article about Abu Hamza al-Masri see page 50.

Many people in Britain believe that it is only a matter of time before the country suffers a major terrorist attack by Islamic extremists, having supported the United States in its war on terror and the 2003 invasion of Iraq.

"Utopians" are idealists who suggest impractical social and political schemes.

Do you agree with the author that we should not try to understand why Islamic terrorists hate the West? How can the problem ever be solved if we do not know the source of their hatred?

YES

An AP report in the Fox News segment on the Internet for Oct 22, 2001 tells us that in London, one Abu Hamza al-Masri, chief cleric (mullah) for the Muslim mosque in London England has declared war on America and his host country, Britain. He came to England in 1984 pleading for asylum from Somalia and his native Egypt. After enjoying the perks and benefits of a true democracy, he now wants to destroy that government. He has previously stated that his goal is to make Great Britain an Islamic state. As far as terrorism goes, Britain is in as deep trouble as we are, except for the World Trade Center attack.

Expelling traitors

What both Britain, who has been our most enthusiastic supporter, and America must do is to enact laws for each country to expel these treasonous people from our respective nations. Immediately, and without due process. Those laws that are on the books now are laws passed by Liberal/Socialists Utopians. And, while well meaning, they are unable to cope with the dedicated violence of Islam. Next, all suspects that are being held by the FBI and Scotland Yard should follow the steps of those who openly preach hatred of our governments. Again, without due process, they should be sent back to their country of origin. If that country refuses to take them, or has promised to execute them, they should be returned forcefully to Afghanistan or any other Islamic country that will take them. There should be no attempt to 'understand' their hatred toward us. The fact that they hate us is enough.

The next step would be to close all Muslim mosques and schools that teach Islam. At that point in time when mosques and schools are closed, the people of Middle Eastern descent will realize that they are being discriminated against and will scream to the United Nations. They should be given a choice: either drop the Muslim faith and dress as Americans or Britons and support our nations as the first order of business. They should be allowed to join any Catholic Protestant or Jewish sect, but they must renounce Islam, which is trying to destroy our respective countries. If they wish to stay here,

Muslim cleric Abu Hamza al-Masri preaches outside Finsbury Park Mosque in London in 2003. The British and American governments suspect that he has links with terrorist organizations.

COMMENTARY: Abu Hamza al-Masri

Abu Hamza al-Masri (meaning Abu Hamza the Egyptian), the imam (prayer leader) at the Finsbury Park Mosque in London, is one of the most radical Islamic figures in Britain. Although he has been questioned by the police about alleged involvement in terrorist activity, he has never been charged. Abu Hamza has declared religious war on both the United States, which he refers to as the "United Snakes of America," and his host country, Britain.

Abu Hamza was born Mustafa Kamel Mustafa in Alexandria, Egypt, about 45 years ago. He came to London in 1979 to become a civil engineer. Abu Hamza worked as a nightclub bouncer in the late 1970s before becoming a radical Muslim. He married a westerner, Valerie Fleming, in 1981 and gained British citizenship. They divorced five years later.

Afghanistan injuries

In the early 1990s Abu Hamza went to Afghanistan, where Islamic rebels, the Mujahideen, were fighting against the Soviet occupation. While he was there, he was introduced to radical Islam. He worked as a civil engineer, studied Islam, and fought with the Mujahideen. He allegedly lost his eye and a hand in a landmine explosion—Abu Hamza's appearance is distinctive since he chooses to use a hook rather than an artificial hand—but some people claim that he lied about how he sustained his injuries and that there is photographic evidence showing him without injury as late as 1993, several years after the conflict in Afghanistan ended.

In 1994 Abu Hamza founded the organization "Supporters of Shariah," a group dedicated to the rule of Islamic law.

Yemen: the cradle of the revolution

In 1999 Abu Hamza was arrested and questioned by British police on suspicion of terrorism in Yemen. He was released without charge after several days and still maintains his innocence. The Yemeni authorities have requested his extradition from Britain to stand trial. Abu Hamza considers Yemen to be the ideal place to begin the Islamic revolution since it is the only country in the Arabian peninsula that has not "surrendered" to the United States. His adopted son served three years in prison in Yemen for his involvement in a terrorist bombing campaign.

The FBI has also requested Abu Hamza's extradition to the United States. Abu Hamza has been linked to Richard Reid, the British "shoe bomber," and Zacharias Moussaoui, the "20th man" held in connection with the September 11, 2001, atrocity. Abu Hamza's comments have provoked much condemnation from moderate Muslims. After being asked in an interview why he did not leave Britain if he did not like it, he replied, "I am living in a toilet with minefields all around." Critics believe that he should be imprisoned for preaching hatred.

they must meet these conditions. If they wish to practice the Mohammedan faith, they will have to leave the country. In no way should these people be tortured or abused. They should be treated with respect, but given the choice firmly and sent away if not agreed to.

> The author says Muslims should be treated with respect. Do you think expecting them to give up their religious belief and "dress as Americans" is respectful?

Enduring oil boycotts

Now … !!! You must be thinking that the Muslims will not stand still for this. After all it is blatant discrimination. You are right. There will be a furious reaction from the Muslim world. They will immediately cut off oil shipments to our two nations. For America, that means 40% of our oil is gone. For England it is not so bad; they will be cut off as well, but they have the huge North Sea basin to use. Some of that surplus oil they were selling to us and may still be able to help. But we will feel the crunch yesterday. Are we so spoiled and soft that we cannot endure discomfort?

We can and should open the Arctic National Wildlife Refuge to drilling. But that will take years in order to make up for the Arab boycott. We can more quickly bring the wells in our own Midwest back on line to help in the crisis. We will pay dearly for our independence from Muslim oil, but that is much cheaper then having to accept a set of values the Muslim would force upon us. Make no mistake, we are in a religious war with the Islamic faith and it will be brutal. The first and most important thing is to recognize this, and then to realize that we might not have all of the luxuries we once had until the war is over.

> For an article about drilling for oil in the Arctic National Wildlife Refuge see Volume 14, International Development, Topic 14 Is the protection of indigenous people more important than economic growth?

Acknowledging America's friends

In America, we may not always realize what another nation is enduring in order to help our country. It should be hailed and admired in every medium that Great Britain has unselfishly tried to 'buddy' us in our hour of tragedy. It should also be recognized that Russia has adopted a much more conciliatory stance in deference to our needs. Even China is trying to remain neutral. This may be the opportune moment to re-align the power structure of the world. But, in any case let us be aware of what England has volunteered to us in an hour of crisis. And let us not try to disguise this power play as anything but a religious war. To do so would be very naive and will have devastating results. Remember, according to Islamic teaching we (meaning Western civilization) are the infidels.

> An "infidel" refers to a person who does not acknowledge your god. The term was coined in the 12th century by Christians as an equivalent for a word used by Muslims to describe nonbelievers at the time of the Crusades.

THE WRONG CHURCHES IN CHINA
Kevin Platt

Kevin Platt is a staff writer for the World Tibet Network News. He wrote this article in December 1999.

Falun Gong, also known as Falun Dafa, is a form of "qigong," an ancient art of exercising mind and body through meditation and special exercises. It differs from other forms of qigong by its emphasis on building moral character according to the principles taught by Falun Gong's founder, Li Hongzhi.

The last census conducted in China in 2000 reported the population to be nearly 1.3 billion. Independent estimates suggest that it is closer to 1.5 billion.

Is there a danger, as the author implies, that if governments have the right in principle to ban one religion, they could extend it to all other religions? Who would decide what religions were acceptable?

NO

X As the West prepares to celebrate the 2,000th anniversary of Jesus' birth, the leaders of the East's communist titan are marking the occasion by intensifying arrests of Christians across China.

The Communist Party is using a new law initially aimed at crushing the Falun Gong spiritual movement to provide cover for attacks on underground Christian groups, say Western diplomats and rights organizations.

Cracking down on Christians

Earlier this month, Beijing's top rulers branded 10 Christian sects as "cults," and "ordered the police to arrest the ringleaders of the groups," says Frank Lu, who heads a human rights watchdog based in Hong Kong.

Mr. Lu says more than 100 Christian leaders have already been rounded up in a nationwide crackdown in the past few weeks. He says the blacklisted fringe groups, with names such as The Shouters and Oriental Lightning, have never committed any acts of violence or shown other traits of groups that might be called cults in the West.

Lu says that "more than 40 million Chinese Christians worship in secret house churches to avoid the tight controls the government places on state-authorized churches," and adds all these followers could eventually be targeted in the current crackdown.

The party's moral legitimacy and popular belief in Communist ideology are evaporating, and Beijing's rulers fear the rise of any group that might claim the allegiance of the masses.

Chinese President "Jiang Zemin is personally leading the crusade against Falun Gong, and the clampdown is being accompanied by a pro-atheism campaign," says a Western diplomat.

The diplomat says that following the detention of tens of thousands of Falun Gong practitioners since a midsummer ban, "It was probably inevitable that the crackdown would be extended to other religions." He says "beatings and arrests are being carried out against Buddhist monks in Tibet, Protestant house churches in Henan Province, and Catholics in Hebei.

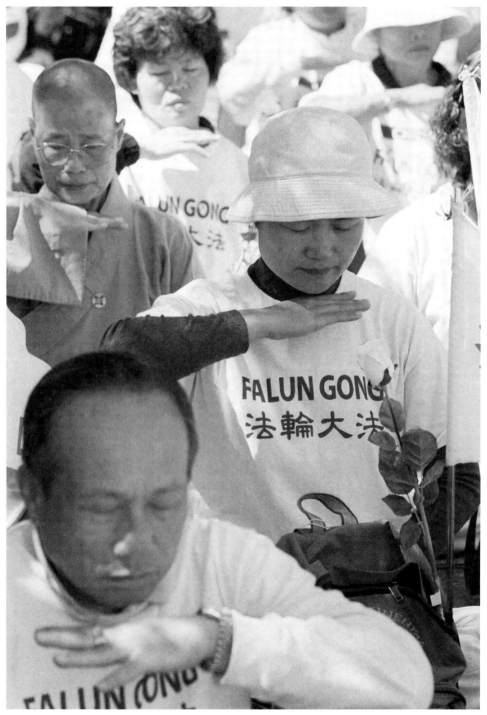

Demonstrators meditate near the United Nations' building in New York to protest China's banning of the spiritual movement Falun Gong.

This religious crackdown is all about independent organizations becoming alternative sources of power," he adds.

Dogma against dogma

A liberal, midlevel official in the Communist Party says he opposes but understands the ongoing battle to stop the spread of Christianity and other religions here.

"The Party saw the Catholic Church join with the Solidarity workers' movement to topple communism in Poland in the 1980s, and it doesn't want to see the same thing happen here," he says.

In its first report on religious freedom and repression worldwide, the US State Department said that Chinese leaders "perceive unregulated religious gatherings as a potential challenge to their authority ... and an alternative to communist dogma." The State Department recently informed Congress that it would continue a ban on the sale of crime-control equipment to China unless Beijing's "serious violations of religious freedoms" cease.

To curtail religious practices, the party and police used "prolonged detention, torture, and reeducation of Tibetan monks and nuns ... [and] some Protestant and Catholic Christians," the department said in a notice to Congress.

Liu Nanhai, a legal scholar at the Chinese Academy of Social Sciences, a government think-tank, says "China is outraged that the US is trying to interfere in our sovereign affairs by imposing sanctions for so-called violations of religious freedoms here." Mr. Liu says "Washington is using US standards on religion to judge us, and is trying to use American law to police the rest of the world."

Meeting Western standards

But an American official here who asked not to be identified says the US is "trying to hold China up to its commitments under the UN's Universal Declaration of Human Rights and Covenant on Civil and Political Rights," which Beijing signed last year. Both those documents provide guarantees on freedom of belief, but China is strengthening rather than abolishing its controls on churches, temples, and mosques. Beijing's rubber-stamp parliament passed new laws on "The Crime of Organizing or Using Evil Religions" in October.

The law defines evil religions as "illegal organizations that use religion, qigong, or other labels to deify their founders, spread superstition and heresy to misguide others, or lead members to endanger society." The vague law "is aimed at

Go to http://countrystudies.us/poland/39.htm for more information about the Polish Catholic Church and the Solidarity movement.

Go to http://www.state.gov/g/drl/rls/irf/2003/index.htm for the 2003 International Religious Freedom Report by the State Department.

The manufacture of "crime control equipment," such as leg irons and electroshock weapons, is big business. Human rights groups say such equipment is used in torture. U.S. companies manufacture and export it even though much of it is illegal in the United States.

For an explanation of "qigong" see the first sidebar on page 52.

putting a legal veneer on a party-ordered attack on religious groups," says the Western diplomat.

The government estimates that China now has 100 million Buddhists, 18 million Muslims, 15 million Protestants, and 4 million Catholics who belong to the sanctioned churches. In its report on religious freedom, the State Department estimates that about 10 million Catholics and 30 to 80 million Protestants worship in house churches.

The report adds that "in certain localities, as many as 20 to 25 percent of party officials may engage in religious activities." This year, Beijing issued an order to its 60 million Communist Party members to abandon religious beliefs, reminding the 2.5-million-strong Army that it is illegal for soldiers to take part in any religious activities.

Lu says that "if the new law and order to arrest members of underground churches is applied across the country, China is going to have to start building a lot of new labor camps to hold all these Christians."

"House churches" are independent groups of lay people who meet in homes, restaurants, parks, and elsewhere. They have no central church organization and no professional clergy preaching to an assembled congregation. This resembles the way early Christians and other persecuted religions have met.

Summary

Dick O'Connor, the author of the first article, believes that a religion should be outlawed if its followers are "treasonous" and trying to destroy the government. In his view present "liberal/socialist utopian" laws cannot cope with the radical face of Islam. Therefore the United States and Britain need to expel foreign religious leaders who preach hatred of their host nations, return foreign terrorist suspects to their countries of origin, close all mosques and Islamic schools, and force American and British Muslims to renounce Islam; if they do not, they should also be expelled. O'Connor admits that such action is discriminatory and would lead to outrage and the possible loss of oil imports from Arab nations, but he concludes that any negative fallout from a ban on Islam would be a small price to pay for no longer having to tolerate the "violence of Islam."

In the second article Kevin Platt uses the example of legislation in China to demonstrate how government action to outlaw one spiritual movement can lead to human rights violations against worshipers of it and other religions. In 1999 Beijing's communist rulers passed a law against the "crime of organizing and using evil religions." Although the legislation was ostensibly enacted to outlaw only Falun Gong, it has led to a general crackdown on "unregulated" religions, including Christianity and Buddhism in Tibet. Platt quotes Hong Kong-based human rights activist Frank Lu, who believes that the legislation has little to do with taking action against cults that might pose a danger to society. Rather, it is about targeting religious organizations that are rapidly becoming a source of power and hence pose a threat to the communist regime, whose legitimacy is increasingly questioned.

FURTHER INFORMATION:

Books:

Hammond, Phillip E., *With Liberty for All: Freedom of Religion in the United States*. Louisville, KY: Westminster/John Knox Press, 1998.

Jenkins, Philip, *Mystics and Messiahs: Cults and New Religions in American History*. Oxford, OH: Oxford Press, 2001.

Useful websites:

http://www.abpnews.com/abpnews/story.cfm?newsId=4074
Article discussing banning of religious symbols in schools.
http://www.falundafa.org/eng/index_en.htm
Site of the Falun Gong or Falun Dafa religion.
http://religiousfreedom.lib.virginia.edu
Site investigating religious freedom around the world.

The following debates in the Pro/Con series may also be of interest:

In this volume:
Topic 13 Does Islam condone terrorism?

Part 3: Religion in the United States

In *The Constitution*:
Topic 9 Does the Constitution protect religious freedom?

SHOULD GOVERNMENTS HAVE THE RIGHT TO OUTLAW RELIGIONS?

YES: Most cults operate outside accepted social, religious, and cultural conventions. They are therefore a potential threat to the existing social order.

YES: Governments are elected bodies and as such always act in the best interests of the people they serve. They would not waste money or resources to ban something that is not a threat.

CULTS
Should cults be banned?

DANGER?
Should governments have the power to decide if a religion is acceptable or not?

NO: Many accepted religions were once seen as dangerous cults because their followers believed in something other than the accepted religion. This is a natural stage of religious development.

SHOULD GOVERNMENTS HAVE THE RIGHT TO OUTLAW RELIGIONS?

KEY POINTS

NO: Governments that do have the authority to outlaw certain religions have shown how they can abuse this right. In China, for example, Falun Gong has been banned, even though many argue that it is a peaceful religion.

YES: Some "doomsday" cults engage in terrorism to hasten an apocalyptic end to the world. Violence is part of their belief system, which makes them a clear danger to society.

YES: Any religious group or movement whose followers engage in violent or terrorist activities should be banned to protect society. They are breaking the law and should be punished.

RELIGION AND TERRORISM
Should governments ban religions involved in violence or terrorism?

NO: Legislation to outlaw a particular cult or religion might threaten the rights of conscience of people who belong to entirely innocent religious or spiritual groups

NO: All religious texts are open to interpretation. It is inevitable that a small minority will misinterpret the Bible, the Koran, and other texts to condone their actions.

THE CHURCH OF SCIENTOLOGY

"A civilization without insanity, without criminals, and without war, where the able can prosper, and honest beings can have rights, and where man is free to rise to greater heights, are the aims of scientology."

—L. RON HUBBARD (1911–1986), FOUNDER

The Church of Scientology has more than 3,200 missions in over 150 countries. It has millions of followers throughout the world, including well-known celebrities like Tom Cruise and John Travolta. Supporters claim that scientology has cured problems ranging from dyslexia and drug abuse to personal crises. Critics, however, believe that it is at best a cult and at worst a money-making scam that deceives and sometimes harms the individuals that follow it.

L. Ron Hubbard and scientology

In 1950 L. Ron Hubbard, a genre-fiction writer, published the bestselling *Dianetics: The Modern Science of Mental Health*, which sought to answer often-asked but previously unanswered philosophical questions such as "What causes humans to behave as they do?" He began to teach dianetics—a form of spiritual healing—and established a foundation. In 1952 Hubbard developed "scientology"—derived from the Latin *scio*, which means "knowing in the fullest sense of the word," and the Greek *logos*, meaning "study of" or literally "knowing how to know." Scientologists define their "religious philosophy" as "the study and handling of the spirit in relationship to itself, universes, and other life."

Scientologists believe in humankind's inherent goodness. They argue that humans develop according to the extent to which they retain their spiritual integrity and values. People are honest and decent; but when this is sacrificed, humans deteriorate. Scientology aims to help people sort out their problems and improve their lives. Many followers argue that scientology, which endorses programs to improve the human condition, has helped change their lives for the better. But if that is so, why has scientology been so heavily criticized?

Definitions

Part of the problem may lie in its definition. Is scientology a science, a religion, or a cult? In 1953 Hubbard established the Church of Scientology. Scientologists claim that they follow a religion because they believe in an ultimate reality, such as a supreme being or eternal truth, that "transcends the here and now of the secular world." Critics, however, view the church with suspicion. Scientology has been investigated in many countries. In 1963, for example, the Food and Drug Administration (FDA) raided the church's office in Washington, D.C. In 1965 the Australian Board of Inquiry proposed banning scientology; there were similar moves in England, where Hubbard lived for several years. Greece, South Africa, New Zealand, and Germany (see below) are also among the countries that have investigated the legitimacy of scientology.

Claims against scientology

Critics allege that the Church of Scientology brainwashes its followers, uses intimidation and threats, and does everything possible to discredit its critics, often by exposing any problems in their past. The use of "disconnection" in scientology has also been criticized. This is the practice of severing ties between scientology members and their family, friends, and colleagues. Critics believe the church isolates members, making them overly dependent on it. Supporters respond that scientology helps dispel negative influences, including physically or mentally abusive partners, and therefore is of benefit to members.

The relationship between Narcoron and scientology is another controversial issue. Narcoron is a drug-rehabilitation program that relies on the use of vitamins and sauna sessions in quantities much greater than many believe are medically acceptable. Although Narcoron advertises a success rate of over 70 percent, critics argue that there is no reliable evidence to support this claim.

Celebrity involvement in the church has brought further criticism. Hubbard formed the Celebrity Church International, which specializes in scientology for celebrities. He believed that artists enrich society and deserve the best care possible. Skeptics, however, say that Hubbard was a starstruck money-grabber.

THE CHURCH AND GERMANY: THE 1997 ADVERTISEMENT

In 1997 a full-page advertisement appeared in *The International Herald Tribune* newspaper. Costing around $56,000, it was signed by 34 members of Hollywood's elite, ranging from director Oliver Stone to actor Dustin Hoffman. It criticized the German Chancellor Helmut Kohl for his government's "shameful pattern of organized persecution" of the Church of Scientology. The campaign was conceived by Tom Cruise's lawyer, Bertram Fields, who said that he became concerned when the youth wing of the Christian Democratic Union, Chancellor Kohl's party, called for a boycott of *Mission Impossible* because of Cruise's links to scientology. The ad controversially stated, "In the 1930s, it was the Jews. Today it is the Scientologists." The comparison to the Holocaust offended many readers; others questioned the fact that it ignored the controversy over scientology itself. A 1991 *Time* cover story, for example, had alleged that the church was a "hugely profitable global racket" that survived "by intimidating members and critics in a Mafia-like manner."

MORALITY AND ETHICS

Morality and ethics are the codes of values on which societies are based. They underlie individual and community notions of right and wrong, or acceptable and unacceptable, behavior. Although many aspects of morality are shared with or reflect religious beliefs, they are not necessarily the same thing. Many people with no religious faith have strict moral standards that they apply to themselves and others; such morals do not necessarily require a belief in a supreme deity. They are a guide to behavior rather than a statement of faith or belief. There are also some questions on which religious teachings provide no specific guidance, partly because in many cases the texts on which they are based originated in the ancient world. Such topics include the development of genetic engineering in the late 20th century or even the eating of meat, which many vegetarians consider immoral, but which is condemned by few major religions.

A matter of conscience?

Morality is considered a matter for individuals, or what is known as an issue of conscience in many nations, both those that have official religions, and those, such as the United States, that do not. In most cases in which a behavior is not deemed illegal, each person is free to make decisions about his or her own behavior and what is or is not acceptable. Although such things as drunk driving and drink-fueled violence are illegal in most countries, most western nations make no rules about whether adults should drink alcohol. It is for citizens to decide whether or not they want to drink and or to get drunk. Some religions do condemn drinking alcohol as immoral, however. Countries with legal systems based on Islam, for example, often forbid the consumption of alcohol or in certain cases limit it to foreigners only.

Although morality is concerned with the behavior of individuals, it also provides the basis for social organization. It is essential for social stability that everyone has largely the same attitudes about what is and is not acceptable. The idea that neighbors should be considerate to their neighbors by, for example, not playing loud music in the middle of the night is a common one. The arrival in an area of someone who does not agree soon causes problems and tension.

Helping young children acquire the moral system that shapes a particular culture is an important part of most education systems. Even preschoolers are taught that it is wrong to lie or to steal—even in circumstances in which lying or stealing might actually benefit them as individuals. In this way societies reinforce their own moral systems and ensure that most citizens conform to them.

In some cases morality takes the form of easily expressed guidelines that often share their sentiments and even their form with religious teaching, such as "Do unto others what you would have them do unto you." Such guidelines are useful because they provide yardsticks for people to judge how to behave even in situations that they have not directly encountered.

The dividing line between morality and religion is sometimes quite blurred because they share so many fundamental principles about what is right and what is wrong. There are those who believe that religious abortion is wrong. Many religions outlaw abortion altogether or place strict limitations on the circumstances under which it is acceptable. Some religious advocates argue that all life is sacred, and that abortion is murder; this attitude infuriates women's and civil rights groups, among others, who argue that abortion is not a religious issue. Topic 6 examines whether it is or is not.

Many religions also believe that using contraception is wrong. It is possible to characterize this question as essentially a debate between a religious viewpoint that sees the use of contraception as

---

"Morality is the theory that every human act must be either right or wrong, and that 99 percent of them are wrong."
—H.L. MENCKEN (1880–1956), U.S. JOURNALIST AND CRITIC

---

teaching provides the yardstick for all morality by defining what behavior is acceptable to God. There are others who maintain that on the contrary, religions embody morality that was evolved by human societies as the best basis for communal living. In their view morality owes more to the need for survival than to the teachings of any deity. They see religions as a codification and explanation of rules for living that already existed. Topic 5 looks at whether religion and morality are linked further.

Personal choice

A criticism frequently leveled at many established religions is that they are intolerant and limit a person's right to make certain choices. One of the most controversial issues raised is whether interfering with humankind's God-given duty to procreate and a more personal decision that involves perhaps lifestyle choices or health considerations. Topic 7 looks at this question.

Changes in society

In today's society increasing numbers of people are choosing either not to get married at all or to end their marriages if they do not work out. Many established religions, however, frown on divorce. Incidences of adultery—a married person having sexual relations with someone who is not his or her spouse—have increased. Adultery is still, however, illegal in a number of places. Topic 8 asks if this should be the case. Topic 9 considers whether divorce is acceptable or whether it is a sign of social decline.

Topic 5
IS MORALITY POSSIBLE WITHOUT A RELIGIOUS BASIS?

YES
FROM "MORALITY REQUIRES GOD ... OR DOES IT?"
FREE INQUIRY, VOL. 17, NO. 3
THEODORE SCHICK, JR.

NO
FROM "MORALITY WITHOUT GOD: A HOUSE BUILT ON SAND"
REASON & REVELATION, NOVEMBER 1995, 15[11]:86
GARRY K. BRANTLEY

INTRODUCTION

Morality is a code of conduct that establishes accepted notions of right and wrong. It is the set of rules created and shared by a society that allows each individual to make decisions about whether particular actions are right or wrong. Although many nonreligious people have a highly developed sense of right and wrong, morality often appears to have a basis in religious teaching; in turn, it often provides the basis for legal codes.

Many people believe that it is necessary for citizens to follow the same moral code, otherwise society would almost certainly descend into chaos. But moral and legal codes do not always correspond: It is widely accepted as being morally wrong to take a life, for example, yet killing is acceptable in certain situations such as war, and some U.S. states have a death penalty for certain crimes. Abortion, meanwhile, is legal in many places, but some people believe that it is immoral.

The moral codes of different societies may also conflict. Islamic and Judaic ritual law, for example, have rules for the live slaughter of food animals that many people in the West believe are immoral since they involve suffering on the part of the animal, which is bled while it is still alive.

Most religions lay down codes of right behavior for their worshipers. In Christianity the most concise version of such codes is the Ten Commandments laid out in the books of Exodus and Deuteronomy. They include injunctions of things that worshipers should do— they should honor their parents—and things that are forbidden, such as committing murder or adultery, or giving false evidence. The Five Pillars of Islam and the Vinaya of Buddhism are similar guidelines for living a devout life within the respective faiths.

Many religious adherents see it as vital that morality has a basis in faith. In some cases they argue that the tenets of religious morality are based on divine rule and are therefore nonnegotiable. In others they propose that the rules of behavior enshrined in religions have been tried and tested over centuries or millennia. They assert that a society abandons such well-proven codes at its peril, and that when society adopts moral tenets that do not have a basis in religion, the result is social decay. For such people the secularization of morality in the 20th century has created a world in which, for example, abortion, teenage pregnancy, and sexually transmitted diseases are the result of greater social acceptance of promiscuous behavior that is frowned on in most religions.

"Morality knows nothing of geographical boundaries or distinctions of race."

—HERBERT SPENCER (1820–1903), ENGLISH PHILOSOPHER

Some observers and policymakers, however, believe that social morality not only *can* be divorced from religion but that it actually *should* be. They argue that religious values are often so absolute that they do not allow moral systems to change to reflect changes in society. In their view a religious-based condemnation of an alcoholic as a sinner, for example, is not an adequate response to a problem that is now widely seen as a medical condition. Numerous religious teachings condemn homosexuality or divorce, but for many people—including those who follow religions—such subjects are

matters for the conscience or morality of individuals. Society, in the shape of either religion or government, should not become involved.

People who believe that morality does not have to be based on religion—including many notable philosophers throughout history—argue that there are plenty of people who are not religious but who are still highly moral in their behavior. They also argue that patterns of right and wrong must have existed in early societies before religions evolved that laid down prescriptive rules of behavior. In their view, therefore, morality is an inherent part of society. It either reflects some kind of innate knowledge of right and wrong with which people are born, or it represents a code of values that have evolved in order to allow society to exist. People largely agree that murder and robbery are wrong, for example: Allowing them undermines the personal safety and property on which stable civilizations are based. That such behaviors are also condemned by the world's great religions suggests more, they argue, that religious teachings reflect human morality than that human morality reflects religious considerations.

In 2002 a Pew Research Center survey showed that about half of Americans believe that people have to believe in God in order to be moral; about the same number, however, see this view as being incompatible with the modern world. They believe that it would be unconstitutional to impose a religiously based moral code on society.

The two articles that follow address some of the key issues in this debate.

MORALITY REQUIRES GOD ... OR DOES IT?
Theodore Schick, Jr.

Theodore Schick,
Jr., is head
of the faculty of
philosophy at
Muhlenberg
College,
Pennsylvania. This
article was
published in 1997
in Free Inquiry, the
quarterly journal of
the Council for
Secular Humanism.

YES

Although Plato demonstrated the logical independence of God and morality over 2,000 years ago in the *Euthyphro*, the belief that morality requires God remains a widely held moral maxim. In particular, it serves as the basic assumption of the Christian fundamentalist's social theory. Fundamentalists claim that all of society's ills—everything from AIDS to out-of-wedlock pregnancies—are the result of a breakdown in morality and that this breakdown is due to a decline in the belief of God. Although many fundamentalists trace the beginning of this decline to the publication of Charles Darwin's *The Origin of Species* in 1859, others trace it to the Supreme Court's 1963 decision banning prayer in the classroom. In an attempt to neutralize these purported sources of moral decay, fundamentalists across America are seeking to restore belief in God by promoting the teaching of creationism and school prayer.

Divine Command Theory

The belief that morality requires God is not limited to theists, however. Many atheists subscribe to it as well. The existentialist Jean-Paul Sartre, for example, says that "If God is dead, everything is permitted." In other words, if there is no supreme being to lay down the moral law, each individual is free to do as he or she pleases. Without a divine lawgiver, there can be no universal moral law.

The view that God creates the moral law is often called the "Divine Command Theory of Ethics." According to this view, what makes an action right is that God wills it to be done. That an agnostic should find this theory suspect is obvious, for, if one doesn't believe in God or if one is unsure which God is the true God, being told that one must do as God commands will not help one solve any moral dilemmas. What is not so obvious is that theists should find this theory suspect, too, for it is inconsistent with a belief in God. The upshot is that both the fundamentalists and the existentialists are mistaken about what morality requires.

To better understand the import of the Divine Command Theory, consider the following tale. It seems that, when Moses came down from the mountain with the ... Ten

Commandments, his followers asked him what they revealed about how they should live their lives. Moses told them, "I have some good news and some bad news."

"Give us the good news first," they said.

"Well, the good news," Moses responded, "is that he kept the number of commandments down to ten."

"Okay, what's the bad news?" they inquired.

"The bad news," Moses replied, "is that he kept the one about adultery in there."

The point is that, according to Divine Command Theory, nothing is right or wrong unless God makes it so. Whatever God says goes. So if God had decreed that adultery was permissible, then adultery would be permissible.

Let's take this line of reasoning to its logical conclusion. If the Divine Command Theory were true, then the Ten Commandments could have gone something like this: "Thou shalt kill everyone you dislike. Thou shalt rape every woman you desire. Thou shalt steal everything you covet...." The reason that this is possible is that killing, raping, [and] stealing … were not wrong before God made them so....

Many would consider this a *reductio ad absurdum* of the Divine Command Theory, for it is absurd to think that such wanton killing, raping, [and] stealing … could be morally permissible. Moreover, to believe that God could have commanded these things is to destroy whatever grounds one might have for praising or worshiping him....

> The Latin phrase reductio ad absurdum *translates as "reduction to the absurd." In terms of presenting an argument it means to make a point — with which you do not agree— seem ridiculous by taking it to its logical conclusion.*

The arbitrary lawgiver

Leibniz's [*Discourse on Metaphysics*] point is that, if things are neither right nor wrong independently of God's will, then God cannot choose one thing over another *because* it is right. Thus, if he does choose one over another, his choice must be arbitrary. But a being whose decisions are arbitrary is not a being worthy of worship.

The fact that Leibniz rejects the Divine Command Theory is significant, for he is one of the most committed theists in the Western intellectual tradition. He argues at great length that there must be an all-powerful, all-knowing, and all-good God and consequently that this must be the best of all possible worlds, for such a God could create nothing less. Ever since Voltaire lampooned this view in *Candide*, it has been difficult to espouse with a straight face. Nevertheless, what Leibniz demonstrates is that, far from being disrespectful or heretical, the view that morality is independent of God is an eminently sensible and loyal one for a theist to hold....

> Gottfried Wilhelm von Leibniz (1646–1716) was a German scholar. In 1686 he published his Discourse on Metaphysics, a philosophical work.

> Voltaire, the pen name of François Marie Arouet de Voltaire (1694–1778), was a French philosopher and author. His satirical novel Candide was published in 1759.

[A] Divine Command theorist might try to deny that the situation described above is possible. He might argue, for example, that God would never condone such killing, raping, [and] stealing … for God is all-good. But to make such a claim is to render the theory vacuous. The Divine Command Theory is a theory of the nature of morality. As such, it tells us what makes something good by offering a definition of morality. But if goodness is a defining attribute of God, then God cannot be used to define goodness, for, in that case, the definition would be circular—the concept being defined would be doing the defining—and such a definition would be uninformative. If being all-good is an essential property of God, then all the Divine Command Theory tells us is that good actions would be willed by a supremely good being. While this is certainly true, it is unenlightening. For it does not tell us what makes something good and hence does not increase our understanding of the nature of morality.

> The author anticipates the likely opposing arguments and undertakes a step-by-step logical destruction of each of them. This is a good way to discredit your opponent.

The Divine Command dilemma

A Divine Command theorist might try to avoid this circularity by denying that goodness is a defining attribute of God. But this would take him from the frying pan into the fire, for if goodness is not an essential property of God, then there is no guarantee that what he wills will be good. Even if God is all-powerful and all-knowing, it does not follow that he is all-good, for, as the story of Satan is supposed to teach us, one can be powerful and intelligent without being good. Thus the Divine Command Theory faces a dilemma: if goodness is a defining attribute of God, the theory is circular, but if it is not a defining attribute, the theory is false. In either case, the Divine Command Theory cannot be considered a viable theory of morality.

> Although often used to mean simply a problem or predicament, the word dilemma has a more specific, technical sense in which it means a choice between two (or more) solutions, neither (or none) of which is appealing.

The foregoing considerations indicate that it is unreasonable to believe that an action is right because God wills it to be done. One can plausibly believe that God wills an action to be done because it is right, but to believe this is to believe that the rightness of an action is independent of God. In any event, the view that the moral law requires a divine lawgiver is untenable.

God the enforcer

There are those who maintain, however, that even if God is not required as the author of the moral law, he is nevertheless required as the enforcer of it, for without the threat of divine punishment, people will not act morally. But this position is no more plausible than the Divine Command Theory itself.

In the first place, as an empirical hypothesis about the psychology of human beings, it is questionable. There is no unambiguous evidence that theists are more moral than nontheists. Not only have psychological studies failed to find a significant correlation between frequency of religious worship and moral conduct, but convicted criminals are much more likely to be theists than atheists.

Second, the threat of divine punishment cannot impose a moral obligation, for might does not make right. Threats extort; they do not create a moral duty. Thus, if our only reason for obeying God is the fear of punishment if we do not, then, from a moral point of view, God has no more claim to our allegiance than Hitler or Stalin.

Moreover, since self-interest is not an adequate basis for morality, there is reason to believe that heaven and hell cannot perform the regulative function often attributed to them. Heaven and hell are often construed as the carrot and stick that God uses to make us toe the line. Heaven is the reward that good people get for being good, and hell is the punishment that bad people get for being bad. But consider this. Good people do good because they want to do good— not because they will personally benefit from it or because someone has forced them to do it. People who do good solely for personal gain or to avoid personal harm are not good people. Someone who saves a drowning child, for example, only because he was offered a reward or was physically threatened does not deserve our praise. Thus, if your only reason for performing good actions is your desire to go to heaven or your fear of going to hell—if all your other-regarding actions are motivated purely by self-interest— then you should go to hell because you are not a good person. An obsessive concern with either heaven or hell should actually lessen one's chances for salvation rather than increase them.

Conclusion

Fundamentalists correctly perceive that universal moral standards are required for the proper functioning of society. But they erroneously believe that God is the only possible source of such standards. Philosophers as diverse as Plato, Immanuel Kant, John Stuart Mill, George Edward Moore, and John Rawls have demonstrated that it is possible to have a universal morality without God. Contrary to what the fundamentalists would have us believe, then, what our society really needs is not more religion but a richer notion of the nature of morality.

An "empirical" hypothesis or explanation is one that can be backed up by observable evidence, in contrast to a hypothesis, which works in theory only.

Do you believe that people have an instinctive desire to do good? When you have to make a decision based on right and wrong, what guidelines do you use to help you decide?

Go to http://www. scholiast.org/ history/histphil.html for links to information on all these famous philosophers.

MORALITY WITHOUT GOD: A HOUSE BUILT ON SAND
Garry K. Brantley

Garry K. Brantley is an author and senior minister at CrossBridge Church of Christ, Birmingham, Alabama. Reason and Revelation, in which this article was published in 1995, is the monthly journal of Apologetics Press, Inc., a publishing house that specializes in Christian literature.

NO

The creation–evolution controversy involves more than a clinically detached discussion of fossils and cosmological theories. The debate inevitably touches each of us on a deeply personal level. Our view of origins is linked inexorably to our own self-concept and how we define our purpose in life. It further exerts a dominating influence on our personal standard of morality. And, despite their opposing philosophical/theological orientations, both theists and atheists agree that some things are "good" or "right," while other things are "evil" or "wrong."

To issue such ethical judgments implies a supreme standard that is both objective and absolute. And, regardless of one's world view, his or her behavior will be directed by some guiding ethical principle. Christians find their highest ethical directive from the personal God of the Bible, while Muslims appeal to Allah's will as expressed in the Koran. Though atheists reject a theistic moral authority, their lives, nonetheless, are governed by some supreme ethical principle. Whether the governing principle is "live and let live," "the good of the many outweighs the good of the few," or "there are no moral absolutes," etc., each serves as the adherents' ultimate standard for personal ethics. Thus, while we might argue over what should serve as our absolute ethical norm, we all acknowledge that there is such an authoritative principle governing our behavior. The question now becomes, "Why do human beings accept as authoritative an absolute moral principle for their lives?"

In response to this question, John Frame has suggested that, ultimately, "the source of absolute moral authority is either personal or impersonal." Which of these two options better explains humankind's sense of moral obligation?

John M. Frame is a theologian and author whose books include Apologetics to the Glory of God: An Introduction, published in 1994. According to www.apologetics index.org, apologetics is "the logical presentation and defense of the Christian faith." Visit the website for a fuller explanation.

An impersonal source?
Atheists, who reject the idea of a personal Creator, contend that the Universe is a natural artifact, and offer purely naturalistic explanations for its existence. To be consistent with this cosmological position, atheists must also attribute

humankind's sense of moral obligation to impersonal, naturalistic processes. Yet, what type of impersonal structure can both create and demand compliance to ethical mandates? What kind of ethical guidance could we determine from the fortuitous combination of subatomic particles? How could blind, purposeless chance demand our ethical allegiance?

Rather than appealing to unpredictable chance, some atheists have attempted to structure their model of morality on the mandates of impersonal, natural laws. Accordingly, "just as what goes up 'must' come down" in the physical realm, there are similar "musts" in the moral realm. The difficulty with this approach to morality is its inability to explain adequately the sense of obligation that is characteristic of moral systems. For, not only do atheists and theists agree that some things are "good" while others are "bad," they also recognize that there are some things that we "ought" and "ought not" do. Yet, how can an impersonal source of moral value explain this obligatory impulse common to humankind? Organic evolution's purposeless, impersonal force that somehow optimizes the preservation of the species is inadequate to create a sense of "ought" in the species it allegedly preserves. In fact, it might be "right" and "noble" to *resist* such a force, especially if we perceive that it is forcing *Homo sapiens sapiens* into extinction. Our personal sense of self-preservation would prompt such a legitimate resistance to the ominous "force."

Or a personal source?

Obviously, appealing to an impersonal source for an authoritative ethical value has insurmountable difficulties. In reality, the basis for morality derives ultimately from personal relationships. Why do we feel obligated to remunerate someone who has performed a service for us? While there may be other factors at work (e.g., civil law with its threat of litigation, family values, etc.), the sense of "ought" in this regard ultimately stems from a previously forged agreement between two persons, both of whom recognize the other as a person. In such a personal arena, the sense of moral obligation is created. Of course, our obligation to pay our bills for services performed is not absolute. We might refuse to pay the full price for substandard work. In that case, a higher moral arbiter, the court, might be involved. But even the court's moral authority is not absolute for it, too, operates according to some guiding principle of ethical value (e.g., "justice for all"). Regardless of our particular place in the hierarchy of moral arbitration, there is a universal

Like the previous author, Brantley employs a form of reductio ad absurdum, in this case implying that a universe without God is nothing but an accident of physics. Does the technique help him make his point?

Homo sapiens is the scientific name for the human species. The species is divided into two subspecies—Homo sapiens sapiens (modern humans) and the now extinct Homo sapiens neandertalensis (Neanderthal man). See Volume 17, New Science, Topic 3 Are Neanderthals related to humankind? for more information.

recognition of moral obligation (the "ought" factor). And
this recognition implies some absolute standard of morality—
a standard that can both create and rightly demand
compliance. Since an impersonal force cannot meet
these criteria, and since moral obligation is created in
personal relationships, it logically follows that the universal
sense of "ought" common to all ethical systems must stem
from an absolute personal Being.

A section of a fresco by Hippolyte Jean Flandrin (1809–1864) shows Adam and Eve facing God after they have fallen from grace in the Garden of Eden (Church of Saint-Germain-des-Prés, Paris).

Thus, the sense of moral obligation unique to the human species argues powerfully for the existence of the personal God of the Bible.... And, practically speaking, without such a standard the lines between "right" and "wrong" not only are blurred, but actually fade into non-existence. In the final analysis, the atheistic attempt to erect a moral superstructure apart from the existence of a personal God will suffer the same fate as a house built on sand—inevitably it will collapse.

The allusion to the house built on sand—which collapsed—is a reference to the parable of the wise and foolish builders (Matthew 7:24–27). A strong conclusion that captures your audience's attention is a good way to end your argument.

Summary

Theodore Schick, Jr., cites believers in God as well as nonbelievers to disprove that morality requires a religious authority. Initially, he outlines arguments for why the divine command theory of ethics—"the view that God creates the moral law"—cannot be viable. The contention here is that it is rationally impossible for God to be all-good without there being some notion of what is "good" separate from God's ethical directives. Schick goes on to argue that God is not even a successful enforcer of moral law. There is no evidence that believers are more moral than nonbelievers—quite the reverse, since criminals are more likely to be believers. He also points out what he sees as a contradiction in Christian morality: If a person is motivated by self-interest to do good—in terms of his or her desire to go to heaven rather than hell—then that person is not strictly moral or good and should really go to hell.

Christian minister Garry K. Brantley contends that "both theists and atheists agree that some things are 'good' or 'right,' while other things are 'evil' or 'wrong.'" He argues that this suggests that there is a "supreme standard." While atheists might argue for the existence of an impersonal moral authority in the form of the naturalistic processes of the cosmos, Brantley asks what ethical guidance can be obtained from a "combination of subatomic particles?" He also argues that impersonal or atheistic laws cannot explain the moral obligation most people feel to do the right thing—even when this might go against self-preservation or the preservation of the human species generally. In Brantley's view, therefore, moral obligation, although "created in personal relationships," "must stem from an absolute personal Being."

FURTHER INFORMATION:

Books:

Broom, Donald M., *The Evolution of Morality and Religion*. New York: Cambridge University Press, 2003.
George, Robert P., *The Clash of Orthodoxies: Law, Religion, and Morality in Crisis*. Wilmington, DE: ISI Books, 2001.
Grayling, A.C., *Meditations for the Humanist: Ethics for a Secular Age*. New York: Oxford University Press, 2002.
Noebel, David A., *The Battle for Truth*. Eugene, OR: Harvest House Publishers, 2001.

Useful websites:

http://www.christiancourier.com/penpoints/religionMorality.htm
"Religion and Morality" by Wayne Jackson.
www.secularhumanism.org
Site of the Council for Secular Humanism.

The following debates in the Pro/Con series may also be of interest:

In this volume:
Topic 3 Does organized religion stifle free thought?

Topic 14 Is the separation between church and state still necessary?

Topic 15 Should Christianity be the official religion of the United States?

IS MORALITY POSSIBLE WITHOUT A RELIGIOUS BASIS?

YES: People have an inherent sense of what is right and wrong; they are either born with this sense or develop it as a result of social conditioning

YES: The existence of a system of morals reflects the fact that people are naturally programmed to cooperate in order to survive

RELIABLE

Is morality possible without God?

EVOLUTION

Is morality the result of evolution?

NO: Morality that is not based on the absolutes of right and wrong laid down by God is purely personal and relative, which means that it is too weak to enforce positive behaviors

NO: The purely impersonal and naturalistic forces that must dominate a universe without God could not have instilled the sense of moral obligation that people generally feel

IS MORALITY POSSIBLE WITHOUT A RELIGIOUS BASIS?

KEY POINTS

YES: It means that if God willed that adultery or murder were permissible, for example, they would be permissible. Morality is not subject to divine whim.

YES: A person may rescue a drowning child with no thought for personal safety, for example: People are inherently good

PARADOXICAL

Is divine command theory an illogical basis for morality?

ALTRUISM

Are people naturally inclined to do good rather than bad?

NO: Because God is inherently good, there is no possibility that he would never sanction an action that was bad

NO: People tend to act from self-interest; in a Christian society that means that all good actions are ultimately conditioned by a fear of hell

Topic 6
IS ABORTION A RELIGIOUS ISSUE?

YES
"POPE CANONISES MOTHER WHO REFUSED ABORTION"
THE GUARDIAN, MAY 17, 2004
SOPHIE ARIE

NO
FROM "BEYOND APOCALYPSE AND APOLOGY: A MORAL DEFENSE OF ABORTION"
AMERICAN CIVIL LIBERTIES UNION
CAITLIN BORGMANN AND CATHERINE WEISS

INTRODUCTION

The issue of elective abortion—the premature expulsion of the fetus by artificially induced means—always causes much heated debate. Many people believe that artificially induced abortion—it also technically includes natural miscarriage—is fundamentally wrong. They believe that it goes against not only the teachings of most religions about the sanctity of life but also more general moral prohibitions on social behavior. Supporters of abortion, however, while they concede that the debate is highly complex, believe that religious objections to abortion are not valid because the fetus has not developed to any stage at which it could be considered to be an individual living being. Some go so far as to argue that there is a moral case in favor of abortion. The reproductive rights of the mother, from this point of view, should take precedence over those of a fetus that does not as yet possess the qualities of "life": consciousness, the ability to survive outside its mother, and so on.

Abortion has existed for millennia. From the ancient world onward the practice was accepted. It was often considered by women to be the only way that they could exercise any control over whether to have children that they might not be able to afford or that might be illegitimate and bring their mothers social ruin, for example. Some people also believed that abortion was justified since the fetus did not acquire a soul until its second trimester of development.

Abortion did not become a criminal offense in the United States until the 19th century. Some critics believe that the ban reflected less religious or moral grounds than the determination of U.S. doctors to take the practice of abortion away from the traditional healers who were often employed to carry it out. When abortion was permitted again after the landmark 1973 Supreme Court ruling in *Roe v. Wade*, doctors controled the abortion decision. The court ruled that abortion law infringed on a woman's constitutional right to privacy.

Most religions condemn abortion, although to different degrees. Some allow it in special circumstances, such as pregnancies resulting from rape or incest, or if the birth threatens the mother's life. The Christian Bible does not mention abortion directly, but the Sixth Commandment is "Thou shalt not kill." Many Christians believe that this covers abortion since they view the fetus as a living being. The Catholic Church condemns all abortion as evil, while Eastern Orthodoxy teaches that abortion is the killing of a child. The Lutheran Church, however, argues that elective abortion is a sin except "in the tragic situation when it is necessary to save the life of a mother."

"There are a number of forces at work in our society that would try to turn back the clock and undermine a woman's right to choose...."
—HILLARY CLINTON (1947–),
SENATOR, NEW YORK

Islam also prohibits abortion apart from when the mother's life is in danger. In Islam the fetus is the creation of God, and no one, not even the mother, has the right to get rid of it under other circumstances. However, many Muslims believe that the soul does not enter the fetus until the fourth month of gestation, and abortion may be permitted before this.

Hindus consider life to be sacred from the moment of conception. The Hindu scriptures refer to abortion as "bhroona hathya," or "killing the undeveloped soul." The practice is again condemned unless the mother's life is in danger. Similarly, although Buddhists believe that an abortion involves taking a life, their religious leader, the Dalai Lama, says that decisions on abortion must be made on a case-by-case basis. In some instances the life of the mother, those of her other children, and their mental and physical well-being must take precedence.

In traditional Jewish law, however, the fetus is not a full human being and has no individual rights. Although Judaism does not sanction abortion on demand, it permits it in cases where not only the physical, but also the mental health of the mother is at risk.

Since 1973 U.S. law has treated abortion as a purely moral issue. There is considerable pressure to change this situation, however, particularly from the religious right. The passing of legislation protecting fetal rights, including the 2001 Unborn Victims of Violence Act, has worried civil rights advocates. Charges brought against pregnant women who have taken narcotics or behaved in ways deemed detrimental to their fetus also alarm them. They are anxious that pressure will eventually lead to abortion being made illegal again. In contrast to those who believe the rights of the fetus to be paramount, birth-control advocates argue that a woman should have ultimate control over her own body. Abortion is not an easy procedure, they claim, and women usually choose it when they feel that they have no other option. It is a difficult enough decision, they assert, without the additional pressure of religious guilt.

The following two extracts examine issues in the debate.

POPE CANONISES MOTHER WHO REFUSED ABORTION
Sophie Arie

Sophie Arie is a journalist for the British-based newspaper The Guardian. *This article was published in the May 17, 2004 edition.*

YES

☑ A mother who refused cancer treatment and died so her fourth child could be born was elevated to sainthood yesterday in a move seen by many as a strong statement from the Vatican against the legalisation of abortion.

Giana Beretta Molla
Pope John Paul II canonised Gianna Beretta Molla, along with five other men and women, before a crowd of 50,000 pilgrims in St Peter's square.

See box on page 78 for more details.

In 1961, doctors advised the 39-year-old paediatrician to abort her fourth child so an ovarian cyst could be removed. She refused, allowing the cyst to grow with the child, and died of the cancer a week after giving birth in 1962.

"I shall accept whatever they will do to me provided they save the child," she is reported to have said.

Pope praises sacrifice
As a giant colour photograph of a woman holding a child was unveiled on St Peter's Basilica, John Paul praised the exemplary mother, doctor and wife for her "extreme sacrifice".

"May our era rediscover, by the example of Gianna Beretta Molla, the pure, chaste and fertile beauty of conjugal love, lived as a response to the divine calling," he said.

First married woman saint in modern times
Beretta Molla is the first married woman to become a Catholic saint in modern times, according to the Vatican.

As a result, her widower, Pietro Molla, 91, was the first man to attend the canonisation of his wife. He is reported to have been overwhelmed by the emotion and the heat.

Beretta Molla's four children, including Gianna Emanuela, 41, for whom she died, were also present.

Some people believe that it is important for children to have two parents. Do you think Molla's actions were justified?

The Pope has described abortion as a "legalised crime" and a "kind of silent and cruel selection which unjustly eliminates the weakest members of society".

Millions have bought photographs of Gianna Beretta Molla with her baby.

COMMENTARY: Gianna Beretta Molla

On May 17, 2004, thousands of people attended the canonization of Gianna Beretta Molla, an Italian woman who rejected life-saving treatment in order to save the life of her unborn child. Molla is now patron of mothers and physicians, but her canonization has been contentious. She has been held up as a symbol of the antiabortion movement, but for others her canonization has set back abortion rights many years.

Background

One of 13 children, Gianna Beretta was born on October 4, 1922, in Magenta, near Milan, Italy, into a strict Catholic household. Along with her brothers and sisters she accompanied her parents to mass and communion each day. As a teenager Molla was a member of Catholic Action, a group of lay persons whose aim was to spread Christian values throughout society. When she was 15, Molla attended a retreat; she wrote a prayer that stated, "I promise You, Jesus, to submit myself to all that You permit to happen to me. Let me know Your Will." She also noted that she would "die rather than commit mortal sin." Her commitment to the Catholic Church was immense and unwaivering, some commentators have reported.

Molla studied medicine and surgery at the University of Pavia, specializing in pediatrics. She remained extremely committed to her religion but also enjoyed life—her interests included skiing and trekking. In 1955 Molla married Pietro Molla but decided to carry on her with her career. They had three healthy children: Pierluigi (1956), Mariolina (1957), and Laura (1959).

During her fourth pregnancy, at the age of 39, Molla discovered that she had developed a fibroma (a large ovarian tumor) in her uterus. The tumor required an operation, and Beretta was advised to have an abortion. She refused and before surgery pleaded with the surgeon to save her baby's life. She stated, "Yes, I have prayed so much in these days. With faith and hope I have entrusted myself to the Lord.... I trust in God, yes; but now it is up to me to fulfill my duty as a mother. I renew to the Lord the offer of my life. I am ready for everything, to save my baby." Both survived; but just days before the baby was due to be delivered in April 1962, she is reported to have said to her husband, "If you must decide between me and the baby, have no hesitation ... save him." Molla died days after giving birth.

Sainthood

In order to become a saint, two miracles need to be attributed to the person. Two Brazilian women are alleged to have been saved after nuns prayed to Molla. Pope John Paul II said, "The extreme sacrifice that took away her life is evidence that only those who have the courage to give themselves completely to God ... can fulfill themselves." His comments, however, drew criticism from many civil and women's rights groups.

How to become a saint

To become a saint, two miracles need to be attributed to the so-called "martyr of maternal love".

In 1977 a sickly Brazilian woman is said to have survived a dangerous labour after nuns prayed to Beretta Molla. In 2000, after similar prayers, another Brazilian woman gave birth to a healthy child despite having lost her amniotic fluid in the third month of pregnancy.

Criticism

Pro-choice campaigners have criticised the canonisation, saying it suggests the church values the life of an unborn child over the health and safety of women.

In the past Vatican officials have said that although the church admires women who sacrifice themselves to save a foetus, it does not oblige anyone to make this choice.

According to Father Brian Johnstone, a bioethics experts at Rome's Alphonsian Academy, the one situation in which Catholic teaching can tolerate the removal of a foetus is if the process is needed to save the mother's life.

Beretta Molla was the most modern of Sunday's new saints.

The other five were all 19th century figures: a Spanish priest, Josep Manyanet y Vives, Italians Luigi Orione, Hannibal Maria di Francia and Paola Elisabetta Cerioli, and a Lebanese Maronite priest, Naamatallah al-Hardini, who is said to have helped cure the lame.

The latest additions bring the Pope's "saint count" to 482, more saints than all the previous popes created together.

John Paul II, who turns 84 tomorrow, has specialised in turning "normal" people into saints.

Look at www.google.com to find out information about other saints with alleged healing powers. Do you think this undermines the importance of modern medicine?

Do you think the church should be able to canonize people for reasons such as this?

BEYOND APOCALYPSE AND APOLOGY: A MORAL DEFENSE OF ABORTION
Caitlin Borgmann and Catherine Weiss

Caitlin Borgmann is state strategies coordinator, and Catherine Weiss is director of the American Civil Liberties Union Reproductive Freedom Project, New York. This article was published in Perspectives on Sexual and Reproductive Health, January/ February 2003.

Around 20 percent of sexually active teenagers contract a sexually transmitted disease (STD). Go to Volume 11, Family and Society, Topic 11 Should teenagers have a right to contraception without parental consent?

Do the circumstances of conception make a difference to the permissibility of abortion? Isn't it always right or always wrong?

NO

... Abortion as a moral choice

... [A] realistic, direct defense ... [of legal abortion] documents the critical role that access to abortion has played in women's lives over the past 30 years. Rather than focusing on whether we are about to lose Roe altogether, it exposes, defends against and attempts to reverse the constant whittling away that diminishes the right to abortion every year. It focuses attention on the unfairness of laws that in effect deny this right to the most vulnerable women.

To defend abortion with confidence, we must first recognize that institutional opposition to the right is part of a broader campaign to undermine women's autonomy and equality. Antichoice leaders see sexuality (especially women's) divorced from procreation as shameful, women as inadequate to make weighty moral decisions and forced childbearing as appropriate punishment for sexual irresponsibility. They approve of requiring women to pay out of pocket for contraception, while ensuring that insurance plans cover men's access to Viagra; reducing sexuality education to a "just say no" mantra and consigning those teenagers who say yes to the deadly risks of unprotected sex; and denying poor women the means to obtain abortions, yet refusing to help them provide adequate food, shelter and education for the children they bear. Abortion is only one piece of the puzzle.

When this puzzle is assembled, the image that emerges is of a woman subjugated, not a fetus saved. For example, it is illuminating that "right-to-life" leaders generally tolerate abortion in cases of rape or incest. The fetus conceived by rape is biologically and morally indistinguishable from the fetus conceived by voluntary intercourse. But in the view of our opponents, the rape victim is innocent while the woman who chooses to have sex is tainted. For them, it is the woman's innocence or guilt that determines whether she should be allowed to have an abortion or forced to bear a child. The impulse to punish women rather than to help children is equally evident in the policies of antichoice states with regard to children already born. If the motivation behind abortion restrictions were really the love of babies, antichoice states should have child-friendly laws. Yet the opposite is so. A comprehensive review of the abortion and child welfare policies in the 50 states demonstrates that the states with the most restrictive abortion laws also spend the least to facilitate adoption, to provide subsistence to poor children and to educate children in general. The study concludes, "Pro-life states are less likely than pro-choice states to provide adequate care to poor and needy children. Their concern for the weak and vulnerable appears to stop at birth." The seemingly contradictory coexistence of "prolife" laws and antichild policies is explained, in significant part, by opposition to women's changing roles in society: The more hostile statewide public opinion is toward women's equality and the lower women's income is relative to men's, the more likely the state is both to restrict abortion and to impoverish children.

For more information on this survey go to pages 153–157 of J.R. Schroedel's Is the Fetus a Person? A Comparison of Policies across the Fifty States *(Ithaca, NY: Cornell University Press, 2000).*

In contrast, our position is prowoman, profamily, prochild and prochoice. This is a moral debate we must have and can win. Such a debate can move doubters to become moral defenders of a woman's decision to have an abortion. Even those who remain personally opposed to abortion may come to support each woman's right to make the decision in accordance with her own conscience, commitments and beliefs. What follows are some of the best reasons to support abortion rights.

Autonomy

A woman deciding whether to continue a pregnancy stands on moral ground. She is entitled to make her decision, and she must live with the consequences. No one else—and certainly not the government—should decide whether she will use her body to bring new life into the world. The decision is too intimate and too important to be taken from her. In everyday life, men and women make decisions that affect the life and death of existing people. They decide whether to join the army; whether to donate blood, a kidney or bone marrow to a child; whether to give money to Save the Children instead of buying a new sweater; whether to decline a lifesaving blood transfusion; whether to drive a small fort on wheels that may protect its passengers in a crash but often kills those in less-substantial vehicles. Few question adults' autonomy to make these decisions, although some may criticize the individual choice made. Yet, our opponents want a different standard to govern

Some people believe that governments should have the right to limit reproductive rights. Do you think this is a good idea?

Do fetuses have rights? And are they more important than the rights of the mother? Go to www.cnn.com and look up recent articles on this subject.

women's decisions about abortion. They portray women who demand the right to make this decision as selfish and immoral, although even many "prolifers" place fetuses on a lower moral plane than existing people (hence their tolerance of abortion in cases of rape and incest, among other inconsistencies). In response, we must staunchly defend women's ability and right to be moral actors, especially when they are making decisions about reproduction.

Equality

Without the right of reproductive choice, women cannot participate equally in the nation's social, political and economic life. Their freedom to decide whether and when to have children opens doors that would otherwise be closed. They may learn to be electricians, librarians, roofers, teachers or triathletes; care for their young children or aging parents; start and finish college; wait until they are financially and emotionally prepared to support a child; keep a steady job; marry if and when they want to.

Perspectives on sexual and reproductive health

Women still do the bulk of the work of raising children and caring for extended families. Whether they experience this work as a privilege, a necessity, a burden or all three, increasing their control over the scope and timing of these responsibilities can only help them to secure a more equal footing on whatever paths they travel. In fact, in countries throughout the world, women's desire and ability to limit the number of children they have go hand in hand with their educational advancement and economic independence....

Some countries—Iran and China, for example—have introduced population-control policies to limit the number of children women can have in the hope that this will help economic growth. Do you think this is right?

Bodily integrity

In virtually all other contexts, the law treats a person's body as inviolable. Prisoners are denied many of their most important personal liberties, yet are protected from unreasonable invasions of their bodies (such as routine body cavity searches). Similarly, the state cannot require a crime victim to undergo an operation to recover evidence (such as a bullet), even if that evidence would help to convict a murder suspect. And no law can force an unwilling parent to undergo bodily invasions far less risky than pregnancy (such as donating bone marrow) to save a living child....

Wantedness and welcome

The decision to have a child—even more than the decision to have an abortion—carries profound moral implications.

Unless a woman is willing to bear a child and give it up for adoption, she should have children when she feels she can welcome them. A mother's freedom to decide whether and when to have an additional child contributes immeasurably to the welfare of the children she already has, as well as any yet to be born. A teenager's decision to delay having a child until a time when she can provide adequate financial and emotional support increases the probability that when she does decide to have a family, it will be healthy and stable. Indeed, many women who decide not to have a child at a particular time do so out of reverence for children.

Do you think having the right to determine when people have children leads to better parents and happier children?

Personal and public health

Finally, the right to abortion promotes personal and public health. We know that criminal bans do not stop women from seeking abortions. The desperate measures women in pre-Roe days felt driven to take to terminate their unwanted pregnancies are testament to how untenable the prospect of childbearing can be. Access to safe, legal abortion ensures that women will not be maimed or killed when they decide they cannot continue a pregnancy. Similarly, access to safe abortion ensures that women can terminate pregnancies that endanger their health. A pregnant woman with a heart condition, uncontrolled hypertension, diabetes or one of a host of other problems must have all medically accepted options open to her. She, her loved ones and her doctor must be able to respond to shifting and serious health risks without having to consult a lawyer.

Roe v. Wade was a landmark case in abortion history. In 1973 the U.S. Supreme Court ruled that existing abortion law infringed on a woman's right to privacy under the Fourteenth Amendment and thus her right to abortion. Go to www.google.com and look up Roe v. Wade.

Conclusion

These reasons to support abortion rights are not new. All of them predate *Roe v. Wade*, some by centuries. Yet, as Roe turns 30 and continues its embattled advance toward middle age, these reasons are as pressing as ever. We state them in different ways to appeal to different audiences at different times, but all provide a basis for persuading people to stand behind abortion rights, both for themselves and for others....

Summary

Any discussion of abortion is an emotional one, causing strong reactions in the people taking part. The preceding two articles look at aspects of whether abortion is a religious issue. In the first journalist Sophie Arie examines the canonization by Pope John Paul II of Gianna Beretta Molla, an Italian woman who gave up her life to save her unborn child. Molla, whose life was dedicated to the Catholic Church, had said on several occasions that she would take whatever God gave to her and would give up her life rather than commit a mortal sin. When Molla found out that she had an ovarian tumor and was advised to have an abortion, she said, "I shall accept whatever they will do to me providing they save the child." The pope, Arie states, has made it clear that he thinks abortion is a "legalized crime" and a "silent and cruel selection which unjustly eliminates the weakest members of society."

Caitlin Borgmann and Catherine Weiss, however, claim that abortion is a moral issue rather than a religious one. It is thus a question of freedom of choice—whether or not to have an abortion is a decision a woman must make in accordance with her own conscience and beliefs. Any woman facing an unwanted or unhealthy pregnancy cannot have the decision to bear that child forced on her by another person, government, or any religious order since she will have to face the consequences alone. Other key issues in this respect are those of equality (women can never be equal in a society where they do not have the right to choose if and when they have children), bodily integrity, whether a child is wanted or not, and personal and public health. These issues should be taken into account when considering abortion.

FURTHER INFORMATION:

Books:

Beckman, Linda J., and S. Marie Harvey (eds.), *The Psychology Culture, and Politics of Abortion.* Washington, D.C.: American Psychological Association, 1998.

Risen, James, and Judy L. Thomas, *Wrath of Angels: The American Abortion Debate.* Boulder, CO: Perseus Books, 1999.

Useful websites:

http://www.aclu.org/ReproductiveRights/ ReproductiveRightslist.cfm?c=224
American Civil Liberties Union site (ACLU) on religious threats to reproductive rights.
http://www.religioustolerance.org/abortion.htm
Site looks at abortion from a religious angle. Examines viewpoints of different faiths.

The following debates in the Pro/Con series may also be of interest:

In this volume:
  Part 2: Morality and ethics, pages 60–61

  Topic 7 Is the use of contraception wrong?

In *Individual and Society*:
  Topic 15 Is abortion a right?

  Abortion in the United States, pages 201–202

IS ABORTION
A RELIGIOUS ISSUE?

YES: Although abortion is not against federal law, it clearly breaks religious and moral injunctions against taking life

YES: Women have the right to make a personal decision about their own bodies based on their own personal morality

CRIME
Is abortion a crime?

MORAL RIGHT
Is abortion a moral right?

NO: U.S. law defines abortion as a legal right, not a crime, and lays down strict guidelines to ensure its legal acceptability

NO: Personal values do not have the same weight as religious codes, which generally prohibit abortion as taking a human life

IS ABORTION A RELIGIOUS ISSUE?
KEY POINTS

YES: The great religions that take issue with abortion have been dominated by male priests and scholars who have interpreted holy scriptures in ways that discriminate against women

YES: Many religions regard the purpose of sex as procreation and see interference with the process in terms of contraception or abortion as immoral

GENDER BIAS
Do attitudes toward abortion reflect an antiwomen bias?

PROCREATION
Is sex just for procreation?

NO: Religious attitudes toward abortion are prolife, not antiwomen. They exist to encourage women to find fulfillment in their natural role as mothers.

NO: Religious limits on sexual behavior reflect social rather than spiritual priorities. Sex is an important part of a loving relationship; people should be able to enjoy it without fear of pregnancy.

CONFLICT RESOLUTION

"The best way to destroy an enemy is to make him a friend."

—ABRAHAM LINCOLN, 16TH PRESIDENT (1861–1865)

Most students have at one time or another found themselves in a difficult or unpleasant situation. Sometimes people react in a volatile or unexpected way, and certain skills are needed to make sure that matters do not get out of hand. Conflict resolution skills have become increasingly popular in schools and colleges during the last 25 years, especially following the rise of harassment and violence. These skills help students resolve problems, such as bullying, in nonviolent ways. Studies have revealed that a peaceful school environment leads to happier, more motivated students. These skills can also be applied elsewhere to help create safe workplaces, homes, neighborhoods, and civil societies.

Reasons for conflict

The most common causes of conflict are: animosity toward others; harassment; jealousy; anger; competition; inequality; a failure to listen; a failure to negotiate or compromise; and a lack of communication with peers/teachers.

Conflict resolution programs provide students with the skills needed to solve problems before they escalate into aggression or violence (see list opposite). Anger management courses, role play, and social skills classes, among other tools, are used to help students both accept and control their behavior, and also to make them understand the consequences of their actions. The programs teach self-control, self-respect, empathy, and teamwork—all skills that are required in negotiation and mediation processes. Conflict resolution enables students to respect their peers both as individuals and as group members. The skills supply students with the basic tools needed to express their opinions in an acceptable way without having to resort to violence. Conflict resolution skills can also help students solve problems for the benefit of the wider community.

Methods of dealing with conflict

Compromise and mediation skills are used to resolve conflicts. Compromise requires that all the parties involved in a dispute discuss their problems and then give up something in order to achieve a settlement. Negotiation is therefore key to compromising. Mediation brings in a neutral person from outside the group to aid people in reaching an agreement. Peer mediation has become widespread in schools. Trained student mediators help resolve disputes amicably. Peer mediation is a voluntary, nonpunitive process that has reduced disciplinary action and violence in schools.

TIPS FOR RESOLVING CONFLICTS

1. Think of a constructive way to deal with the situation before you speak
2. Agree on some ground rules for behavior:
- No interrupting.
- No name-calling, swearing, or personal criticism.
- No shouting. Try to speak in a soft, even tone.
3. Communicate: talk and listen.
This involves each party telling his or her view of the situation in turn. A useful way to do this is by "I-messages." This can include the following:
- Stating how you are feeling using the words "I feel ..."
- Describing the behavior of others by saying, for example, "When you do this I feel ..."
- Detailing the effects of the other person's behavior by saying, for example, "Because of this/As a result of this I feel ..."
- Stating clearly what you think would correct the situation for you: "I would like ... to happen ..."
The other people in the group should then restate what they understand the problems are by paraphrasing what has been said. This prevents misunderstandings. Each person goes through the same process until everyone has been heard.
4. Negotiate and compromise
- All those present suggest and list possible solutions to the problem/s.
- Everyone discusses and agrees on a resolution by choosing a possible solution from the list.
The above involves actively listening to other people in the group. This requires:
- Clarifying anything that is not clear by asking questions.
- Restating information: This avoids confusion or misunderstandings.
- Encouraging others to speak by using neutral or nonaggressive language to help others explain what they feel about a certain situation.
In situations in which the above is not possible, mediation may be necessary.

NATIONAL CENTER FOR CHILDREN IN POVERTY REPORT

In 1999 the National Center for Children in Poverty published a report called *Teaching Conflict Resolution: An Effective School-Based Approach to Violence Prevention*. The report examined the success of the New York-based Resolving Conflict Creatively Program (RCCP), a school program aimed at facilitating constructive conflict resolution and positive relations between students of all ages. The report assessed the effect of the RCCP program on students' behavior by comparing the data on a group of students before and after they had participated in the program with data on those who did not take part. The results highlighted the fact that RCCP is able to help reduce, if not actually prevent, the rate of increase in aggressive behavior that participating students experience during a school year.

Topic 7
IS THE USE OF CONTRACEPTION WRONG?

YES
"THE HARMS OF CONTRACEPTION"
WWW.OMSOUL.COM
ONE MORE SOUL

NO
FROM "THE CIVILIZING FORCE OF BIRTH CONTROL"
SEX IN CIVILIZATION
MARGARET SANGER

INTRODUCTION

The term "contraception" refers to any method used to prevent pregnancy. Many different types of contraceptive are available, including condoms, the diaphragm, the birth-control pill (the Pill), and intrauterine devices (IUDs). There has long been much debate about whether the use of contraception is right or wrong. Some commentators argue against it on religious or moral grounds. They say it is God's will that humans reproduce, and that sex should be reserved for procreation. Other critics believe that some forms of contraception are simply abortion under another name because they effectively prevent the formation of a bond between a living sperm and a living egg. Opponents of such a view argue that neither the sperm nor the egg are living by any meaningful definition of the word. Many also propose that sex is a natural biological function that is not exclusively for reproduction: It also provides enjoyment and strengthens

bonds of tenderness and love. They claim that the world is overpopulated, and that contraception is essential to control birthrates. Many also point out that using condoms can prevent the spread of HIV/AIDs and other sexually transmitted diseases (STDs).

Historically people have always used birth control. The Old Testament story of Onan tells how he spilled his sperm onto the ground in order to avoid fathering a child. Cleopatra, the queen of Egypt, is said to have taken herbs to prevent pregnancy. Ancient Egyptians also used condomlike linen sheaths for protection against disease. It was during the 16th century that people first realized that sheaths—then often made from animal intestines—worked as a contraceptive. The development of vulcanization in the mid-19th century made possible the mass production of cheap rubber condoms.

As the use of contraceptives became more common, critics began to campaign against birth control. In the United States Anthony Comstock (1844–1915), a devout Christian, believed that the availability of contraceptives promoted immorality. Offended by advertising for birth-control devices, he drafted a bill that Congress made law in 1873. The Comstock Law defined contraceptives as obscene and illegal. It made it a federal offense to distribute any sexually related material or devices through the mail or across state lines.

"An armor against pleasure, and a cobweb against infection."

—16TH-CENTURY DESCRIPTION OF CONDOMS

The Comstock Law remained largely unchallenged until Margaret Sanger (1879–1966), a nurse working with poor immigrants, vowed to make contraceptives and information on birth control (a term she coined) available to women. She was arrested in 1916 after she opened a birth-control clinic in New York. Her court case led to a ruling in 1918 that established a doctor's right to provide women with contraceptive advice for "the cure and prevention of disease." A further ruling in 1936 permitted doctors to mail contraceptives across state borders.

In 1960 the Food and Drug Administration approved the first birth-control pill to go on sale. By the middle of the decade the Pill had become the most popular form of contraception in the United States—despite the fact that several states still banned the sale of contraceptives. Critics objected that the Pill made society more promiscuous by encouraging women to have multiple sexual partners. Advocates countered that every woman should have ultimate control over her reproductive rights.

The attitude of religions toward contraception varies. In 1930 the Lambeth Conference, the world assembly of Anglican bishops, backed limited acceptance of birth control. That year, however, the Catholic Church declared that birth control was a sin. In 1951 Pope Pius XII (1939–1958) sanctioned the use of the rhythm method (whereby a couple abstains from sex during the woman's fertile period each month) as a form of natural birth control. In 1968 Pope Paul VI (1963–1978) stated categorically that the Catholic Church remained opposed to all artificial birth control—a position it still holds. Critics argue that the time has come for the church to adopt an approach more suited to today's society, but supporters insist that sex should remain essentially for procreation, making contraception unnecessary. Both Islam and Judaism permit the use of birth control in some circumstances, such as if a woman's health would be at risk if she were to have a child.

Many humanitarian organizations promote contraception as a way to stabilize population growth and reduce poverty, as well as to slow the spread of HIV/AIDS and prevent other STDs. Critics contend, however, that using birth control is itself not without health risks. For example, some medical studies have linked the Pill to blood clots and breast cancer.

The following extracts by the One More Soul organization and Margaret Sanger discuss these issues in depth.

THE HARMS OF CONTRACEPTION
One More Soul

One More Soul
(www.omsoul.com)
is an organization
"dedicated to
spreading the truth
about ... the harms
of contraception."

Norplant® is a
contraceptive
consisting of six
matchstick-size
capsules inserted in
a woman's arm. The
capsules release
small amounts of
the hormone
progestin over a
five-year period.
Depo-Provera® is a
contraceptive
administered by
injection every
three months. An
IUD (intrauterine
device) is a small
T-shaped device
that is inserted
in a woman's
uterus. It works
by preventing
sperm from
meeting an egg
or by stopping
the embryo
from nesting
in the lining
of the uterus.

Viagra® is a drug
used to treat
impotence. It first
became available in
the United States
in 1998. Within
three years annual
sales exceeded
$1 billion.

YES

There are several reasons why we believe that the use of contraception harms everyone involved. The first reason is that the use of contraception leads to abortion. Several "contraceptives" are in fact abortifacients. That is, they cause early abortions. All oral contraceptives, Norplant, Depo-Provera, and IUDs cause abortions before a woman even knows she's pregnant. According to Dr. Bogomir Kuhar, in *Infant Homicides Through Contraceptives*, these forms of birth control take an estimated 8.1 to 12.75 million lives each year in the US alone. Contraceptives also cause abortions through their failures. All contraceptives fail, some quite often. Even surgical sterilization has a failure rate. Each "failure" results in a new human life, a new baby, an actual woman facing an unplanned and often unwanted pregnancy. These pregnancies are at risk for abortion.

The sexual revolution

The invention of the birth control pill was revolutionary and, in fact, caused the sexual revolution. Once people thought they could have sex without the possibility of pregnancy, or with a greatly reduced risk of pregnancy, they began to disregard the traditional structures that had protected children and sex for centuries. Contraceptive pills were soon prescribed for younger and younger unmarried women. Since contraceptives fail, this led to an upsurge in the numbers of out of wedlock and teenage pregnancies, and the number of single parent families. With the increase in premarital and extramarital sex, and the number of partners one person might have, the rate of infection from sexually transmitted diseases [STDs] skyrocketed. Even the number of serious sexually transmitted diseases soared, from about twelve known diseases thirty years ago to over fifty today. This plague has even struck our senior citizens as, empowered by Viagra, they have contact with multiple sex partners. Several retirement communities now report epidemics of STDs. Nature is telling them that even after fertility is naturally gone, the marriage vow is still sacred. The diseases themselves have changed, from easily treatable, known diseases, to more and more destructive ones, including the AIDS virus. Some contraceptives, especially hormonal contraceptives, even make the user more susceptible to STDs.

Contraceptives can help destroy marriages. Only four years after contraceptives were first tested, researchers found that marriages in which contraceptives were used were twice as likely to end in divorce than marriages in which there was no contraceptive use. Why this huge difference? Well, using contraceptives means that a couple's fertility is suppressed, and treated like a disease. They are no longer able to share themselves with each other totally in the sex act. There is a barrier that is not just physical or chemical, but also emotional, erected between them. They are closing one part of themselves off from each other, and from God. Often the couple begin to be dissatisfied. The wife starts to feel that the husband does not desire her, only her body. The husband begins to feel that his wife doesn't really want to have sex with him, that she is cold and tired. These attitudes can poison their whole relationship. With this crucial part of their marriage gone bad, soon other problems develop. Before they know it, the couple is in divorce court, dividing up their mutual property.

Treating children like a disease

Contraceptives treat children like a disease. We take medicine or have surgery done to prevent them. When a couple does become pregnant in our modern culture, it may be seen as an occasion for condolences rather than congratulations. A pregnancy after a couple has one or two children may be treated as an unfortunate mistake. As Christians, we know that this attitude is wrong. The Bible tells us that children are a gift from God. They are His blessings. Universally, children are seen and treated as blessings after they are born. Every child certainly brings his or her set of challenges, but most parents will say that their children are a blessing, even when a child is a "problem" child. An abundance of children is an expression of God's special favor. What right do any of us have to refuse a gift from God? Instead of the world's attitude that children are bothersome nuisances that prevent us from enjoying our hard-earned wealth, we need to see each child as a marvelous assist to full human life. We believe that all children are good and beautiful. Although some pregnancies may occur under tragic circumstances, each child is an occasion for celebration.

Ellen Grant, a British doctor who prescribed the Pill in the 1960s, noted that some patients said that their marriages broke up after they started taking the Pill.

When contraception became widely available, many couples felt liberated that they were able to make love without fear of pregnancy. Do you think that it creates or removes barriers between men and women?

Some people believe that the world's population is growing at such a rate that the planet will not be able to sustain it, and that population control is essential for humankind's survival. Others see the current low birthrates as leading to dangerously unbalanced demographics. What are your thoughts?

Supporters of contraception argue that far from degrading women, it empowers them to take control over their bodies and their sexuality.

Why do you think most contraceptives are designed to be used by women? Do you think there should be more contraceptives available for men?

The National Cancer Institute reports an increased risk of breast cancer in women under 35 who have recently used an oral contraceptive. See http://cis.nci.nih.gov/fact/3_13.htm for details.

Do you think it is unethical for a doctor to prescribe hormonal contraceptives if he or she considers contraception harmful, even if the patient requests it?

Degrading to women

Contraceptives degrade women. From the day in junior high when a woman menstruates for the first time, a woman's fertility is a huge part of her life. If her constantly changing hormones were not enough, for five to ten days every month she gets powerfully reminded again and again that this body of hers was designed to conceive and bear children. When a woman uses contraceptives, she and her partner are actively rejecting this essential fact about herself. Her ability to become pregnant, one of the greatest blessings of her life, is treated as unacceptable and a burden. Because most contraceptives are designed to be used by women, when they fail, and a pregnancy occurs, it is "her fault." She is expected to "deal with" her mistake, usually by having an abortion. The father of the child, although he is as responsible for this child as the mother, feels free to abandon both of them. After all, since the contraception wasn't his responsibility, why should he be responsible for the result of the contraceptive failure?

Side effects of hormonal contraception

Hormonal contraceptives, besides being abortifacient, can have horrific side effects for the women who use them. From high blood pressure to blood clots, to heart attacks, to migraine headaches, to menstrual problems after you quit taking the drug, hormonal contraceptives (the pill, Norplant, and Depo-Provera, etc) can wreak havoc on a woman's body. It is no coincidence that the rise in breast cancer followed ten to fifteen years after hormonal contraceptives first became readily available. It is also no coincidence that many women who have been on the pill for years and now want children, find they are now infertile. Infertility has become a national epidemic, with couples spending hundreds of thousands of dollars trying desperately to conceive. Unethical doctors continue to become wealthy prescribing contraceptives and then treating the side effects.

What the Roman Catholic Church teaches

Finally, we believe that the use of contraception is wrong, because that is what our Church teaches. Although it has come under serious fire both from within and without, the Roman Catholic Church has never changed its centuries-old teaching that contraception is morally wrong, and that its use is immoral. Many Catholics have been deceived into believing that the Catholic Church has changed its teaching, or that it doesn't matter anymore. The truth is that the church cannot change the Creator's design clearly linking procreation to sexual intercourse. Separating the unitive and procreative ends is to violate the meaning of the conjugal act and thus contrary to nature. What is intrinsically immoral will always remain so. We challenge all believers to find out the truth, examine their own consciences, and live up to the standard that our church set for us. It's never too late to make a change.

Do you think something can be "instrinsically immoral"? See Topic 5 Is morality possible without a religious basis?

A CIVILIZING FORCE OF BIRTH CONTROL
Margaret Sanger

Margaret Sanger (1879–1966) was a pioneer of birth control. This extract is from an essay that appeared in a book called Sex in Civilization *(1929). Go to http:// historymatters. gmu.edu/d/5082/ to read the full text.*

Charles-Louis de Secondat de Montesquieu (1689–1755) was a French philosopher whose ideas on the separation of powers greatly influenced the U.S. Constitution. See Volume 2, Government, page 18.

Compare Sanger's account of how contraceptives can affect married life with the views of the One More Soul organization on page 91. Is one argument more convincing than the other? Why?

NO

X … The birth control program is not concerned with the fruits of culture, but with sowing the "seeds" of civilization. It does not insist that men and women be educated by books or the arts; but upon the basis of their innate, though possibly, undeveloped, intelligence, it does seek to awaken them to a consciousness of their responsibilities toward each other, to their children and children-to-be, and thus to the community of the present and of the future. Thus it seeks to fulfill the requirement expressed by Montesquieu: it renders intelligent beings yet more intelligent!…

Equipped with the instrument of birth control, the mother regains not only mastery of her procreative function, but an immeasurably increased sense of power over life itself. Thus quite aside from its economic and eugenic aspects— the importance of which I am in no sense seeking to minimize—the practice of birth control brings with it inestimable psychic benefits. A whole sphere of life—the sexual—is elevated from the level of the purely instinctive and fortuitous and submitted to intelligent direction. Mystery and ignorance are banished. Married love is enriched and greatly reinforced by completely fulfilled sexual communion which has been emancipated of the destructive restrictions and mutilations of unexpressed fears. And so between husband and wife mental and spiritual bonds are strengthened and vitalized.…

Responsibility

The technique of birth control dissociates two ideas: the ritual of physical and spiritual communion and the process of reproduction. Its opponents say that its advocates overvalue the former and undervalue the latter. They fail to recognize that, by placing the implement of this dissociation into the hands of husbands and wives, it places with them the responsibility of using that implement with intelligence and discrimination. But such has ever, since the discovery of fire, been the serene, untroubled way of civilization. It has placed in men's hands the sharp-edged knife, the razor, the harnessed powers of steam and electricity, alcohol, gunpowder, firearms, radio-activity and now the power of flight. Do not tell us that he will abuse these powers, that he will misuse them to his own destruction. We know that already. He has; he does; he will. But out of his own experience, his own trial and error, his own mistakes, by suffering his own self-inflicted punishments and his own hard-earned rewards man slowly but certainly advances on the path of civilization. Like every other great instrument of civilization, birth control is making men and women face a new responsibility, and forcing their intelligence to the solution of problems they had for ages deliberately avoided.

Catholic Church and morality

Because of its misuse and abuse by reactionaries and defenders of the status quo, the term "morality" has come to connote, in this twentieth century of ours, practically everything that is distasteful to the spirit of progress. As a matter of fact, however, we cannot evade the problem of morality; and such ideas as may be advanced as instruments of an emergent civilization must be tested from the point of view of ethical integrity. Birth control has been denounced as inimical to the mind and morals and health of the younger citizens to whom we look for the future growth and upbuilding of civilization. Its opponents claim that it will permit the "dissemination of immoral and salacious literature under the guise of information, and will give unlimited opportunity to the purveyors of the obscene in newspaper, magazine and every other form of advertising." Marriage without the desire and responsibility of parenthood, [Sanger's footnote: "Yes, according to Mr. P. J. Ward of the National Catholic Welfare Conference, Washington, D.C."] and not lived in strict continence, is "immoral and sinful." The authority on which this opposition of the Roman Catholic Church against birth control is based is the conception that there is only one true church, and subsequently only one true morality. It is claimed that the Catholic Church is the depository of eternal truth, the Kingdom of God on earth. The Catholic Church, according to Father Ward, is therefore responsible for the morals of the entire human race. It is the duty of the church, therefore, to interfere with and to block all legislation that may adversely affect the "morals" of non-Catholics as well as Catholics. Though we have been led astray by ethical error, we are still all her children. The Catholic Church never loses the hope that non-Catholics will some day be counted in the fold. The church therefore considers it her duty to supervise all social and moral legislation.

Does the fact that some individuals abuse or misuse the "powers" Sanger lists mean that their use should be limited for everyone? How else could abuse be prevented?

"Inimical" means hostile, or harmful.

The National Catholic Welfare Conference was created in 1922 to address issues such as education and social action.

Do you think it is still considered "immoral" for a married couple not to want to have children?

The position of the church, as enunciated by this executive of the National Catholic Welfare Conference, exemplifies by its very exaggeration the concept of a "closed system" of morality that is far more prevalent than might at first be suspected. From this point of view there no longer exists any living moral problem. Right and wrong in the realm of ethical action have been decided once and for all time. No choice is offered the individual. He may submit to the dictates of the higher authority, and be saved; or he may decide his own problems for himself, and be eternally damned. He cannot question the laws of the ecclesiastical authorities concerning his sexual behavior. He—or preferably, she—is offered the choice between uninterrupted procreation or rigid continence. Unquestioning obedience, submission to ecclesiastical law, and the reference of all intimate personal and sexual problems to the nearest representative of the church—such are the ready-made solutions to all moral questions of the adherents of this type of ethics....

"Continence" means restraint, especially from sexual intercourse.

Against such "morality," the spirit of Western civilization is revolting with ever-increasing vigor.... We are no longer living in a little closed completed universe of which God's plan was revealed once and for all time to a little group of delegates. The center of our universe has shifted from Heaven to earth.... This new world, this emergent civilization, is one of experimentation, of trial and error. The revealed and dogmatic basis of morality, as expressed by the Roman Catholics, and as accepted by so many other unthinking religious organizations, by so many so-called educators, by so many limited members of the medical profession, and even by some who call themselves sociologists, has lost its old authority....

At the time Sanger wrote this piece, she faced strong opposition not only from the Catholic Church but also from many doctors. See the biography of Sanger at http://www. nyu.edu/projects/ sanger/msbio.htm for details of her struggle to find support for birth control in the United States.

Supreme importance of child-life

Instead of operating as a menace to the foundations of marriage, birth control is actually one of the surest means of assuring the fulfillment of its inherent promises. It recreates the very pattern of the marriage relation, perforce substituting intelligence and common sense for shame and the half-guilty consciousness of sin; of consideration for brutal selfishness; and of foresight for reckless irresponsibility. In all of these prevision is unquestionably a force working with and not contrary to the spirit of civilization as we understand it.

Its greatest value, however, is to be found in its assertion—and not its denial, as its enemies claim—of the supreme importance of child-life. One incontrovertible fact we cannot escape: among families into which a large number of children are born, there is apt to be a correspondingly large infantile mortality. The unwelcome child has an appreciably smaller chance of survival than the child brought into the world by desire.... The mental and physical condition of the mother, both before and after birth, is of paramount importance to the whole life of her child. Whether we be partisans of heredity or of environment as the chief factor in the life of an individual, there can be no denying this factor—since the mother is both environment and heredity. Now that we realize that the first five years of a life are the most plastic and are those in which the whole psychic pattern of maturity is set, the importance of the surrounding and enveloping motherhood can scarcely be overestimated....

According to Education Week magazine—www. edweek.org— evidence suggests that the first five years of life are key to a child's long-term development. Children who have good early care and learning activities do better at school and in life.

Biological freedom

The changing attitude toward contraception, which is evident everywhere when men and women are thinking deeply about the constant problems of human existence— in Europe, in Asia, and in America—is one of the eloquent indices of the triumph of the new, scientific morality. It indicates the laying of a solid foundation for the civilization of the future. This, I venture to prophesy, will differ from the so-called civilization of the East, which has erected its structure on the ugly basis of human slavery and misery. It will be a civilization of a healthy and happy worldliness, demanding no blood sacrifices and permitting to each individual the full realization of his innate potentialities. We shall reach spiritual communism through the blossoming of the self.

The Planned Parenthood Federation of America, an organization that Sanger founded, admits that some of her views— including this view of Asian societies— are out of keeping with modern ideas and are used by critics to discredit Sanger. Go to http://www. plannedparenthood. org/about/thisisppl sanger.html for more information.

Women in the past have been confronted with the empty victories of political freedom, of economic freedom, of social freedom. But with the winning of *biological freedom*, women and men and children will enter triumphantly into an era that will be in every sense of the word civilized....

Summary

The first article by One More Soul, a prolife organization, argues that contraception is wrong for a variety of reasons. The author asserts that some contraceptives are abortifacients—they induce termination even before a woman knows she's pregnant. Other abortions are caused by contraceptives that fail, resulting in unwanted pregnancies. The author argues that since contraception was made freely available, more people are having sex out of wedlock, teenage sex has increased, and sexually transmitted diseases have become more prevalent. Birth control destroys marriages, the author claims, because it creates an emotional barrier between partners. It also encourages society to treat children as a kind of disease. Furthermore, it degrades women by taking away their primary function—to procreate. Finally, the author says that contraception is wrong because it is against the Catholic Church's teachings, which state that it is intrinsically immoral.

The second piece, which is taken from an extract by reproductive rights pioneer Margaret Sanger, argues that birth control aids civilization—it makes intelligent beings more intelligent by giving them choice. Sanger contends that the Catholic Church has no right to dictate whether a woman should have a child if she is unwilling and claims that a rebellion has taken place against this kind of enforced morality. She argues that birth control helps marriages by allowing couples to enjoy sex without feelings of sin or shame and, most importantly, prevents unwanted children from being born.

FURTHER INFORMATION:

Books:

Bullough, Vern L. (ed.), *Encyclopedia of Birth Control*. Santa Barbara, CA: ABC-CLIO, 2001.

Maguire, Daniel C. (ed.), *Sacred Rights: The Case for Contraception and Abortion in World Religions*. New York: Oxford University Press, 2003.

Useful websites:

http://www.catholic.com/library/birth_control.asp
The Catholic Church's view on artificial contraception.

http://www.nyu.edu/projects/sanger/
The Margaret Sanger Papers Project, with a detailed biography of the birth control advocate.

http://www.pbs.org/wgbh/amex/pill/index.html
History of the development of the Pill and other forms of birth control.

www.plannedparenthood.org
Site of the Planned Parenthood Federation of America, the world's largest reproductive health care organization.

The following debates in the Pro/Con series may also be of interest:

In this volume:
Topic 6 Is abortion a religious issue?

In *Family and Society*:
Topic 10 Does sex education work?

A history of contraception, pages 136–137

Topic 11 Should teenagers have a right to contraception without parental consent?

IS THE USE OF CONTRACEPTION WRONG?

YES: It is natural that sex leads to conception; this process should not be prevented

YES: Several contraceptives work by inducing early abortions. Like abortion, this contravenes the commandment not to kill.

PROCREATION

Is sex just for procreation?

ABORTION

Is contraception abortion under another name?

NO: Sex is a natural and enjoyable expression of emotional closeness that people should be allowed to enjoy without fear of pregnancy or STDs

NO: Most contraceptives are used as preventive precaution; they do not "kill" anything that is living by any meaningful definition of the term

IS THE USE OF CONTRACEPTION WRONG?

KEY POINTS

YES: People have become used to thinking that they can have sex at any time; this has led to a great increase in promiscuous behavior

YES: People who use contraception are not prepared to take the consequences of their actions; they are also potentially damaging their emotional and physical health

IMMORALITY

Has contraception led to a more immoral society?

IRRESPONSIBLE

Is the use of contraception irresponsible?

NO: Contraception does not make people have more sex with more partners; it simply gives people more choice and encourages them to act responsibly

NO: Contraception allows parents to wait to have children until they are ready to love and care for them and be responsible for their needs

Topic 8
SHOULD ADULTERY BE A CRIMINAL OFFENSE?

YES
"UNCONSTITUTIONAL ADULTERY"
CAIRO TIMES, JULY 25–31, 2002, VOLUME 6, ISSUE 21
ABDALLA F. HASSAN

NO
"SHARI'AH LAW, ADULTERY AND RAPE"
WWW.ISHR.ORG, GERMANY
INTERNATIONAL SOCIETY FOR HUMAN RIGHTS

INTRODUCTION

Adultery is voluntary sexual intercourse between a married person and someone other than his or her spouse. Most societies frown on adulterous relationships, and in many adultery is considered a grounds for divorce. Current research estimates that between 25 to 33 percent of married men and between 17 and 25 percent of married women are likely to commit adultery at some time during their married lives. Cases of adultery involving celebrities feature constantly in newspapers and TV shows.

Some people argue that the fact that adultery is so common in modern society shows a lack of moral discipline; they suggest that making adultery a crime would force people to take their marriage vows more seriously. Others argue that adultery has always existed and will always exist, and that this kind of personal behavior is a matter for the moral judgment of the individual, not the law courts.

Most of the world's religions disapprove of adultery; the Seventh Commandment in the Christian Bible is "Thou shalt not commit adultery." The Talmud and the Koran, holy books of Judaism and Islam, respectively, both condemn adultery, as does Hindu law. There are some societies in which adultery is not automatically condemned, however, including various traditional peoples of the South Pacific, Africa, and the Arctic Circle.

In some countries—and in more than 20 U.S. states—adultery is, however, a civil crime. As long ago as the 18th century B.C. Babylonian law established the punishment for adultery of death by drowning. In Islamic law adultery can still in some cases be punished by death. An international outcry followed the 2003 death sentence passed on a young Nigerian woman, Safiya Husaini, for example. Husaini was found guilty of adultery under Islamic Sharia law. Many critics of antiadultery laws point out that women generally tend to be punished more often for the crime than men. This reflects, they argue, male dominance of society and legal systems, and is yet another argument against the existence of antiadultery laws.

"Moral disapproval is not sufficient reason to criminalize such conduct [adultery]."
—REBECCA K. GLENBERG, ACLU OF VIRGINIA LEGAL DIRECTOR (2004), ON STATE ADULTERY LAWS

While many people disapprove of adultery on moral grounds, some acknowledge that adultery statistics may show that people are not naturally suited to having one mate for life. Some commentators claim that existing legal proscriptions against adultery are not necessarily a reflection of spiritual or moral considerations but arose instead out of social organization. In the past the outlawing of adultery served to help establish cohesive communities by preventing sexual competition. It was also vital in societies based on primogeniture, in which property and titles were inherited by the eldest son. Before blood tests and other ways to establish paternity, the outlawing of adultery was necessary so that men could be sure that they had fathered their wife's offspring. But such considerations are now outdated, they argue, in a world in which morality and sexual behavior are widely seen as matters of personal conscience. Legal proscriptions on such subjects are no longer necessary or desirable.

In 2003 many Americans focused on whether or not adultery should be a criminal offense when lawyer John Bushey, Jr., was tried for adultery in Virginia. He pleaded guilty and was fined $125, but he reserved the right to challenge the state law on constitutional grounds (see page 104). Bushey's case came as a shock to some Americans by reminding them of the existence of such laws. Most people believed that any attempt to lay down regulations on sexual behavior by the government or the courts was an unacceptable infringement on civil rights, and was unconstitutional. Nearly half of the state governments, however, still have adultery laws that date from centuries ago. The English common law adopted by numerous American colonies made illegal such sexual acts as adultery, fornication (sex between unmarried people), and sodomy (oral and anal sex). When states wrote their own legal codes in the second half of the 19th century, they incorporated these laws, although the exact definition of these crimes can vary substantially from state to state. Some codes define adultery as sex outside of marriage, for example, while others define it as occurring when a married person lives with someone other than his or her spouse. In West Virginia adultery is defined as "lewdly and lasciviously" associating with anyone other than one's spouse. Adultery is also a criminal offense in the military, but parties are only brought to trial if a case harms "good order and discipline."

Should adultery be a criminal offense? The following articles examine many of the main issues in the debate.

UNCONSTITUTIONAL ADULTERY
Abdalla F. Hassan

Abdalla F. Hassan is an Egyptian journalist. This article appeared in the Cairo Times, July 25–31, 2002.

According to Egyptian law, prostitution is illegal. While a man caught with a prostitute cannot be imprisoned, he can testify against the prostitute in court. Go to "Prostitution and the law" at http://www.newint.org/issue252/facts.htm to see how Egyptian law compares to that of other countries.

The Egyptian Constitution has 211 articles. Go to http://www.sis.gov.eg/egyptinf/politics/parlment/html/constit.htm to look at it. How does it compare to the U.S. Constitution? Is it more comprehensive or less so?

YES

There have long been complaints about inequalities between the sexes in Egyptian society, but the provisions in the penal code for adultery seem especially jarring. A married woman convicted of adultery can be sentenced to up to two years in prison, while the maximum sentence for a man is six months. In addition, the man has to be discovered in flagrante delicto inside the family home while a woman can be charged for the practice anywhere. Finally, a married man found with a prostitute is not breaking any laws, but rather a material witness in the case against the prostitute herself. For the past four years, civic groups and women's organizations have been campaigning to repeal these discriminatory laws on adultery and on 17 July they just drew a step closer.

Constitutionality of adultery laws

The constitutionality of laws against adultery became the main issue in a trial at the Kasr Al Nil Court of Misdemeanors, where a woman is being charged by her husband of engaging in an illicit extramarital affair. Her defense argued that the law is unconstitutional because it metes out different penalties for men and women convicted of the same crime. This is a violation of Article 40 of the constitution, which states: "All citizens are equal before the law. They have equal public rights and duties without discrimination due to sex, ethnic origin, language, religion, or creed."

The Arab Office of Law, a private volunteer organization, took up the case of the alleged adulterous women in the Kasr Al Nil Court of Misdemeanors, using the case as a springboard to launch a constitutional challenge of the adultery laws. "One cannot go directly to the Supreme Constitutional Court (SCC). The constitutionality of a law must be challenged through a case currently in the courts," explains Yasser Abdel Gowad, president of both the Arab Office for Law and the Center for Egyptian Women's Legal Assistance.

Presiding judge Muhammad Abdel Karim found enough merit in the defenses' arguments to refer the matter to the

In Nigeria in 2002 Amina Lawal (above) was sentenced to death by stoning after being found guilty of adultery under Sharia law.

> ## COMMENTARY: Adultery, privacy, and Virginia
>
> In February 2004 the American Civil Liberties Union (ACLU) announced that it was taking on the case of Virginia attorney John Bushey, Jr. Accused the previous year of having sexual intercourse with someone other than his wife, Bushey had pleaded guilty to violating Virginia's adultery code. The maximum fine for the offense is $250: Bushey was fined $125 plus court costs, but retained his right to challenge the law on the grounds that criminalizing adultery violated the constitutionally guaranteed right to privacy. The ACLU will assist with the legal challenge. The case has wide significance: Virginia is one of several states that still have statutes making adultery a criminal offense.
>
> ### Bushey and the right to privacy
>
> Bushey is the first person in many Virginians' memory to be charged with adultery. Many of his peers were shocked not just to discover that adultery was still a criminal offense in the state, but also because Bushey had been a model citizen—a 65-year-old attorney who had held his position in the Shenandoah Valley town of Luray, Virginia, for 32 years. The accusations of adultery had first been leveled at the attorney by his former lover after Bushey had returned to his wife.
>
> Bushey did not fight the charge but made it clear that he believed the law to be wrong. "[T]he government has no right to criminalize the behavior of consenting adults in the privacy of a bedroom," he stated. Many Americans agree. They see a positive parallel in the Supreme Court's 2003 decision to strike down Texas's antisodomy law on the grounds that the state cannot make private sexual conduct a crime. Supporters, however, disagree: They believe that such acts work as deterrents and prevent what they see as the moral degeneration of society.

Sharia (literally "the path to the watering hole") derives from the teachings of the Koran and from Sunna (the practice of the Prophet Muhammad). Hadd offenses—such as unlawful sexual intercourse—are punished by specific penalties.

than the spouse may file an official complaint. According to Article 274 of the penal code, a married woman convicted by a court of committing adultery is imprisoned for a period not to exceed two years. Following her conviction, her husband may choose to absolve her sentence. But according to Article 277 of the penal code, a married man commits adultery only if he is found to have engaged in the sinful act in the "marital home." Moreover, if found guilty, he only receives a prison sentence not to exceed six months, which his spouse may not exonerate.

Not only is the law concerning adultery viewed by legal activists as a plain violation of Egypt's constitution, but it also goes against Sharia law, which equally punishes both men and women found to have committed adultery.

"The laws typically favored men over women. Legislators who crafted the laws may have thought the crime of adultery for women is a greater crime than it is for men," says Magdi Helmi, a journalist with the opposition daily Al Wafd who has been involved in the campaign.

In cases of prostitution involving a married man, Article 240 of the penal code imprisons the woman but no punishment is levied again the man, who is merely a material witness. "This dates back to English rule when British soldiers were protected when they frequented houses of prostitution," offers Helmi.

Still, a SCC ruling on the constitutionality of the adultery laws will take time. "Generally, the case in front of the Supreme Constitutional Court takes years—two, three or four years—depending on the specific details of the case" says Abdel Gowad. "I don't think the SCC will reach a decision before a year."

But if the SCC declares the articles concerning adultery in the penal code to be unconstitutional, a legal void would exist, which the legislative branch would have to address. Helmi asserts that the government may propose a law in the next parliamentary session to equalize the punishment between men and women in crimes of adultery, even before the SCC makes its ruling. Abdel Gowad believes the legislature may not be prompted to act just yet. "I believe the People's Assembly will wait for the SCC ruling."

> If adultery is a crime, should both sexes be punished equally? Is one sex more to blame than the other?

Due to social constraints, adultery cases rarely make it to court and the issue is usually solved away from the limelight. Still, if the cases that do make it to court are few, Abdel Gowad still sees that the unevenness in the law should be remedied. "Equality should be present in the law. The right of equality has a value, irrespective of how often women are subject to this law."

> See Volume 1, Individual and Society, Topic 3 Are women still the second sex?

SHARI'AH LAW, ADULTERY, AND RAPE
International Society for Human Rights

The International Society for Human Rights (ISHR) is an international nongovernmental organization that bases its work on the Universal Declaration of Human Rights. This article was published by the German branch of the ISHR in 2003.

NO

The fate of the Nigerian woman Safiya Husaini once more led the world to pay attention to the practice of Islamic law (shari'ah) in Islamic countries. Despite all attempts to promote a dialogue between the different cultures, for many people in the West, Islam and specifically the implementation of shari'ah jurisdiction remains a book with seven seals.

There are different interpretations and applications of shari'ah in the four different Sunni schools of law. By far not every Muslim country applies the most severe regulations of shari'ah. However, the increasing number of states that are introducing shari'ah law into their jurisdiction, such as in the Northern states of the federal state of Nigeria, is alarming.

Shari'ah is more than a criminal code. It may be described as a code of conduct for every Muslim, which regulates everything from business relations to private behaviour. The radical features of shari'ah are especially evident in the cruel forms of punishment the shari'ah prescribes for non-adherence to regulations, such as amputation, lashing and stoning. The latter form of punishment has caused an uproar of indignation in the cases of Safiya Husaini and Amina Lawal. It is less known in the West that those who break away from Islamic faith are also threatened with death by stoning, alas the number of these cases is very difficult to establish.

In cases of adultery, shari'ah resorts to particularly drastic measures. Rape creates an especially difficult burden of proof for the victim. Shari'ah law only provides for punishment in cases of adultery if both parties admit to have committed the "crime". If this is not the case, four independent witnesses have to be found; however, the witnesses must be male. In cases of rape, shari'ah rules that a rapist is to be punished with 100 lashes, if unmarried, or with death by stoning, if married, since this would then constitute adultery.

A pregnancy as a result of rape first of all counts as evidence of adultery committed by the woman. The rape victim then has to prove that she really was raped. In case the man—which is very likely—denies that he has raped the woman, the woman has to name four male witnesses to prove the rape. In case the woman does not find these four

Many human rights groups have criticized countries that have adopted Sharia law. Is it unfair to judge Sharia by the standards of non-Islamic societies?

male witnesses—which again is very likely—she will be charged with slander.

For the crime of slander, shari'ah prescribes a punishment of 80 lashes. On top of that, the woman will be charged with adultery, and is thus threatened with the death penalty, if she is married. In case, she is unmarried, the "adultery" counts as immoral behaviour and is punished with 100 lashes. This is at least what the criminal code of January 2000 of the Nigerian state Zamfara says.

The victim carries the burden of proof

In the case of rape it may thus happen—and in most cases this is what seems to happen—that the victim has to prove that she was raped. One can argue about moral attitudes. In our world it sometimes, too, is difficult to find a consensus of what is right and what is wrong. In the West, too, until a couple of years ago, a rape victim had difficulties to assert herself in court. As in: She must have provoked it with her behaviour. Here, too, there are contentious issues concerning the burden of proof and the rule of presumed innocence to the disadvantage of the victim. However, this does not lead to the death penalty for the women. And even, if one believes that s/he has the right to judge over the morality of someone else, the type of punishment, i.e. death by stoning, remains absolutely unacceptable. Regardless of the fact that it should be the rapist who should be punished in the first place, and not vice versa.

Shari'ah even prescribes the size of the stones with which the convict is to be killed: not too small, because then they would not cause death, but not to large either, because then the convict probably dies as soon as the first stone hits. By the way, the Qur'an does not even have that kind of punishment for adultery: The Qur'an speaks of 100 lashes and that is that, though cruel enough (see Sura 24,2 and 24,3).

At the beginning of 2002, four stoning verdicts against women in Islamic states were announced: two in Nigeria, one in Sudan and one in Pakistan. Each woman had been charged with adultery.

Go to http://www. submission.org/ suras/sura24.html to read the Koran on adultery. How does it compare to other religions? Go to www.google.com to find the Bible online and the Bhagavad Gita.

The case of Safiya Husaini

35-year old divorcee Safiya Husaini from the Northern Nigerian state Sokoto had been reported to the police for extramarital sexual intercourse during her pregnancy. Consequently, she was sentenced to death by stoning by the Islamic court of the town of Gwadabawa on 14 October

Do people have a right to disobey laws that they feel are wrong? For further information on this go to Volume 9, Criminal Law and the Penal System.

Should the international community impose sanctions on countries that do not adhere to the international laws that they have ratified?

Representative Betty McCollum (Democrat, Minnesota) was among those politicians who objected to Husaini's sentence. McCollum is trying to get the practice of stoning people to death banned.

Katsina is a Sharia-run state in the northwestern part of Nigeria.

2001. It would have been the first case ever in Nigeria of an execution under Islamic law. This sentence and this type of punishment quite clearly violates the International Covenant of Civil and Political Rights as well as the Convention against Torture and Other Cruel, Inhuman or Degrading treatment or Punishment, both ratified by the Republic of Nigeria.

At the beginning, Safiya Husaini had testified that she had been raped by a 60-year old man of her village. The man was acquitted for lack of evidence. Later Safiya, who has five children, changed her testimony and declared that her divorced husband was the father of the child.

Safiya Husaini's fate led to world-wide protests, amongst which protest by 77 MPs of the European Parliament and by a parliamentary assembly from 130 countries in the capital of Morocco, Rabat. The protests had the effect that the Nigerian Minister of Justice declared in his letter of 18 March 2002 to the governors of the federal states which had introduced shari'ah law that shari'ah was unconstitutional, because it officially was only applicable to Muslims. Furthermore, shari'ah stood in contradiction to the constitutional principle of equality. As a response, the governor of Zamfara, Ahmed Sani, who is an advocate of the strict application of Islamic law, argued that, on the contrary, shari'ah was an expression of the constitutionally guaranteed freedom of religion. Nevertheless, on 25 March 2002, Safiya Husaini was acquitted by the Islamic court of appeal in Sokoto on the basis of juridical procedural errors.

Other verdicts

The protest and discussion of the case of Safiya Husaini did not lead to an overall reassessment of the application of this type of punishment for adultery, as some might have hoped. On the contrary, shortly before Husaini's acquittal, on 22 March 2002, 35-year old Amina Lawal was sentenced to death by stoning for the same "offence" by a shari'ah court in the Nigerian federal state of Katsina. The court in Bakori considered the extramarital sexual relationship of the divorced women a proven fact. Amina Lawal, too, had been reported to the police while pregnant. The charge against the man who has been named as the father was dropped. Amina Lawal had given birth to a child one and a half years after her second divorce. A women's organisation announced the appeal was to be brought before an appeals court in the beginning of April 2002. In the meantime, the government of Katsina announced that protests will neither influence the trial nor the government.

International protest helped in the case of 18-year old Christian Abok Alfa Akok in the West Sudanese town Darfur who was charged with adultery and sentenced to death by stoning on 8 December 2001. In March 2002 the verdict was transformed into 75 lashings to be carried out immediately. Interesting here is the fact that by convicting a Christian this case stands in direct contrast to statements by Islamists that shari'ah is not applicable to non-Muslims. This is a tendency which can also be observed concerning issues such as alcohol prohibition, dress codes and gender separation on public transport.

In April 2002 a stoning verdict was reported in south-western Pakistan. Apparently, Zafran Bibi who originally had accused her brother-in-law of rape, had been convinced by the police to admit that she had committed adultery. In order to prove the rape, four male witnesses would have been necessary as well. After protests from human rights groups, the supreme court of Pakistan allowed an appeal and ordered the temporary suspension of the execution in the beginning of May. So far, death penalties in accordance with the respective Pakistani law have not been carried out. However, "lynch-law" is known to have been applied to adulterers.

Generally, alongside the revival and re-politisation of Islam, a tendency of introducing shari'ah law has been recorded in recent decades. This mainly concerns countries such as Sudan, Nigeria, Pakistan, Iran, Saudi Arabia and Bangladesh. For most Muslims, shari'ah is an indispensable part of their faith in connection with the revelations of the Qur'an and other fundamental Islamic sources of law. A contradiction is felt between the understanding of the UN declarations and the regulations of shari'ah, particularly concerning issues such as religious freedom, gender equality and cruel and inhuman forms of punishment. In religiously mixed countries such as Nigeria these tensions divide the nation.

When 18-year-old Abok Alfa Akok, a Christian living in Nyala, Southern Darfur, became pregnant, she claimed that she had been raped. She was sentenced to death, but this was commuted to 75 lashes. The sentence was carried out while she was still pregnant, resulting in international criticism.

Should international law take precedence over religious law?

Summary

The preceding articles discuss whether adultery should be a criminal offense. In the first extract Egyptian journalist Abdalla F. Hassan, writing about the legal situation in Egypt, argues that it should be only if practiced according to Sharia law, which "equally punishes both the men and women found to have committed adultery." Hassan continually draws attention to the unfavorable sentences given out to Egyptian women found guilty of the crime of adultery. The author cites Article 40 of the Egyptian constitution as well as Articles 274 and 277 of the penal code as corroborating evidence for a repeal of the discriminatory laws that seem to allow male adulterers more forgiveness than women. The "No" article, published by the German branch of the International Society for Human Rights, disagrees. It argues that Sharia law has an unfair attitude toward adultery. Under Sharia law, unless both partners are prepared to admit to the "crime" of adultery, a conviction can only be secured on the testimony of four independent *male* witnesses. This system is prejudiced against women, the authors argue. A pregnancy resulting from rape can also be taken as evidence of adultery; the burden of proof is on the victim to counter such a charge. She must prove that she has been raped by producing four male witnesses, which the authors again argue is highly unlikely. If the victim cannot produce witnesses, she will be charged with slander and also faces the possibility of being sentenced to death for adultery. The International Society for Human Rights argues that this is grossly unfair.

FURTHER INFORMATION:

Books

DeSalvo, Louise A., *Adultery*. Boston, MA: Beacon Press, 1999.

Useful websites:

http://www.newadvent.org/cathen01163a.htm
Adultery article from the Catholic Encyclopedia site.
http://www.probe.org/docs/adultery.html
Adultery and society article.
http://www.twopaths.com/faq_adultery.htm
Analysis of adultery and the Bible.
http://www.upi.com/view.cfm?StoryID=25022002-053430-4979r
Article examining the flogging of a Sudanese Christian pregnant woman accused of adultery.
http://writ.news.findlaw.com/grossman/20031216.html
Findlaw article on adultery law and Virginia.

The following debates in the Pro/Con series may also be of interest:

In this volume:
Topic 9 Is divorce ever acceptable?

In *Individual and Society*:
Topic 3 Are women still the second sex?

In *Family and Society*:
Topic 1 Does society support family values?

Topic 3 Is marriage essential to the modern family unit?

SHOULD ADULTERY BE A CRIMINAL OFFENSE?

YES: Most societies promote monogamous relationships; adultery is wrong since it leads to betrayal and deceit, and undermines social stability

YES: Practically every religion states that adultery is a sin. It is forbidden in the biblical seventh commandment, for example.

MORALITY
Is adultery immoral?

RELIGION
Is adultery an offense against God?

NO: Moral codes vary in different societies, some of which accept adultery. Also, in societies where divorce is not acceptable, what other choice do unmarried people have who love each other?

NO: There are no absolute definitions of what constitutes adultery. In some interpretations of scripture, for example, rape might strictly be interpreted as adultery.

SHOULD ADULTERY BE A CRIMINAL OFFENSE?
KEY POINTS

YES: As written in scripture and in many legal codes, adultery laws apply equally to men and to women. Their application may be biased against women, but their principle is fair.

YES: Adultery laws underline the moral basis of society and help prevent the degeneration of the values on which civilization depends

FAIRNESS
Are adultery laws fair?

PURPOSE
Do adultery laws serve a purpose?

NO: Adultery laws often penalize women more than men. This is discrimination.

NO: Up to 33 percent of men and 25 percent of women are unfaithful at one time or another. Although such cases may cause individual heartache, they do not threaten society and thus should not be subject to law.

Topic 9
IS DIVORCE EVER ACCEPTABLE?

YES
FROM "IS DIVORCE EVER RIGHT?"
PASTORAL POSITION PAPER, WWW.CHRISTKIRK.COM
DAVE HATCHER

NO
FROM "THE UNHEALED WOUND: THE DAMAGE OF DIVORCE TO CHILDREN"
CRISIS MAGAZINE, APRIL 7, 2003
JOHN OMICINSKI

INTRODUCTION

Divorce is the legal dissolution of a marriage. During 2001 some 2.3 million Americans, or about eight people in every one thousand, got married. According to estimates, around half of those marriages will end in divorce—a rate that is among the highest in the world. National Center for Health Statistics figures reveal that four Americans per thousand also got divorced in 2001. Divorce has long been condemned by both governments and religions. Governments disapprove of it because it threatens the main building block of a stable society, the family. Religions criticize divorce because marriage is in many societies a holy sacrament; its dissolution therefore represents humans breaking a union sanctioned by God. However, some commentators argue that divorce has now become so commonplace that it is fully accepted by society. It might be unfortunate, but human nature makes it necessary. Other people believe that divorce is wrong no matter what the circumstances.

The institution of marriage in the United States developed from three related but different Christian traditions: the Roman Catholic view that marriage was a sacrament that could not be ended by divorce, only by annulment (a declaration that a marriage is invalid); the English view that divorce was a legal matter and could be obtained through Parliament (eventually through the courts); and the Protestant view that both marriage and divorce were secular matters to be handled by civil authorities—divorce was allowed, but only on the specific grounds of cruelty, desertion, or adultery.

The Constitution does not limit the rights of the states to enact their own laws governing marriage and divorce. Despite efforts to amend the Constitution to permit federal legislation on divorce, the states retain separate laws. In the past, when many states still outlawed divorce, this gave rise to "migratory divorce." Couples would move temporarily to a state where divorce was easier to obtain.

From the 1960s popular attitudes toward divorce changed as the United States became more secular. Its increasing acceptance was reflected in reinterpretations of existing laws and in new state legislation. The English and Protestant traditions merged, enabling the establishment of easier grounds for divorce, although Roman Catholics still saw marriage as indissoluble. The focus of divorce legislation shifted from specifying legal grounds for divorce—such as adultery—to criteria defining the breakdown of the marital relationship. This shift could be seen in provisions that allowed divorce on the grounds of alcoholism, drug addiction, or nonsupport.

"The possibility of divorce renders both marriage partners stricter in their observance of the duties they owe to each other."

—DENIS DIDEROT (1713–1784),

FRENCH PHILOSOPHER

Another growing trend was to allow divorce if both parties voluntarily lived apart for a certain period. Thus in 1967 New York allowed divorce for couples who had been legally separated for two years. In 1969 California permitted divorce when "irreconcilable differences" arose in a marriage; it thus became the first state with a "no-fault" divorce law. Most other states soon followed suit.

Some commentators argue that divorce must be acceptable to Americans because they have made it legal. They also point out that divorce is not a modern practice: Moses accepted the possibility. In Jewish law a wife did not have the right to divorce her husband, but she did have the right to remarry if her husband divorced her. Such a view, however, is contradicted by the New Testament teachings of Jesus. In Matthew, for example, one of the main scriptural texts on which Christian marriage is founded, Jesus says, "Therefore what God has joined together, let man not separate" (19:6).

Today many people believe that if a couple have tried to make their marriage work, they should be allowed as painless a way out as possible. Most societies now have some provision for divorce. While they discourage it, many religions—including Protestantism, Judaism, Islam, and Hinduism—permit the dissolution of a marriage.

Some critics counter, however, that marriage demands a lifelong commitment regardless of any change in circumstances. Divorce, they say, should not be provided as an easy option. One justification for this attitude is the consequence for children of broken homes. Its supporters claim that children need to grow up in a stable family environment with two parents. Others object that children will be less unhappy if their parents divorce than if they continue to live with parents who no longer enjoy a loving relationship. Other people interpret the same evidence in exactly the opposite way: Children whose parents divorce are always damaged; but if divorce was not permitted, the husband and wife would have no option but to make the marriage work.

The following two articles address both sides of this debate.

IS DIVORCE EVER RIGHT?
Dave Hatcher

Dave Hatcher is the pastor of Eastside Evangelical Fellowship in Kirkland, Washington.

YES

When it comes to the issue of divorce and remarriage, several prefatory remarks should be made. First, the issue should not be discussed as though it was a scientific research project, where, after gathering all the facts, the cold conclusions are declared. Marriage is a covenant relationship filled with powerful symbols and mystery, along with blessings and curses. It is the only relationship created for mankind on this earth which binds two individuals together as one, satisfying deep longings for intimacy, servanthood, and family. Marriage is both reality and symbol. People really do get married, but this covenant act is symbolic of something even greater and more profound. When a man and a woman marry, they are proclaiming the gospel of the love of the Lord Jesus Christ for His Bride, the church.

Then, throughout their marriage together, they continue to proclaim this, either truthfully, or fallaciously. Whenever lies are proclaimed and lived without the grace of repentance, they eventually destroy both the reality of the marriage and the symbol becomes hollow and empty. The result is deep emotional and spiritual damage, effecting not only the two involved, but also the people around them, and the culture at large. On every level, marriage is a potent thing.

The strict view

Because the topic of marriage is a sacred one, many zealous Christians try to argue that to strive for anything less than the most "conservative" views on divorce and remarriage is to compromise the truth, and trifle with it. But the "moral high ground" is not attained by being more tight-shoed than the opposition. We are never commanded to come up with the most conservative position. Rather, we are required to understand and obey the biblical view. We are not to add to or subtract from the Law. Doing either is sinful. Only Scripture can give us the right perspective on divorce and remarriage. Scripture is our standard.

So we begin by looking at the teachings of Jesus in Matthew 19.... In Matthew 19, Jesus is answering a question posed to Him by the Pharisees in an attempt to test Him.

This statement reflects a Christian perspective. Does it imply that a civil or non-Christian marriage is not as legitimate as a church wedding?

Many historians point out that early marriages were often not sacred or based on love. They were alliances between families, arranged to protect property rights, gain political favor, and so on.

The Pharisees were a major religious and political Jewish sect that emerged in the second century B.C. and remained active until the first or second century A.D.

In the first century, the Jewish teachers fell into two basic camps with regard to the issue of acceptable divorce. Those who followed Hillel were sort of like our modern day liberals. Divorce for them should be allowed on any grounds at all. They interpreted the phrase "some uncleanness" in the Deuteronomy 24:1–4 passage to mean something as little as ruining the dinner. The other group, the followers of Shammai, held the ultra-conservative position that this passage taught that one could only divorce on grounds of fornication. In an attempt to pigeon-hole Jesus into one of these two camps, the Pharisees ask Jesus to comment on this controversy.

> *Hillel and Shammai were Jewish scholars who were born in the century preceding the birth of Christ.*

But Christ transcends these trick questions, and takes the teachers back to the creation account. Christ reemphasizes that marriage is something that was instituted by God. It is a holy institution. It is not something to be tampered with by men.

Yeah, but … they reply. Moses, you see, had given regulations for divorce. But Jesus quickly points out that these provisions were provided because of the hardness of their hearts. It had never been God's ideal. Sin always brings about evil consequences, and hardness of heart still exists. So Jesus states, "… whoever divorces his wife, except for sexual immorality, and marries another, commits adultery; and whoever marries her who is divorced commits adultery."…

Interpretation

Let's deal with the first part—"whoever divorces his wife, except for sexual immorality, and marries another, commits adultery.…" Who is the one committing adultery here? He is one who has 1) divorced his wife and 2) married another. So to whom does the exception refer? To the same person; the one who has divorced and remarried. You cannot argue that the exception clause is limited to the one who divorces but not to the one who remarries. The point of the verse is in regard to the same person. He is one who has been divorced, except for a clause, and been remarried. That one, if he remarries, commits adultery. Consequently, the exception—one who was divorced because of sexual immorality on the part of his spouse and then remarries— does not commit adultery.

> *Hatcher's argument revolves around the word "except." Translation of the Bible is notoriously difficult. Do you think that it is safe to base so much of a case on a single word?*

In essence, Jesus was dealing with the same problem that we see in our culture today—serial polygamy legislated through bureaucracy. There were those who believed that as long as you had all the paperwork (for divorce and remarriage) in place, you were free to have sex with this

> *"Polygamy" is a form of marriage in which a person is allowed to have more than one husband or wife. The opposite is monogamy, which is marriage to only one spouse at a time.*

Why do you think "sexual immorality" is regarded as such a serious offense in a marriage? Where does it rank in your view? Would you place it above physical cruelty, for example?

woman now, and then someone else later if things didn't work out. The mystery and symbolism was destroyed, and with it, so was the blessing.

But as Jesus rebukes this thinking, He is careful not to make the institution of marriage a sacred thing unto itself. There were in fact times that divorce would be allowed. Sexual immorality is considered to be such a heinous sin that it breaks the very covenant of the marriage. Jesus seems to say that the fidelity of the marriage relationship is more important than the formal institution itself, as if to say, "Marriage was made for man, and not man for marriage" —as if to say, "Which is more important, fidelity or the thing which requires fidelity?" Which is more important, the gold or the temple?

Put another way, it is the validity of the divorce that governs the determination of the permissibility of remarriage. Sexual immorality breaks the very heart of the covenant of marriage, and consequently frees the innocent party, if he or she chooses, to put the guilty party away.

This exception clause also provides the innocent person with the opportunity to remarry if he or she so chooses. The second part of this verse clarifies this, but must be understood in relation to the same exception. The second statement "and whoever marries her who is divorced commits adultery" makes no sense otherwise. If the one who was divorced, even if the former spouse was guilty of sexual immorality, caused his or her new spouse to commit adultery, then there is really no freedom at all, and the whole verse is meaningless. Jesus is clearly allowing for a husband or wife to put away a spouse for sexual immorality, and this may be done in such a way that allows the innocent spouse the freedom to remarry without consequence....

To "put away" is an archaic usage, meaning to divorce. Used in this sense it does not mean to incarcerate or confine to an institution.

The Pauline teaching

There are times when what God has joined together is separated, by the Word of God. Sexual immorality on the part of a spouse is one occasion. The innocent party is duly freed to remarry if he or she so chooses, because he is no longer bound to the covenant. This is the same freedom Paul assumes in his illustration in Romans 7, where a spouse is no longer bound to a marriage covenant when his partner has died. There, he is free to remarry.

This understanding of release from the previous covenant is important when looking at the other possibility for divorce and remarriage in Paul's teaching.

In his letter to the Corinthians, Paul answers a number of sex and marriage questions which had apparently been asked of him. One of these questions appears to have been: "What if, having become a believer myself, my unbelieving spouse wishes to leave me?" Paul answers that when an unbelieving spouse deserts a believing partner the believer is to let the spouse go (1 Cor 7:12–16). When Paul says to let the deserter go, he describes the state of the believer: "a brother or sister is not under bondage in such cases" (1 Cor 7:15).

What is his point? It can't be simply that he is not bound to stay with the spouse, because the spouse already left. Paul had already said let him depart. "Not under bondage" must refer to the marriage vows. One is no longer bound to the marriage covenant if one has been truly deserted. And if one were no longer bound by a marriage vow, it would follow that one is free to remarry. 1 Corinthians 7:27–28 must be read with the local context in mind (Paul is arguing that for the present, it is better that the Corinthians not be married), and the exception clauses stated in Jesus' declaration (which do not appear in this passage …): "Are you bound to a wife? Do not seek to be loosed. Are you loosed from a wife? Do not seek a wife. But even if you do marry, you have not sinned…"

So, desertion by an unbelieving spouse looses the believer from the previous marriage covenant and frees him or her for remarriage. This is because, in these special circumstances, God rather than man, separates what He has joined together.

The confession

These are some of the reasons why the Westminster Confession teaches: "In the case of adultery after marriage, it is lawful for the innocent party to sue out a divorce: and, after the divorce, to marry another, as if the offending party were dead … nothing but adultery, or such wilful desertion as can no way be remedied by the church, or civil magistrate, is cause sufficient of dissolving the bond of marriage …"

It is true that God says that He hates divorce (Mal 2:16). But it is equally true that God hates infidelity and covenant breaking as well. So much so that at times God Himself has commanded divorce. He told Abraham to divorce Hagar. He commanded through Ezra that men divorce their pagan wives on a particular occasion. Even God himself is represented as divorcing Israel in Jeremiah 3:8.

So marriage certainly is a powerful thing. May God grant us a clear mind in the administration of this glorious blessing, and may He deliver us from the evil of blatant disregard as well as overzealous misunderstanding.

The Westminster Confession was drawn up in 1646. It is the confession of faith, or creed, of English-speaking Presbyterians. See http://www.bible-researcher.com/wescon01.html for more detail.

Hagar was the servant of Sarah, Abraham's wife, and became Abraham's concubine, bearing the prophet a son, Ishmael. See http://www.bartleby.com/65/ab/Abraham.html and links to find out more.

THE UNHEALED WOUND: THE DAMAGE OF DIVORCE TO CHILDREN
John Omicinski

John Omicinski worked in newspaper journalism for more than 40 years, retiring as a national correspondent for the Washington bureau of Gannett News Service.

Do you think that the pope has the right to comment on issues such as divorce? Is it a difficult enough decision to come to without this extra guilt?

More than 27 percent of children in the United States reside with just one parent. Recent research shows that this percentage will grow. If more than a quarter of children do not have two-parent families, is it likely that they will feel like second-class citizens?

NO

… There is nothing good to say about divorce. Those who divorce do great damage to themselves but more so to their children, who neither understand divorce nor know how to "adjust" and "bounce back." Divorce is an unmitigated disaster, a social earthquake for children, affecting them mentally, spiritually, socially, and, except perhaps among the rich, financially for the rest of their lives. And its fault lines are spreading across U.S. society.

The social fabric of our "Divorce Nation" has been as badly torn by marital splits as it was by the Vietnam War and segregation. On January 30, Pope John Paul II, in a speech to the judges of the Roman Rota, declared that the divorce crisis spreads because, too often, family matters are seen through the prism of secular values, which are often twisted by the mass media. Modern men and women, he suggests, quickly reject faith as a mast in a marital storm, preferring popular culture's messages. "Today's mentality, highly secularized, tends to affirm the human values of the institution of the family," he said, "by separating them from religious values and proclaiming [them] altogether auto-nomous from God."…

Marriage—for ever?

Permanence in marriage is largely a thing of the past in America, making it at the same time a pearl of great price, worth far more than the glamour, luxury, and false freedom often sought by divorcing parents. Judith Wallerstein, who shocked America with her 2000 book, *The Unexpected Legacy of Divorce*, a detailed account of divorce's debilitating effects on about 100 children studied over 25 years, says she was stunned by what she found. Perceptively, Wallerstein notes that children of divorce end up "feeling like second-class citizens compared with [their] friends in intact families." That feeling doesn't go away. Before she did the study, Wallerstein, a University of California–Berkeley social scientist, was naively sucked in by a culture run by parents, not children. And those parents want to be pardoned of any culpability for damaging their children. They want divorce laws fashioned by "assumptions congenial to adult wishes," Wallerstein now says....

Wallerstein's book finds the surviving children's wounds surprisingly similar: Children of divorce are less trusting, more aggressive, inclined to depression, more ready to accept failure easily, and confused about many things, including sex. I second all those motions. More than 54 years after my parents divorced, it still stings, affecting me every day. Its effects run the gamut, from emotional to practical. Many of us try to teach ourselves to love and trust and to be friends because we weren't taught much about those things by any parent. "Love" wasn't a word bandied about in my house....

Not only do I wish my parents never divorced, I'll go a step further. If I had to live my life over knowing it would happen again, I wouldn't.

Does this suggest that more investment should be put into counseling children whose parents are divorcing?

Does such an emotional statement detract from or add to the author's argument?

No-fault divorce

My parents divorced in the early 1950s, placing me and my two sisters in the vanguard of the armies of children of divorce, who now make up 25 percent of those 46 and older in the United States. Not only did we have to live with divorce but also with the stigma of it in a nominally Roman Catholic family in the 1950s. Most people treated us as if we had three eyes. Adultery or criminal behavior were among the only grounds for divorce in those days. But more than a decade later (1969), when the "Me Generation" demanded it, then–California governor Ronald Reagan signed the first no-fault divorce law, and the wildfire spread, burning down families across the country. (Significantly, Reagan himself had a nasty divorce from Jane Wyman under the old laws and probably was more than willing to scribble his signature.)

As a result, says Maggie Gallagher in her 1996 book, *The Abolition of Marriage: How We Destroy Lasting Love* from a formal, legal standpoint, marriage is no longer an enforceable commitment.... Marriage has been reconceived as a purely private act, not a social institution.... Thanks to no-fault divorce and the attitudes, norms, and policies that support it, getting married now more closely resembles taking a concubine than taking a wife. Once couples stayed married "for the sake of the children," she says, but in the last 30 years they have come to divorce "for the sake of the children." Parents conveniently assume that their children cannot be happy if they are unhappy, but never that they cannot be happy if their children are unhappy. No surprise that America has the highest divorce rate in the world, 20 or 30 times greater than some countries. Another so-called "great

See Volume 11, Family and Society, Topic 3 Is marriage essential to the family unit? What do you think?

American liberal social policy breakthrough" has caused a disastrous avalanche of social problems, and no amount of billions in government programs is going to clean that up....

Damage

Damaged by divorce, kids aren't sure what to do about the opposite sex—whether to love it or leave it. Wallerstein's cohort of divorce flotsam avoided the altar: Only 26 percent married, though many had several relationships that led to nothing.

My response was the reverse. After the coldness of home, I wanted to get married and have a nice, warm family. Looking back at the years, I see that I was casting about for someone who would be loyal and trustworthy and would stick to a marriage. I found her in high school, dated her through college on and off, and married her while I was in the army. Kids followed quickly. She came from a strong, hardworking family that seemed to laugh a lot together and at life, and I liked that. There wasn't a lot of laughing at life at my house growing up; the smallest problem could become a great conundrum because we didn't work together very well.

Do you think people try harder to make relationships work if they are married? Should there be courses in how to be and stay married?

Over our 41 years of marriage, my lack of marital "training," so to speak, has caused severe strains in our family circle. Many times, divorce would have been the easy way out, but for some reason, neither of us took the fatal step. There are still many differences between us, but none seems irreconcilable. Some are simply forgotten. It happens, if you let enough time go by. My wife comes from a family where there are several strong marriages, and perhaps she had people who could talk her through difficult landings. I had no one to advise me and often talked to bartenders or bottles about my "troubles." I know now that a priest would have been a better option, because I use them now as sounding boards as well as confessors. As a result of a lot of praying to the Blessed Virgin Mary in the 1980s, the burden of drinking was, almost miraculously, lifted, and I have been sober for a long time. That's helped my relations with friends and family, but the veil of my parents' divorce still blurs my vision.

The author uses very emotional language to put his argument across. Is it effective?

There is very little literature geared to the children of divorce. But Stephanie Staal's 2000 book, *The Love They Lost*, is one of few by a child-survivor. She and I share the belief that all children of divorce change in some way; some more, some less. Her word-picture is effective: "Divorce plants a splinter in our minds, and in response, we assemble our identities around it. When we forge ahead in our own intimate relationships, the splinter twists, and we are often forced to … challenge the lessons learned from our parents' breakup."

Over the years, I consciously or subconsciously sought out surrogate fathers. I believe it is a commonplace reaction by male children of a divorce, who usually end up with the mother and lack male bonds. In the process, I found some delightful men who taught me how to write, how to play golf, how to get out of myself, how to enjoy others' company, and, not least, how to pray. All were wonderful and great role models, but at the end of the day, they went home and so did I.

Nowadays on weekends, when I'm sipping a coffee at malls or rummaging through bookstores, I find myself watching the dads and sons go by, wondering if it's a weekend custody visit or the real family thing. If they're in a big hurry, I always suspect I am watching a split family trying to make up for lost time. In an era when the words "I feel your pain" have been cheapened, as so many emotions have been, I feel a genuine sympathy for these custody-wanderers, filling the hours until it's time to go "home." Especially for the kid. Maybe he's getting "quality time," but he's not getting quality love, and though he may go home with an armload of packages, he will feel emotionally short-changed. Family love, of course, cannot operate on timelines. Some of the happiest families I know lead very slow lives, but they are lived together in peace. As Dickens pointed out, happy families are all the same; it is the unhappy ones that are different. And I can't help wondering about the guilt-ridden father, especially if he is in a second marriage, that so-called triumph of hope over experience. If there are kids in the second marriage, where does he draw his lines of love? The emotional calculus of divorce is too complicated, especially for children, no matter how suave and sophisticated the players may be, no matter how driven the adults are to "make things work." God's arithmetic—one on one—works best for all concerned.

> Can these two things—quality time and quality love—be separated?

> The author ends on a strong note, but is his argument convincing? Can love be compartmentalized in this way?

Summary

Dave Hatcher, a pastor from Kirkland, Washington, begins the first article by emphasizing the practical and symbolic importance of marriage: It is a unique relationship "which binds two individuals together as one." Those who enter marriage make a solemn undertaking, not only to each other but also to Jesus and the church. Having established his view that marriage is not to be taken lightly, however, Hatcher explains why it should be possible, in certain circumstances, to end it. He says that it is better to divorce than to persist in a relationship that proclaims a love that the husband and wife do not feel. It is also wrong, he argues, for one partner to be forced to stay in a relationship that is meant to be exclusive if the other partner has been unfaithful. Hatcher supports his opinions with quotations from the Bible.

   The second article looks at at the pain divorce causes, especially to children. Journalist John Omicinski draws on his own experiences as the child of divorced parents to argue that divorce is never acceptable. He even goes so far as to say that if he could live his life over with that same experience he would choose not to. Omicinski draws on many books discussing divorce to argue that people give up far too easily on marriage. Citing Maggie Gallagher's 1996 book *The Abolition of Marriage: How We Destroy Lasting Love*, he argues that "Thanks to no-fault divorce and the attitudes, norms, and policies that support it, getting married now more closely resembles taking a concubine than taking a wife." He claims that divorce is an "unmitigated disaster, a social earthquake."

FURTHER INFORMATION:

Books:

Adams, Jay E., *Marriage, Divorce, and Remarriage in the Bible: A Fresh Look at What Scripture Teaches.* Grand Rapids, MI: Zondervan, 1986.

Instone-Brewer, David, *Divorce and Remarriage in the Bible: The Social and Literary Context.* Grand Rapids, MI: W.B. Eerdmans, 2002.

Medved, Diane, *The Case against Divorce.* New York: D.I. Fine, 1989.

Whitehead, Barbara Dafoe, *The Divorce Culture.* New York: Alfred Knopf, 1997.

Useful websites:

http://www.divorcereform.org/stats.html
A collection of statistcs on divorce from Americans for Divorce Reform.
www.divorcesource.com
A legal resource for divorce, including state divorce laws.

The following debates in the Pro/Con series may also be of interest:

In this volume:
Topic 8 Should adultery be a criminal offense?

Topic 10 Should the Bible be interpreted literally?

In *Family and Society*:
Topic 1 Does society support family values?

Topic 4 Is the two-parent family best?

IS DIVORCE EVER ACCEPTABLE?

YES: In today's world it is increasingly difficult for people to be sure of their choice of partner, so divorce is bound to occur more

YES: Marriage is a relationship that depends on love and trust. A spouse should have the right to end an abusive marriage

OLD-FASHIONED
Is the idea that "marriage is for life" old-fashioned?

ABUSE
Is divorce acceptable in cases of abuse?

NO: Maintaining a marriage has always required effort on both sides; the rise in divorce rates simply reflects people's unwillingness to work at something

NO: Some people use abuse as an easy excuse to give up on marriage; most cases can be resolved with the help of guidance

IS DIVORCE EVER ACCEPTABLE? KEY POINTS

YES: The Old Testament book of Deuteronomy suggests that a man may divorce his wife

YES: St. Paul says that in the case of a believer being deserted by his or her spouse "a brother or sister is not under bondage" (1 Corinthians 7:15)

SCRIPTURE
Does the Bible approve of divorce?

NO: Jesus said, "Therefore what God has joined together, let man not separate" (Matthew 19:6). That means divorce is wrong.

NO: In the Old Testament book of Malachi God calls divorce "treachery"

PART 3
WORLD RELIGIONS

There are many religions in the world, and most people follow some religious faith. Christianity claims the most adherents, with followers in all parts of the world. But large numbers of worshipers also practice folk religions, particularly in China and Africa, as well as East Asian religions such as Taoism that are more concerned with philosophy and codes of behavior than with belief in a supreme being, or deity. In 2000 the estimated numbers of followers for the major established world religions were: Christianity 2.1 billion (33.4 percent of the world population), Islam 1.2 billion (18.5 percent), Hinduism 840 million (13.4 percent), Buddhism 366 million (5.9 percent), Sikhism 21.5 million (0.3 percent), and Judaism 17.5 million (0.3 percent).

Complex histories

All of the world's organized religions have long and complex histories. Judaism and Hinduism, the majority religion of the India, are two of the oldest established faiths, both dating back over 3,000 years. The youngest are Islam, founded in the seventh century A.D. by the Prophet Muhammad (about 570–632), and Sikhism, founded in the Punjab, northwest India, in the late 15th century by Guru Nanak (1469–1539).

Religions have evolved over centuries, not just in their rituals and the structure of their churches but also in their beliefs. There are long traditions of interpretation of scriptures—the sacred texts of a religion. Among a number of world religions the changing interpretations have led to a fracturing of the chief church into various branches. Islam, for example, is divided into the majority Sunni branch and the minority Shi'ah; the Sufis are a small mystical sect related to Islam. Similarly, in Buddhism there are differences between the conservative Theravada tradition, or the Way of the Elders, and the Mahayana, or Great Vehicle, a more diverse tradition; Zen Buddhism is a derivative of the Mahayana branch.

Christianity, which is based on the life and teachings of Jesus Christ, arose in the first century A.D. and grew to become the official religion of the Roman Empire. Theological disputes developed between the centers of the church in Rome and in Constantinople (now Istanbul in Turkey), with the two formally dividing in the 11th century into eastern and western branches that became the Eastern Orthodox and Roman Catholic churches. As protest grew against the increasing power and wealth of the Catholic Church in the 15th and early 16th centuries, the Reformation brought the creation of a new branch of Christianity known as Protestantism. Many Protestant denominations have emerged, including Baptists and Methodists.

Religion and conflict

As religions have evolved, they have come into conflict both with other religions and with diverse traditions within their own faiths. An example of the former type of conflict is the Crusades, religious wars waged by Christians against Islamic Turks in the Holy Land from the 11th to the 13th centuries. Some observers view aspects of the current War on Terrorism, with its U.S.-led attacks on Afghanistan and Iraq, as similar to a war between Islam and Christianity. In the 20th century there was also conflict between Muslims and Hindus in South Asia.

majority of adherents acknowledge that the world's major faiths need to coexist. Much of the time this is not particularly difficult since most religions emphasize values such as peace, tolerance, charity, and forgiveness. Moreover, many religions share the same problems, such as adapting ancient beliefs to suit the modern world and learning to function in multifaith, multiracial societies. Such problems may well be more effectively solved by faiths acting together.

The first two topics in this section examine issues at the heart of modern Christianity. Topic 10 considers whether the Bible, the sacred writings

---

"I am a sort of collector of religions; and the curious thing is that I find I can believe them all."

—GEORGE BERNARD SHAW (1856–1950), IRISH PLAYWRIGHT

Religions have also turned to violence to enforce established doctrines against new, or heretic, interpretations. Shi'ah and Sunni Muslims, for example, have been on opposing sides in many conflicts, most recently the Iran–Iraq War of the 1980s. The emergence of Protestantism within Christianity was the cue for centuries of war that was more or less motivated by the desire of Catholicism to suppress the new faith. The Catholic Church also launched the Inquisition, a court charged with protecting the faith, which it did by means including torture and execution.

Religious tolerance

Although some people still believe that religion is exclusive, and that their own faith should try to win converts from and suppress other religions, the

of both the Jewish and Christian faiths, should be interpreted literally. A literal reading of the texts is most often associated with various fundamentalist Protestant denominations. Topic 11 looks at how the Catholic Church has coped with allegations of child sex abuse involving priests in America and other countries.

Topic 12 asks whether monotheistic religions—those that worship a single deity, including the Abrahamic faiths (Judaism, Christianity, and Islam)—are less tolerant than faiths that worship many gods. Some observers have been debating this issue since the September 11, 2001, attacks on the United States carried out by Islamic fundamentalists. Islam is also the subject of Topic 13, which considers whether Islam is a religion that condones violence.

Topic 10
SHOULD THE BIBLE BE INTERPRETED LITERALLY?

YES

FROM "IS THE BIBLE LITERAL?"
HTTP://WWW.GEOCITIES.COM/HEARTLAND/WOODS/8255/LITERALPFV.HTML
JAMES H. BOYD

NO

FROM "SOME REASONS WHY HUMANISTS REJECT THE BIBLE"
WWW.HUMANISMBYJOE.COM
JOSEPH C. SOMMER

INTRODUCTION

The Bible is the sacred book, or rather collection of books, of the Jewish and Christian faiths. The sacred writings of Judaism—the Hebrew Bible—consist of the books known to Christians as the Old Testament. Its different sections were written in Hebrew between the 12th and 2nd centuries B.C. The Christian Bible also includes the books of the New Testament, which were originally written in Greek during the first and second centuries A.D.

Some Jews and Christians believe that the Bible is God's word and should be accepted as literal truth; they are known as literalists. Others argue that the Bible cannot be God's literal word. It was written at different times by many different authors in different cultures. It is part a history of certain communities, part a collection of moral fables and guidelines. It even contradicts itself. Teachings such as "An eye for an eye" and "Turn the other cheek" are mutually exclusive, so how,

critics ask, can both be interpreted as God's infallible word? There are also problems caused by the difficulty of translating the Bible or establishing its original form.

Although the ancient Jews believed that their scriptures were inspired by God and intended to be taken literally, they accepted that some passages seemed to require interpretation before their true meaning became apparent. Scholars provided it in the form of critical commentaries known in Hebrew as *midrash*.

The earliest adherents of Christianity also believed in the literal truth of their scriptures, but again began to interpret that truth at an early stage. One of the greatest early theologians, Origen of Alexandria (about 185–254), wrote a critical text of the Old Testament and the gospels of Matthew and John in the third century. However, after that there was very little consensus about the meaning of almost any part of the

Bible—many people had different explanations for the events described and for the symbolic or the literal meanings of the text. Many of the great splits in the Christian church—most notably that between Roman Catholicism and Protestantism in the 16th century—have been based at least partly on different interpretations of the Bible.

Literalists believe that certain passages in the Bible may be metaphorical, but that they are clearly indicated; the rest is either prediction or history. Literalists believe, for example, the account in Genesis of the creation of the universe in seven days. A calculation based on the information in the Old Testament suggests that this creation occurred in only 3760 B.C. Scientists, however, argue that the geology of the earth and the theory of evolution prove that the earth is millions of years old. Some literalists still believe that evolution should not be taught in schools, or that creationism—belief in the biblical account—should be taught alongside it.

"The Bible is literature...."

—GEORGE SANTAYANA

(1863–1952), PHILOSOPHER

The majority of practicing Christians today admit that the distinction in the Bible between historical truth and literary metaphor is sometimes less than completely clear. For example, Jesus may not literally have defied the laws of science by walking on water, as described in Matthew 14:25; the image might have symbolized the strength of Jesus's own faith and the faith he demanded from his disciples. Nearly all Christians, however, still believe in the literal resurrection of Christ.

Reform Judaism—a movement that began in the 19th century—challenged many traditional Jewish beliefs and practices in an effort to adapt to the social, political, and cultural conditions of the modern world. Reform Jews responded to scientific theory with their own "science of Judaism," which aimed to show that their religion had changed over time to accommodate new theories of knowledge. They developed a theology that rejected the literalist understanding of the Hebrew Bible and the timeless authority of the *halachah*—"the way," a term referring to the body of laws and customs that has evolved since biblical times. As opposed to Orthodox Jews, who uphold that the laws presented to Moses on Mount Sinai represent God's revelation given once and for all time, Reform Jews believe that the will of God needs to be reinterpreted by each generation. They argue that scientific knowledge and modern insights all form part of his revelation. Therefore, while the Bible may be an authoritative text, it is not a fixed authority but is subject to constant reinterpretation.

Some Christians agree that many of the attitudes reflected in the Bible cannot be applied to contemporary society, and that people who read the texts literally often hold attitudes incompatible with modern life and knowledge. They point out, for example, that it is possible to read into some Bible passages encouragement for prejudice, intolerance, and violence.

The following extracts present very different views about whether or not the Bible should be interpreted literally.

IS THE BIBLE LITERAL?
James H. Boyd

YES

Three chefs were working in a restaurant one day, when their kitchen supervisor approached them with an order, and instructions on how to properly prepare it. The first chef … said "You can show a recipe to 100 different people, and each of them get a different meaning. You can't understand recipes, so why even read them?"

The second chef took a slightly different angle. He said "I don't believe this recipe to be the literal directions of our supervisor. I believe the ingredients all have hidden meanings. I think the meat represents one thing, the spices and other ingredients symbolize something else, and the time and cooking temperature are some sort of mysterious allegory."

While the other two were engaging in their debate, the third chef simply took the recipe, and prepared the dish according to instructions…. This chef was rewarded for following directions properly, while the other two were reprimanded, or worse.

While this little story may seem somewhat silly, it sadly illustrates the attitude that many people take toward God and His Word, the Bible, which is to be OUR instructions, our "recipe," for how to live our lives.

The author sets the scene with a modern-day parable. Do you think that the parallel he draws is helpful or distracting?

Origen, the "husk," and the "kernel"
As we will examine shortly, Jesus and the Apostles took the Bible quite literally. The tendency to allegorize and spiritualize Scripture was popularized around A.D. 250 by a man named Origen. Origen was a prolific author, and a valiant evangelist in the early church. He suffered brutal persecution, and eventually martyrdom for his beliefs. Although his courage and zeal were certainly commendable, he unfortunately embraced several false and heretical doctrines, which stemmed from his unorthodox views of Scripture. Rather than affirm the Apostolic teaching that the Scriptures were the infallible Word of God, he taught that they were merely the "husk" which hid the "kernel" of Truth, and thus, began replacing the plainly revealed teachings of Scripture with enigmatic, allegorical interpretations. As a result of this teaching, the floodgates were open to a devastating deluge of confusion and division, from which the

Origen of Alexandria (about 185–254) was one of the foremost early Christian scholars. Go to http://www.iep.utm.edu/o/origen.htm to find out more.

Literalists believe that biblical events such as Christ's crowning with thorns—here in a painting by Titian (Tiziano Vecellio; about 1488–1576)—record things that really happened in history.

church has never fully recovered. In order for the church as a whole to function as God intends, there MUST be a re-discovery of the foundational, literal Truth of the Bible.

The character of the Bible

To understand the intended meaning of Scripture, let's look at what the Bible says about itself. The Bible is a REVELATION, which means "to reveal, to unveil, to lift a curtain for all to see." God gave us the Bible to REVEAL Truth, not to CONCEAL it. The Bible is written in simple terms, for simple people (Matthew 11:25; 13:19–23; 2 Corinthians 4:1–6; 2 Timothy 3:16–17). 80% of the Bible is simply history, promises, and guidelines for living. The other 20% consists of prophecies about future events.

Understand that when we refer to the Bible being literal, we are not denying that it does contain some figurative language. However, we need to keep two important facts in mind;

1) When figurative language is being used, it is obvious.

2) The figurative language is always intended to convey a literal truth.

For example, when Jesus referred to Himself as a "vine" (John 15:1), He obviously didn't mean that He had leaves and grapes growing out of His arms! Rather, He was illustrating the literal truth that His relationship with His disciples can be compared to a vine's relationship with its branches.

Statements of Jesus and the Apostles

Whenever Jesus, the Apostles, or any other New Testament figure quoted from Scripture, they quoted it as literal, historical, and authoritative. An example of this would be creation. Both Jesus and Paul affirm that Adam and Eve were literal, historic figures (Matthew 19:4; 1 Timothy 2:14–15). The doctrine of original sin, which Paul so powerfully teaches in Romans 5, would be meaningless if there were not a literal fall. In addition, the Bible gives us the general location of the Garden of Eden, near the Pishon, Gihon, Tigris, and Euphrates rivers (Genesis 2:10–14). This would place it around modern Iraq or northern Syria.

Other examples of Old Testament events quoted as literal history include; Cain and Abel (Genesis 4; Hebrews 11:4; 1 John 3:12), the flood (Genesis 7; Matthew 24:39), the call of Abraham (Genesis 12–13; Hebrews 11:8), the destruction

Citing authoritative sources is a key tool in presenting an argument. Throughout the article the author provides detailed biblical references in support of his points.

If the author is prepared to concede that some parts of the Bible are not literal, how is it possible to tell whether other parts are? If Jesus "obviously" did not really sprout leaves, is it also possible that he "obviously" did not really walk on water?

Mention of the Tigris and Euphrates rivers points to a Middle East location for the Garden of Eden. However, it is difficult to give an exact position since the identities of the Pishon and Gihon rivers of the Bible remain open to doubt.

of Sodom and Gomorrah (Genesis 18-19; Luke 17:29), the exodus from Egypt (Exodus 14:22; 1 Corinthians 10:1-2), Jonah and the great fish (Jonah 2; Matthew 12:40), and Daniel in the Lion's den (Daniel 6; Hebrews 11:33).

Fulfilled prophecy

Another example of the literal character of the Bible is the literal fulfillment of prophecy. Although prophecy does sometimes use figurative language to convey its point, such as the dream of King Nebuchadnezzar in Daniel 2, and much of the Book of Revelation, the prophecies all point to specific, literal events. Let's look at a few of them;

The flood Prophesied in Genesis 6:3, literally fulfilled in Genesis 7:10.

Joshua and Caleb's entry into Canaan (Numbers 14:24, 30) Literally fulfilled in Joshua 3:7,17;14:6-12.

The destruction of the temple (1 Kings 9:7; 2 Chronicles 7:20-21; Jeremiah 7:14) Literal fulfillment— 2 Kings 25:9.

The fall of Jericho (Joshua 6:1-5) Literally fulfilled in Joshua 6:20.

The destruction of Tyre (Ezekiel 26:3-5, 12, 14) Literal fulfillment—When King Nebuchadnezzar attacked and laid siege to the city, tearing down the walls and towers. Then, in 332 B.C., Alexander the Great took the city after a seven month siege. TO THIS DAY this area is used by fishermen as a place to lay their nets, just like it says in verse 14.

As you can see from these, and many other examples, Bible prophecy is fulfilled, literally, and in very meticulous detail. As is the case for all of the Bible, the God who created us also knows how to communicate with us. God is not trying to confuse us, as He is not the author of confusion (1 Corinthians 14:33). He WANTS to make Himself known to us because He loves us, and wants to have a relationship with us. He gave us the Bible to show us how to establish and build that relationship. The Bible reveals to us the heart of God, what does and doesn't please Him, and how we are to worship and follow Him. Above all, He gave it to us to reveal Jesus to us, who is the one who made it possible for us to have this relationship....

Babylonia had a number of kings named Nebuchadnezzar. The one in the book of Daniel was Nebuchadnezzar II, who lived from about 630 to 561 B.C. He twice laid siege to Jerusalem, destroying the city in 586 and taking many of its inhabitants into captivity in Babylon.

Alexander the Great (356–323 B.C.) was one of the commanding figures of ancient history, conquering most of Asia before his death in his early thirties. Go to http:// ancienthistory. about.com/cs/ alexander for a range of links on Alexander and his career.

SOME REASONS WHY HUMANISTS REJECT THE BIBLE
Joseph C. Sommer

Joseph C. Sommer is an author, attorney, and humanist (see sidebar below). This article appears in full on his website (www.humanismbyjoe.com).

NO

... In the United States, the Bible is commonly hailed as a divinely inspired book. Television and radio media often carry religious programs praising the Bible as the holy and infallible word of God. Religious organizations also distribute vast quantities of books, magazines, tapes, pamphlets and other materials....

The Bible is also extolled by many politicians. For instance, in 1983 President Ronald Reagan signed into law an Act of Congress proclaiming that year to be the "Year of the Bible." The law declared the Bible to be the "Word of God" and asserted that there is "a national need to study and apply its teachings."...

The massive and incessant promotion of the Bible significantly influences the beliefs of millions of people....

"Omniscient" means all-knowing, or being possessed of complete knowledge.

When people accept the claim that the Bible contains absolute truth as revealed by a just and omniscient God, and attempt to mold the laws and social practices of a nation to reflect biblical teachings, there is potential for serious error and harm if the Bible is actually a product of fallible humans who lived in an unenlightened era. In that case, the Bible would not be a guidebook for attaining human happiness and well-being, but would instead perpetuate the ideas of an ignorant and superstitious past and cause humanity to not progress beyond that level.

Those results would be tragic because ignorance and superstition, as even most supporters of the Bible would probably agree, have caused humankind to suffer immense amounts of misery throughout history....

Humanists see the point of human existence as seeking human progress and the betterment of the human situation through science and rational thought. They reject the supernatural and the existence of a divine purpose.

Cruelties

Humanists also reject the Bible because it sanctions the most outrageous cruelty and injustice imaginable. In civilized legal systems, a fundamental principle is that the suffering of the innocent is the very essence of injustice. Yet the Bible teaches that God repeatedly violated this elementary moral precept by harming numerous innocent persons....

God's violence incites human violence

A major problem with the violence and injustice in the Bible is that, all too often, the teachings and example set by the biblical God have incited and been used to justify cruel acts by his followers. Many of them reasoned that since God, who is considered just and loving, committed or approved of the most brutal acts of violence, good Christians need not have qualms about behaving similarly. It is likely that this logic was, at least in part, what the American patriot Thomas Paine was referring to when he said, "The belief in a cruel god makes a cruel man."...

Teachings inconsistent with the laws of nature

A further reason that Humanists reject the Bible is that it contains numerous claims that are inconsistent with the laws of nature. Humanists believe that the promotion of those claims as being true has caused tremendous harm to humanity....

The Bible and supernatural events

Biblical teachings about supernatural beings intervening in this world are diametrically opposed to the scientific principle that natural laws operate uniformly and unvaryingly. Belief in the Bible is, therefore, inconsistent with a scientific outlook and discourages development of a scientific approach to problems....

Harms of the supernatural outlook

A terribly harmful effect of believing that supernatural beings intervene in the world is that people have often misdirected their energies in attempting to solve problems. Instead of studying this world to discover facts that could be used to develop scientific solutions to problems, they engaged in religious activities in an effort to obtain the assistance of benevolent supernatural beings or thwart the influence of malicious preternatural agents....

Based on biblical teachings, Christian theologians during [the Middle Ages] believed that the plagues were caused by the anger of God or the malevolence of Satan. The Bible gave them ample support for that belief....

Due to these beliefs about the supernatural causes of disease, theologians taught that plagues could be averted or alleviated by seeking God's aid and protection. The method of obtaining this supernatural assistance, they thought, was to perform religious acts such as repenting from sin; providing gifts to churches, monasteries and shrines;

The political theorist Thomas Paine (1737–1809) was born in England and emigrated to America in 1774. His writings were influential in the American Revolution (1775–1783). See www.thomaspaine. org for a biography.

There is a modern parallel to the plague in the spread of HIV/AIDS. Some religious commentators see the disease, which is largely transmitted through sexual behavior or narcotics abuse, as being a punishment for humanity's immorality. Do you think that such a view can help solve the problem?

participating in religious processions; attending church services (which often only increased the spread of disease); and killing Jews and witches (since it was believed that Satan used them as his agents in causing illness). The theologians largely ignored the possibility of physical causes and cures of diseases....

Teachings inconsistent with the physical world

Humanists also repudiate the Bible because it contains many teachings that are inconsistent with the structure of the physical world.... A classic example of an incorrect Bible teaching is seen in the opposition that Christian theologians mounted against Galileo's proof of the theory, which was expounded by Copernicus in the sixteenth century, that the earth rotates on its axis and revolves around the sun. In the seventeenth century, Galileo's telescope proved that Copernicus had been right. In opposing the Copernican doctrine and attempting to show that the earth remains stationary while the sun moves around it, the Catholic Church pointed to the tenth chapter of the book of Joshua. There we are told that Joshua, in order to have a longer period of daylight in which to carry out the Lord's command to slaughter the Amorites, told the sun to stand still—not the earth....

Because of Galileo's advocacy of the unbiblical Copernican doctrine, the Inquisition threatened him with torture, forced him to recant his support for that theory and sentenced him to imprisonment. Moreover, for nearly two hundred years the Catholic Church's Index of Forbidden Books condemned all writings that affirmed the idea of the double motion of the earth. And for generations the major branches of Protestantism—Lutheran, Calvinist and Anglican— denounced the Copernican doctrine as contrary to scripture.

A flat earth resting on pillars

The Bible supports the primitive idea that the earth is flat. In the sixth century, a Christian monk named Cosmas wrote a book titled *Topographia Christiana* that describes the structure of the physical world. Basing his views on the Bible, Cosmas held that the earth is flat and surrounded by four seas.

One of the reasons for Cosmas' belief in a flat earth was the statement, at Revelation 1:7, that when Christ returns, "every eye shall see him." Cosmas reasoned that if the earth were round, people on the other side would not see Christ's second coming....

Galileo Galilei (1564–1642) was an Italian astronomer, mathematician, and physicist. Nicholas Copernicus (1473–1543) was a Polish astronomer, clergyman, and medical doctor. Go to http://galileo.rice.edu for an in-depth treatment of Galileo and his work. The site also contains a section on the Inquisition, the religious tribunal responsible for investigating heretics, or those whose views diverged from Catholic orthodoxy.

Cosmas of Alexandria, also called Cosmas Indicopleustes, was a merchant and traveler who became a monk later in life. Go to http://www.henry-davis.com/MAPS/EMwebpages/202mono.html for more information about Topographia Christiana (Christian Topography).

[T]he view of the world contained in Cosmas' book was accepted for several centuries as orthodox Christian doctrine. Even in the fifteenth century, when Christopher Columbus proposed to sail west from Spain to reach the East Indies, the biblical notion of a flat earth was a major source of opposition to him....

False prophecies

Prophecies contained in the Bible provide further support for the Humanist position that the book is not the word of God. Because many of the prophecies turned out to be false, they are clear proof that the Bible is not inerrant.

> *"Inerrant" means free from error or incapable of being wrong.*

The Bible itself contains a test for determining whether a prophecy was inspired by God. Deuteronomy 18:22 states: "When a prophet speaketh in the name of the Lord, if the thing follow not, nor come to pass, that is the thing which the Lord hath not spoken, but the prophet hath spoken it presumptuously: thou shalt not be afraid of him." Applying this test to the Bible leads to the conclusion that the book contains many statements that were not inspired by God....

Inaccurate statements about history

Another reason that Humanists view the Bible as untrustworthy is that it has erroneous statements about history. The findings of historians and other scholars show that many assertions in the Bible are historically inaccurate....

Other problems with the Bible

Harm that the Bible causes to personal lives should also be mentioned as a reason to reject the book. Few persons seem surprised when the media carry reports about the Bible inciting believers to commit bizarre and harmful acts. Some people use Bible verses to justify beating children, withholding medical treatment, handling snakes, drinking poison, chopping off body parts, plucking out eyes, driving out demons, withdrawing from the affairs of this world, renouncing the pleasures of life, and expecting the imminent end of the world. These actions would occur much less often if the Bible were not viewed as the word of God....

> *Use the Internet or other reference tools to try to discover instances of the Bible being used to justify some of the acts referred to here. Do you agree with the author that such acts would happen less often if people did not interpret the Bible as God's word?*

Conclusion

We should reject the views of those who say that the Bible contains infallible answers to today's problems. Science is a much more reliable source for the answers.

Summary

According to the author of the first article—a born-again Christian from Tennessee—the Bible is like a recipe for life: Those who put in the right ingredients and stick to the instructions will get the best results. He explains that the practice of interpreting the Bible—instead of reading it literally—began only in the third century A.D. and was followed by "confusion and division." To see what the Bible really means, he argues, we should read it in the same way as Jesus and the Apostles read it: without any attempt to attach symbolic meanings to the words on the page. According to the author, God loves people and wants to make Himself known to them; He is not trying to confuse or mislead them. The Bible should therefore be taken at face value in almost every detail. The few exceptions—metaphors, for example—are clearly signposted and need not cause confusion; even they are merely devices to help express the truth.

The second article is written by Joseph C. Sommer, a humanist—someone who bases his philosophical outlook on human values rather than on religious belief. While acknowledging that large numbers of Americans believe that the Bible is the word of God, Sommer argues that there is too much doubt about the book's authorship and content for its precepts to be followed slavishly. He believes that many of the Bible's teachings are cruel and unjust by modern standards, and the practice of ascribing often violent teachings and acts to a supposedly just and loving God has given Christians license to behave in a similarly brutal fashion. Moreover, besides its moral shortcomings, the author accuses the Bible of being historically inaccurate, steeped in the supernatural, laced with unfulfilled prophecies, and also out of step with modern science to a large extent.

FURTHER INFORMATION:

Books:

Borg, Marcus J., *Reading the Bible Again for the First Time: Taking the Bible Seriously But Not Literally*. San Francisco, CA: HarperSanFrancisco, 2001.

Geoghegan, Jeffrey, and Michael Homan, *The Bible for Dummies*. New York: Wiley Publishing, 2003.

Johnson, Phillip E., *Defeating Darwinism by Opening Minds*. Downers Grove, IL: InterVarsity Press, 1997.

Sheler, Jeffery L., *Is the Bible True? How Modern Debates and Discoveries Affirm the Essence of the Scriptures*. San Francisco, CA: HarperSanFrancisco, 1999.

Useful websites:

http://bible.gospelcom.net
Multiple versions of the Bible online.

The following debates in the Pro/Con series may also be of interest:

In this volume:
Topic 1 Does evil exist?

Topic 3 Does organized religion stifle free thought?

Topic 16 Has the religious right isolated the United States from the rest of the world?

SHOULD THE BIBLE BE INTERPRETED LITERALLY?

YES: The Bible is the word of God in simple terms and should be taken at face value

YES: The Bible should be used as a guidebook for all aspects of our daily lives. It teaches us to be moral and compassionate.

HOLY WRIT
Is the Bible authoritative?

TEACHINGS
Should we follow the teachings of the Bible?

NO: The Bible is full of contradictions and inconsistencies—it follows that not everything in it can be true

NO: The Bible sanctions violence, cruelty, and injustice. It was written in an unenlightened era, and its teachings do not reflect modern life.

SHOULD THE BIBLE BE INTERPRETED LITERALLY?

KEY POINTS

YES: Many biblical prophecies, such as the flood and the fall of Jericho, were fulfilled literally

YES: Many scientists, including those who support evolutionism, find it possible to reconcile scientific facts with a careful reading of the biblical account

RELIABILITY
Did the prophecies of the Bible come to pass?

RATIONALITY
Does the Bible stand the test of science?

NO: Many of the prophecies made in the Bible turned out to be false, proving that its creators were neither omnipotent nor omniscient

NO: The stories and teachings of the Bible often contradict the laws of nature, proven science, and rational thinking

Topic 11

HAS THE CATHOLIC CHURCH DEALT PROPERLY WITH SEXUAL ABUSE ALLEGATIONS AGAINST PRIESTS?

YES

"A TIME FOR REDEMPTION"
SUNDAY OREGONIAN, MARCH 31, 2002
DAVID REINHARD

NO

"SIN CITY: HARBORING SINNERS AND CRIMINALS"
NATIONAL REVIEW ONLINE, JANUARY 31, 2002
JOHN O'SULLIVAN

INTRODUCTION

In December 2003 the U.S. singer Lauryn Hill shocked the Vatican when she told a crowd gathered there for a Christmas concert, "Holy God is a witness to the corruption of your leadership, of the exploitation and abuses which are the minimum that can be said for the clergy." Hill was referring to the revelation, following an exposé by *The Boston Globe* newspaper in 2002, that hundreds of U.S. Catholic priests had been sexually abusing children for many years, possibly with the knowledge of the Vatican. Episodes such as this have led commentators to question whether the Catholic Church takes seriously enough sexual abuse allegations against priests.

Allegations of sexual abuse against Catholic priests are not new. Priests are bachelors whose positions of trust bring them into contact with a wide range of young people, and they have often been subjects of suspicion. Some people believe, however, that the extent of the problem has only begun to be fully understood in the last 20 years, following highly publicized cases such as that of Boston priest John Geoghan in 2002.

In the past Vatican policy has been to deal with accused priests within the church structure, through counseling, institutions set up to deal with sex abusers, and transfers. These methods, supporters say, give priests the opportunity to defend themselves and also protect victims' identities, which prevents them suffering from further shame. Critics allege, however, that this is merely a convenient way for the Catholic Church to avoid dealing properly with a problem that could have long-term effects on the church. More importantly, they claim, it also leaves perpetrators free to reoffend.

Following *The Boston Globe* articles, which focused on child abuse by Catholic priests in the Archdiocese of Boston, the problem came to international attention. Some observers began to wonder whether the church had been complicit by failing to take appropriate action against the members of its clergy accused of abuse.

> *"I wonder what else we could have done."*
>
> —REV. ROBERT W. BULLOCK, PASTOR OF OUR LADY OF SORROW CHURCH, SHARON, ON SEX ABUSE

Dan O'Shea, a Texas attorney representing some of the victims of abuse, revealed the existence of a confidential 1962 Vatican document, *Crimen Sollicitationes* ("On the Manner of Proceeding in Cases of Solicitations"), which detailed how sexual allegations should be handled by the church. The document, which was meant to have been sent to every bishop in the world, asserted that allegations should be kept secret to protect the identity of both the accused and the accusers. Some commentators, such as the Reverend Thomas P. Doyle, have criticized this approach. Doyle, a canon lawyer—a specialist in church law—believes, "The secrecy has been justified to avoid scandal when in fact it has enabled even more scandal."

Doyle has been equally critical of proposed new tribunals to deal with alleged abusers. He argues that priests could be tried unfairly since the identity of their accuser would be protected,

leaving the "door open for egregious abuses." Supporters counter that it is better to be safe than sorry, especially if the church is failing to protect children. Even the Charter for the Protection of Children and Young People, advocated by the church in 2002, was passed only after the Vatican modified it, leading critics to argue that it was again failing to confront the issue.

After the sentencing of priest John Geoghan in 2002, an ABC News poll showed that Americans believed that the Catholic Church was not doing enough to deal with the sex abuse allegations. Around 55 percent of those polled thought that the church's ban on priests' marrying contributed to the problem, suggesting a possible link between abuse and celibacy.

Other commentators point out that similar problems exist in the Protestant Church, which allows its priests to marry. James Cobble, director of the Christian Ministry Resources (CMR), an organization that surveys 75,000 congregations nationwide, suggests that the "problem is even greater in the Protestant churches simply because of their far larger numbers."

Whether this is true or not, some commentators accept that the Catholic Church is working hard to address abuse allegations. CNN reported in 2004 that an audit commissioned by the U.S. Conference of Catholic Bishops' Office of Child and Youth Protection to assess the church's response to sex abuse among priests indicated "solid progress." While this might seem like good news, it was countered by fresh allegations of sexual abuse by priests in other countries, such as Great Britain and Ireland.

The following articles look at the debate in further detail.

A TIME FOR REDEMPTION
David Reinhard

David Reinhard is a columnist for the newspaper The Oregonian. Go to http://www.oregonlive.com/news/oregonian/ for online articles from the newspaper.

YES

I think the Roman Catholic Church has turned the corner on its priest sexual abuse scandal. Yes, turned the corner.

True, the stories about pedophile priests—the crimes and cover-ups—will fill the news and fuel the outrage of Catholics, non-Catholics and anti-Catholics for some time to come. The courts, civil and criminal, will continue to mete out some measure of justice in these cases for a good while.

And commentators of all stripes, faiths and motivations will offer their opinions on what ails the Catholic priesthood. But, in recent weeks, the church has finally moved to right itself, and not because of any recent statements from the Vatican or American bishops, welcome as they may be. I've seen the first fitful steps at two churches in Portland [Oregon], and I'm sure many other Catholics have witnessed the same thing at their churches. It happens when a priest breaks from discussing the daily scripture readings and devotes his homily to today's all-too-routine headlines. It happens when a priest marshals the courage and grace to speak about the unspeakable—a priest's sexual abuse of children, what Philadelphia's Cardinal Anthony J. Bevilacqua calls "the most depraved of moral aberrations."

Speaking the unspeakable

How difficult it must be for these priests to address this with their congregations, particularly with altar boys or girls and other youngsters in attendance. It must be uncomfortable as, well, hell. Certainly, it is for the most faithful Catholics.

Although pedophilia cases dominate news headlines, over 90 percent of reported sexual abuse by the clergy is perpetrated against women rather than children.

But silence will not suffice. Screening out unfit candidates for the priesthood and maintaining zero-tolerance for priests who have sex with minors—a category that extends beyond pedophilia, which is about adult sexual attraction to prepubescent children—are important. It's encouraging that most dioceses have taken action. But sometimes talk is as important as action, particularly when the actions have occurred in the church's bureaucratic warrens and within secret legal settlements.

Was the Catholic Church wise to settle with victims in secret?

Facing this scandal head-on—finally speaking about the unspeakable—is, I think, vital for the priests and their parishioners, not to mention the church. Priests and parishioners need each other now more than ever. Their responses to the scandal are probably not so different.

That became clear—painfully and comfortingly—on a recent day when Father Paul Peri stood in the center aisle at St. Michael's in downtown Portland and poured out his heart. He wanted to talk about the proverbial elephant in the living room, the Catholic topic everyone and no one was discussing at church services. So he talked to the congregation.

He talked about how sad he was for the victims of this abuse. He talked about how angry he was at those who had brought shame on the church and, yes, the media's hyping this story out of proportion. He talked about the shame he feels and his worry that this scandal will turn away men seeking the priesthood. He talked, as well, about the priests he knows.

They're probably not so different from the [nation's] 40,000 other priests. They get up each day, celebrate Mass, teach and minister to the poor, the lonely, the dispossessed. They're not without sin, but they are without scandal. They live in the light, not the darkness. Yet they are not the public face of the Catholic clergy these days—Boston's defrocked priest John Geoghan is—and the scandal of this maddening reality was Peri's own cross to bear this Lent.

He ended on an upbeat note that day, but it was not Peri's hopeful words that seemed to move his flock. It was the mere discussion of "the issue" and the fact that his feelings—his sorrow, anger, shame, and frustration—mirrored their own. Did the tears come from witnessing Peri's pain or from a relief that our common scandal was brought out of the darkness and into the light?

The burden of scandal

Parishioners, of course, cannot know what it means to be a priest these scandal-filled days. If you're a priest, how does anyone know you haven't molested a child? How do you defend yourself against suspicions when the crime itself occurs in private? You almost have to prove something didn't happen; you almost have to prove a negative.

It's an impossible burden that makes an often lonely calling lonelier. In the current atmosphere, the clerical collar becomes a kind of choker. As one priest told me, "You stand up there and feel people who don't know you suspect you of being a child molester."

This has been a season of suffering for the Catholic clergy and laity. You hear or read the stories of clerical sexual abuse,

> Irish novelist Bernard MacLaverty (1942–) referred to the Irish Catholic–Protestant conflict, or "Troubles," as "The elephant in our living room, no one mentions it because it's just so enormous."

> Do you think that the church's reaction to the scandal should begin with individual priests, like Father Peri, or should it begin with the church itself?

> Father John Geoghan (about 1935–2003), a Boston Catholic priest, was imprisoned in 2002 after being convicted of molesting a 10-year-old boy at a public swimming pool. Geoghan was later murdered by a fellow prison inmate.

as well as reports that molester-priests were shuffled from one parish to another. You're outraged on almost every level. You know this goes on in other institutions. The news is full of reports of abuse in other religions and helping professions. There's scant evidence that pedophilia is any more prevalent in the Catholic Church than in the larger population.

Outrage at the church

But the gap between the church's moral teaching and these acts—the hideous behavior and the church hierarchy's apparent tolerance of it—is great. It makes the church a natural and legitimate target of special outrage. You know these pedophile priests are a relative handful of men who've served in the priesthood over the years. You know these cases most often go back decades when pedophilia was seen more as a moral failing—"go and sin no more"—than an intractable psychological pathology.

But you also know that a single instance of sex abuse is one too many, particularly when it's committed by an alleged man of God and facilitated by the church's actions; particularly when it alienates a young person or family from God's love.

Fr. Emmerich Vogt, a Dominican priest, is now director of the Shrine of St. Jude in San Francisco.

If Peri's homily put the current scandal in human context, Father Emmerich Vogt's homily a few days later at Portland's Holy Rosary Priory placed today's news in a historical and cultural context. This is not the first time that scandal has rocked the church. In fact, said Vogt, the church was born in the scandal of Judas. "Judas priests" have been with the church throughout history and continue to this day—not only in today's pedophile priests, but in priests and other religious figures who soft-pedal the church's moral teaching on abortion, homosexuality, adultery, illegitimacy and pornography. Even the papacy has had its scandal. Pope Alexander VI's four illegitimate children in the 15th century are but one example.

Judas Iscariot was the apostle who betrayed Jesus prior to his crucifixion. Go to http://www.newadvent.org/cathen/08539a.htm for an article about Judas.

This certainly isn't the first time Catholics have been called on to speak out against scandalous clerical behavior. As Vogt noted, St. Francis de Sales was asked to do so in his day. "Those who commit these types of scandals are guilty of the spiritual equivalent of murder," said the 17th-century bishop. Their terrible example destroys the faith of others in God.

St. Francis de Sales (1567–1622) was the bishop of Geneva from 1602. He spoke out against the sexual scandals of the Catholic clergy. He is the patron saint of journalists because of the books and tracts that he wrote.

The church might be a divine institution, but it's filled with imperfect humans who are inevitably products of their time and culture. And look at our era's sexed-up atmosphere. What should we expect? Our priests come from our culture's families. Vogt said it's mystifying to witness a secular culture that celebrates or tolerates today's degradation now zeroing in on the church's sex scandal. Yes, the stories of abusive priests command attention. Nobody's more eager to bring justice to these priests than the parishioners who love their church and children, or the priests who are unfairly tarred.

Catholic Church being singled out?

But, as a Catholic, the attention often seems outsized to me. Is the church being singled out for special scrutiny here? Is it because the church has resisted the postmodern moral order? Is it because the church maintains an unshakable belief in absolute truth and opposes all of today's media-friendly hobbyhorses—abortion, relaxed sexual mores and all the rest? Is it because there are many other agendas at work?

Do you think that Reinhard might have grounds for thinking that the Catholic Church's unshakable belief on a number of issues—such as contraception—means that it comes in for particular criticism in the modern world? What other reasons might there be?

What else to conclude when Catholics and non-Catholics offer up as fixes such things as ending priestly celibacy or opening the Catholic priesthood to women? In New Jersey, an Orthodox rabbi will soon go to trial on charges of groping two teen-age girls. In South Carolina, a Baptist minister is serving a 60-year prison sentence for sexually abusing 23 children. In Maryland, a former Episcopal priest was convicted recently of molesting a 14-year-old boy. In Portland, the Mormon Church announced last fall a $3 million settlement in a lawsuit brought by a man claiming he was abused by a high priest in the early 1990s. Celibacy and the all-male clergy didn't lead to the sins of these [people].

Do you think that religious clergy should be celibate? Catholic priests are, but generally ministers of other faiths can be married.

And yet, however disproportionate the current targeting of the Catholic Church may be, this sad reality remains: Some Catholic priests violated their vows and their parish's children, and the hierarchy didn't respond in the best interests of its children. Priests and parishioners together must say, "Enough." Today's Judas priests must find no sanctuary in the Catholic Church.

Past scandal, Vogt assured his flock, has always produced good men and women to renew the church. We've seen the first stirrings of this in places like St. Michael's, Holy Rosary and other parishes across the country. Yes, the sex-with-minors scandal is infuriating, depressing and embarrassing. But there's worse to endure. As St. Francis de Sales also said about scandal in the church, "While those who give scandal are guilty of the spiritual equivalent of murder, those who take scandal—who allow scandals to destroy their faith—are guilty of spiritual suicide."

Do you think that adjectives such as "depressing" and "embarrassing" are strong enough to describe the scandal facing the Catholic Church?

Yes, the church will have to carry this cross well beyond Lent. But Catholics are ever a hopeful people who believe in the redemptive power of suffering. We are, this day reminds us, an Easter people.

SIN CITY: HARBORING SINNERS AND CRIMINALS
John O'Sullivan

NO

The author of this article, John O'Sullivan, is editor at large of the National Review Online.

X Those who think of Christ as "Gentle Jesus, meek and mild" have read the New Testament very selectively. Christ had many words of comfort for the afflicted; but He also uttered harsh words of condemnation to the impenitent. And there is no judgment more terrifying than His warning to anyone who attacked the innocence of children that "it were better for him, if a millstone be tied around his neck and he be cast into the depths of the sea."

The word "defrock" means to deprive a priest of his position or office. It is the greatest dishonor for a priest.

But there was apparently a shortage of millstones in Boston over the last three decades. In that time, the Catholic Church harbored several priests who repeatedly molested young boys. One priest, now defrocked, John Geoghan, has been convicted of serious assaults in that period and awaits sentencing. Other names are surfacing now that the courts have ordered the Boston archdiocese to disclose its internal documents on Geoghan. And newspapers speculate that as many as fifty priests may eventually be accused. That is almost certainly a large exaggeration. But suppose that the true figure is five. Would that not be shocking enough?

The real scandal

Do you think the hierarchy of the Catholic Church should bear the greatest responsibility for this scandal?

As the church documents have already shown, however, priestly sexual abuse is the lesser scandal. What has shocked Catholic Boston still more has been the apparent willingness of church officials, including two cardinals and five bishops, to allow priests whom they knew to have abused children to return to their parishes, or to be assigned to new ones, after the most cursory period of psychological "treatment" and

Do you believe that pedophiles should receive medical treatment rather than be punished?

without informing either the police or, on one occasion at least, the parish priest who would be supervising their pastoral work. And in Geoghan's case, the bishops committed this extraordinary blunder—one might call it by harsher names—on repeated occasions, never apparently deterred by their past disappointments or by his almost flamboyant recidivism.

One reason for this, given by the current Bishop of Brooklyn, was fear of "scandal." But that defense surely

Cardinal Bernard Law was archbishop of Boston when the sex-abuse scandal emerged in 2002. He is the highest-ranking figure to be brought down by the problem in the Catholic Church.

falls on both moral and prudential grounds. It was imprudent to conceal priestly child abuse at the risk, now realized, of provoking the far greater scandal of an ecclesiastical cover-up. And, morally, it set Father Geoghan free to corrupt more innocent children.

No worldly cynic would have behaved as stupidly as the elders of the Church did. He would have handed Geoghan over to the cops and sought the moral credit of dealing honestly with the Church's most embarrassing problems. And everyone, including Geoghan, would have been better off.

So weak is the argument of avoiding "scandal" in this case that one is inclined to treat it as the rationalization of a deeper failing. And that failing is a bishop's lack of faith in their own religious mission and message.

What, after all, did they think pedophilia was? Was it a sin, a crime or a medical condition? Child sex abuse certainly is a crime—and a very serious one at that. Handing its perpetrators over to the authorities therefore falls under the injunction: "Render unto Caesar the things that are Caesar's." Yet the Church bureaucracy did not treat it as a crime. At no point did the various bishops and monsignors seriously seem to think of calling in the police even though they knew Geoghan was committing a series of felonies that carry heavy prison sentences. If you or I sought absolution for murder in confession, it would be granted only on condition that we admitted our crime to the authorities. For a priest, child sex abuse is an act of similar magnitude. Faced with a crime in its own house, however, the Church acted to a lower standard than those it imposes on the faithful.

The sin of pedophilia

Nor, however, did they treat what Geoghan did as a sin. To be sure, the bishops occasionally used the language of sin, repentance and renewal in their correspondence with him about his new postings or brief hospitalizations. But there is little sign of the stern moral condemnation that a serious sin invites; nor of any demanding inquiry for evidence of Geoghan's "firm purpose of amendment." On the contrary: after one sordid episode, he was given $2,000 and a trip to Rome. All in all, he was treated more tenderly than the parents of the children he abused.

What emerges from the internal documents is that the Church truly believes in psychiatry. Its belief in psychiatry, indeed, is as the belief of little children or of primitive tribes or of early twentieth century intellectuals. It regarded Geoghan's pedophilia almost blithely as a medical condition

> Even though the church has its own laws, why shouldn't priests who do wrong be subjected to the criminal law of the land, like everyone else?

> The Vatican press office director, Dr. Joaquin Navarro-Calls, is a psychiatrist who formerly taught at Barcelona and Granada universities. Go to http://www.nopsychs.org/blameshame.html for an article about "Psychiatry's Responsibility in the Current Pedophilia Scandal."

which a good psychiatrist might cure. Admittedly it did not employ good psychiatrists to do so, merely those it could trust to be discreet. (One of them, as luck would have it, has been accused by a woman patient of sexual abuse. It's been a bad week at the Bishopric.)

No cure for pedophilia?

But even a good psychiatrist would have made little headway with Geoghan because, as good psychiatrists know, pedophilia is one of those conditions that can be "cured" only if the patient desperately wishes to recover from it (and perhaps not even then.) Psychiatry can cure those mental and emotional illnesses that are the result of physical causes such as a chemical imbalance in the system. But it can only assist the patient to overcome those conditions such as alcoholism and pedophilia which, even if they arise from genetic predispositions or early childhood experiences, are nonetheless embedded in the mind and will. And there was little clear evidence that Geoghan ever really wanted to be "cured" and was prepared to embark on the hard business of disciplining his own will. His illness was more a moral failing—that is, a sin—than a medical fact. It was therefore in the Church's own territory of sin, repentance and reform. But the Bishops lacked the faith to see that or to propose their own hard spiritual remedies.

Christ himself would have spoken far more harshly to John Geoghan and the other priests who destroyed the innocence of those in their care. Yet in speaking harshly He would have loved them more. For He might have turned them away from the sins that corrupted their souls and attacked the bodies of children in their charge. Geoghan himself can only hope to find in prison the stern but loving Christ whom he evaded all too easily in the Boston Archdiocese.

Do you think that pedophiles can ever be cured? Go to http://www.theawarenesscenter.org/offendersarticles.html for a list of online articles about this question.

Geoghan was murdered by a prison inmate at the beginning of the 10-year sentence he was serving for his crime. Do you think he got what he deserved?

Summary

In the first article editor and writer David Reinhard argues that the Catholic Church has done enough to deal with the sex abuse allegations against priests. He says that the church has turned a corner and has begun to sort out its problems, regardless of guidance sent from the Vatican. Silence is not enough, Reinhard claims; and although zero-tolerance of sexual misconduct and screening of priests will help, talking is one of the best solutions to the problem. He recounts stories of two priests in Portland, Oregon, talking directly in public to their parishioners about the issue. However, he concludes that the Catholic Church is being singled out and that other religions and churches also have clergy that are subject to allegations of abuse.

In the second article journalist John O'Sullivan focuses on the events in the Archdiocese of Boston as exposed by *The Boston Globe* newspaper in 2002 and argues that the church there did not act in the best interests of the children. He refers in particular to the case of priest John Geoghan, whose sexual misconduct was repeatedly covered up by the church. He points out that at one time the church even gave Geoghan money for a trip to Rome as its way of dealing with the problem. O'Sullivan asserts that the church viewed pedophilia as a treatable medical condition and employed psychiatrists who would keep quiet. He concludes that "Christ himself would have spoken far more harshly to John Geoghan and the other priests who destroyed the innocence of those in their care."

FURTHER INFORMATION:

Books:

Weigel, George, *The Courage to Be Catholic: Crisis, Reform, and the Future of the Church*. New York: Basic Books, 2002.

Useful websites:

http://www.beliefnet.com/story/102/story_10276_1.html
Multifaith site containing news coverage and articles on the clergy sexual abuse scandals.
http://www.biblia.com/christianity/clergy/htm
"Clergy Abuse Scandals" by J. Dominquez.
http://www.boston.com/spotlight/abuse/
Full coverage of *The Boston Globe's* investigation of sexual abuse in the Catholic Church.
http://www.usccb.org/bishops/charter.htm
Revised edition of the Catholic Church's Charter for the Protection of Children and Young People, 2002.
http://www.usccb.org/comm/restoretrust.htm

U.S. Conference of Catholic Bishops 2003 press release, "Restoring Trust: Response to the Clergy Sexual Abuse."

The following debates in the Pro/Con series may also be of interest:

In this volume:
Part 3: World Religions, pages 124–125
The Archdiocese of Boston: The Catholic Church and child abuse, pages 150–151

In *Criminal Law and the Penal System*:
Topic 16 Should sex offenders be castrated?

HAS THE CATHOLIC CHURCH DEALT PROPERLY WITH SEXUAL ABUSE ALLEGATIONS AGAINST PRIESTS?

YES: Numerous authorities believe that pedophilia should be treated as a disease that needs counselors rather than accusers

YES: Secrecy provided protection for the victim and gave the accused a chance to defend themselves before a witch-hunt began

A TREATABLE CONDITION?
Did the church act appropriately in sending offending priests to special therapists?

SECRECY
Was dealing with abuse allegations in secrecy the best way to handle the issue?

HAS THE CATHOLIC CHURCH DEALT PROPERLY WITH SEXUAL ABUSE ALLEGATIONS AGAINST PRIESTS?

KEY POINTS

NO: Any priest guilty of sexual abuse had broken the law; it is for state and federal courts to decide what should happen to them

NO: Secrecy left the church open to allegations that it was covering up the problem. It was not aimed at protecting the victim but at saving the church from embarrassment.

YES: The church believed this was the best action for everyone involved. It paid out millions of dollars to help the abused move on from their suffering.

YES: Sex abusers include many people who are not celibate, including priests of other religions, such as Protestantism or Judaism

SETTLEMENT
Was the church right to settle with victims of abuse out of court?

CELIBACY
Is it simplistic to argue that celibacy is the cause of the problem?

NO: The fact that offenders were not punished shows that the church's financial settlements were not an acknowledgment of being in the wrong; they were attempts to brush the problem under the carpet

NO: The church requirement that its clergy are celibate means that priests are not able to conduct open relationships; it is inevitable that some become involved in abusive ones

THE ARCHDIOCESE OF BOSTON: THE CATHOLIC CHURCH AND CHILD ABUSE

"The harm done by some priests ... fills us all with a deep sense of sadness and shame...."
—POPE JOHN PAUL II, JULY 28, 2002, CANADA

In early 2002 *The Boston Globe* published a series of articles alleging that some Catholic priests in the archdiocese of Boston had been sexually abusing children for many years. Increasing numbers of people then emerged with stories of abuse. Records showed that the church had known about individual cases but had dealt with alleged offenders on a case-by-case basis. All over the United States survivors of abuse came forward to reveal their own experiences. The Catholic Church was accused of failing to deal appropriately with the widespread problem. Although the church adopted a Charter for the Protection of Children and Young Adults in 2002, some commentators believe that the issue of sexual abuse in the church has still not been properly addressed.

Exposing the Boston scandal

In January 2002 *The Boston Globe* printed an article that accused former priest John J. Geoghan of abusing children in the archdiocese of Boston over a period of many years. The *Globe* further asserted that Cardinal Bernard Law, the archbishop of the area, had been aware of Geoghan's sexual activities since 1984, yet Geoghan had not been removed permanently from duty until 1993. The article caused a public outcry as the church and general public struggled to deal with the implications of the newspaper's accusations. International attention suddenly became focused on the archdiocese. As the days passed and the extent of Geoghan's abusive activities became known, it also became evident that the problem did not stop with just one priest. Many people began to accuse other members of the church in the archdiocese of abuse, leading some observers to conclude that Cardinal Law had not only been aware of some of these cases, but that he had also tried to cover up the magnitude of the problem.

Cardinal Law: dealing with abuse—or not?

Cardinal Law believed in treating each case separately. He kept detailed files on the accused; and while some cases were dismissed, others were taken seriously. Records showed that alleged abusers were sometimes transferred to different parishes where they found a new source of potential victims. Others were sent to church-approved institutions set up specifically to deal with sex offenders, after which some were reinstated in their former positions—where they continued to abuse young boys and girls.

Law had already been criticized for his handling of the abuse allegations against Reverend James Porter in 1993. After this he publicly stated that the church pledged "to report such incidents to civil authorities in accordance with the law and to alert complainants of their right to do this in all other instances." However, Law's own documentation, along with other records, showed that the archdiocese had spent millions of dollars in settling abuse cases privately. Some commentators, including a number of lawyers, argue that the church was right to deal with each accusation on an individual basis, preserving the anonymity of the victim. Others counter that this method enabled offenders to carry on the abuse unchallenged.

Cardinal Law and his colleagues were also accused of misleading priests in other dioceses. An example of this occurred in 1990 when Bishop Robert J. Banks, then deputy to Cardinal Law, wrote a letter to the California diocese of San Bernardino, endorsing the transfer of priest Paul R. Shanley, in which he stated that there was nothing in Shanley's past that could be construed as problematic. At the time both Banks and Law were aware that Shanley had been accused of molesting a boy in the diocese. The diocese of San Bernardino later sued the archdiocese of Boston for "active misconduct and negligence" in withholding the information after several young men accused Shanley of abuse, rape, and sexual misconduct.

By the end of 2002 a study conducted by *The New York Times* indicated that more than 1,000 U.S. priests had been accused of abuse, and that five senior church figures, including Cardinal Law, had resigned in the ensuing scandal, bringing the total who had resigned in similar circumstances since 1990 to nine. Over 500 people had made claims of abuse by priests—this included 86 claims against Geoghan alone. Several priests, including Geoghan, were tried and imprisoned for their crimes. Geoghan was later murdered by an inmate who said that he did it on behalf of all the priest's victims.

Making amends

Many civil suits by survivors of abuse have been brought against the Catholic Church from all over the world. By January 2004 the archdiocese of Boston had paid out around $85 million in damages. Some people, however, argue that the church's failure to deal with pedophiles years ago has had a negative effect on all members of the community. Although the archdiocese mortgaged its Brighton headquarters and sold off property to make settlements, it also cut back on vital social service work, including residential programs for victims of HIV/AIDS.

Some commentators think that the cost was justified because the Catholic Church received a wake-up call to bring it into the 21st century, as shown by its endorsement of the Charter for the Protection of Children and Young Adults. Others respond that the charter itself illustrates how much further the church has to go: The Vatican only agreed to it after a provision for the removal of priests convicted of abuse from the priesthood was taken out. Since the Boston scandal other cases involving Catholic priests and nuns have been reported in Ireland, Britain, and elsewhere. This, critics say, proves that the matter is far from closed.

Topic 12
ARE MONOTHEISTIC RELIGIONS MORE INTOLERANT THAN OTHER RELIGIONS?

YES
FROM "THE ROOT CAUSES OF RELIGIOUS ATROCITIES"
THE REJECTION OF PASCAL'S WAGER: A SKEPTIC'S GUIDE TO CHRISTIANITY, 2002
PAUL N. TOBIN

NO
"PM DECRIES MISUSE OF RELIGION BY TERRORISTS"
THE HINDU, FEBRUARY 10, 2003
NEENA VYAS

INTRODUCTION

"Monotheism" means belief in the existence of a single god. It is distinguished from "polytheism," or the belief in many gods. Christianity, Judaism, and Islam share a tradition of monotheism. They believe in one supreme deity, respectively God, Yahweh, and Allah. The world's many polytheistic faiths include Hinduism, which is the majority religion of India, the Japanese religion Shinto, and most African traditional religions. Theologians have long debated whether monotheisms are by their very nature more inclined to be intolerant of other beliefs than polytheisms. At the start of the 21st century high-profile terrorist actions in the name of Islam gave new life to the debate.

The three great monotheisms —Christianity, Judaism, and Islam—are all related. They are Abrahamic faiths, which means that they trace their roots back to the prophet Abraham. Jews and Christians view this Old Testament patriarch as a model of supreme faith for his willingness to offer his son Isaac to God as sacrifice, while Muslims believe that the Arabs are descended from Ishmael, Abraham's other son. The Koran claims that Ishmael and his father rebuilt the Kaaba, the Muslim holy site in Mecca. Of the three faiths Judaism was the first to appear, more than 3,000 years ago, followed by Christianity in the early years A.D. Islam emerged in the seventh century.

Despite close links between these three faiths, there has long been conflict between them, including the Crusades waged by Christians against Muslims in the Middle Ages and the Arab–Israeli conflict that has dominated the Middle Eastern region since the early 20th century.

Some critics claim that the nature of monotheism itself is a key element in the friction between these religions: Each faith believes that its god is the one true deity. Critics suggest that this belief leads to the conclusion that all other gods must be false and all other religions at best misguided. Some people assert that further evidence of this is found in the infighting within these religions between those who hold orthodox views and those who have nonorthodox, or heretical, ideas. The two main branches of Islam—Sunni and Shi'ah—regard one another as heretical. In the Middle Ages the Roman Catholic Church instituted the Inquisition, a type of religious court, to seek out and prosecute heretics, and in the 17th century bitter differences between Catholics and Protestants triggered the Thirty Years' War (1618–1648) in Europe. Commentators also stress that Christianity and Islam are proselytizing religions—that is, they seek to convert others to the faith. That means that they are a threat to other religions by trying to recruit their worshipers.

"[G]erms, geography, printing, sailing ships, steel, and climate have mattered, but probably none of them so much as human ideas about God."

—RODNEY STARK,

U.S. SOCIOLOGIST (2001)

Religious commentators sometimes contrast the histories of the Abrahamic faiths with the apparent tolerance of polytheistic religions. Although polytheism is defined as the worship of many gods, each of whom has its own function—such as the god of fertility or goddess of wisdom—it can take a number of forms. For example, polytheists may admit the existence of numerous gods but worship only one, as sometimes occurred in ancient Egypt. Or they may believe in a chief god and numerous lesser deities—such as Zeus and the Olympian gods of ancient Greece, or Odin and the gods of Asgard in early Scandinavian religion. A third type of polytheism, which prevails among some Hindus, respects a number of gods but views them all as part of a single divinity.

Whatever the form of polytheism, it is its inclusive nature that its advocates claim is responsible for a tolerant outlook. The ancient Egyptians, for example, far from having an "I am right, you are wrong" attitude, welcomed new gods and developed a huge and complex pantheon (set of gods).

Some critics of this view, however, suggest that advocates of polytheism overstate their case. They point to historical examples of polytheistic intolerance, such as the persecution of the early Christians by pagan (polytheistic) Roman emperors and the suppression of Christianity in 16th-century Buddhist Japan. Discussing the Roman persecutions, James Hitchcock, a professor of history at St. Louis University, has asserted that "polytheism can tolerate any religion except monotheism." Commentators also cite more recent examples of intolerance among polytheistic faiths. For example, some critics have accused the Hindu nationalist movement in India of inciting violence against Muslims and Christians.

The following articles examine the debate further.

THE ROOT CAUSES OF RELIGIOUS ATROCITIES
Paul N. Tobin

Paul N. Tobin, who claims to have gone "from being a believing Christian into a convinced atheist," is the author of the website "The Rejection of Pascal's Wager: A Skeptic's Guide to Christianity" (http://www. geocities.com/ paulntobin/index. html). This article, available on the site, is dated 2002.

YES

✓ … In his book *One True God: The Historical Consequences of Monotheism*, the University of Washington sociologist Rodney Stark postulated that the root causes of intolerance seen in monotheistic religions are the exclusiveness and particularism that are embedded within its very definition.

Monotheism, by its very nature, is the antithesis of polytheism. Note that polytheism is the belief in many non-exclusive deities. A person can go to one temple to ask a favour from the goddess of love and go to another the next day asking for help with money issues from the god of wealth. Polytheistic deities offer specialized services and are thus, by their very nature, non-exclusive. Thus there is never a need for adherents to a certain deity in polytheism to actively seek the overthrow or suppression of other gods.

Monotheism, however, is the belief that there exists only one God. All other gods are, by definition, either false or attempts by the devil to fool their adherents. Embedded within this belief is an automatic contempt for polytheistic gods. This tells us why monotheism will always be intolerant of polytheism.

In the theological sense "particularism" means the belief held by members of a religion that only they have been chosen by God for redemption.

Furthermore, in defining the attributes of their one God, [they] include the concept of immutability, that God does not change. Thus the God of the monotheists communicates only one consistent message. In this sense, monotheism is also particularistic. Not only is there only one God, there is only one true message and only one true religion. This leads to both internal and external conflicts.

Orthodoxy vs. heresy

In trying to find and understand the one true message, theologians read and interpret scriptures. Yet this is the very cause of heresy. For heresy, by definition, is an interpretation of the same message in a method different from the group which ultimately won the battle (and the right to call their interpretation "orthodoxy"). All monotheistic religions show this tendency to splinter. In first century Judaism we find such factions as the Essenes, the Pharisees and the Sadducees. The Jewish Talmud noted that there were twenty four different factions altogether. In Islam we have the Sunnis, the Shiites and the Sufis. In Christianity we have from the earliest days various groups … Even today we find Christianity splintering into more than 20,000 denominations.

Obviously if monotheistic beliefs could not even reconcile themselves with factions who share the same scripture (but a different interpretation of it), their attitude towards other monotheistic religions with different scriptures are even worse. For if God is said to convey only one consistent message, competing sacred scriptures, with different and sometimes contradictory messages, cannot be reconciled within a particular monotheistic paradigm. Classic examples of these [failures of reconciliation] are the various crusades between Christendom and Islam.…

While intolerance plays a major role in the historical horrors perpetrated by Christians and Christianity, two more tenets of Christian theology are required to make the cocktail really explosive.

The Talmud, which literally means "learning" or "study" in Hebrew, is a body of writings that record the study and interpretation of Jewish oral traditions and the Hebrew scriptures.

The inscrutability of God's mind

Another basic tenet of many monotheistic religions, including Christianity, is that God is all wise and his wisdom is impenetrable to the human mind.…

The message was well understood by Christian theologians. Martin Luther (1483–1546), for instance, asserted that if God asked him to go to the field and eat corn, he would do it no matter how ludicrous it would seem.

Luther's Catholic rival, St. Ignatius Loyola (1491–1556), has the same teaching.… [The] founder of the Society of Jesus or Jesuits, in his book *Rules for Thinking Within the Church* taught a simple rule for believers to follow when their reason contradicts their faith: "If the church should have defined anything to be black which to our eyes appear white, we ought in like manner pronounce it black."

Thus whether God is speaking through the Bible or through the church, his commandments are not to be questioned but to be followed.…

Martin Luther was a German priest. Disillusioned with the Roman Catholic Church, he claimed that the authority of the Bible was higher than the authority of the pope. He became leader of the reform movement in Europe known as the Protestant Reformation.

Do you think most religions demand unquestioning faith from their adherents?

The ultimate moral yardstick

Although Christians do believe that some moral values are "built-in" to the human psyche (see for instance Romans 1:19, 20; 2:14, 15); in the final analysis, an act is moral or ethical only because God commands it. This is clearly stated in the

See Topic 5 Is morality possible without a religious basis?

The author refers to M.G Easton's The Illustrated Bible Dictionary, originally published in the late 19th century. Go to http://www.ccel.org/e/easton/ebd/ebd.html for an online version.

section of Moral Law in *The Illustrated Bible Dictionary*: "The Scripture … taken as a whole, is our rule, our only rule, of faith and practice, and as a revelation of God's will, is binding on the consciences of all Christian men."

We know from the Bible that God has commanded actions which under any circumstances would be considered barbaric and rivalling the achievements of Hitler and Stalin. One case to point is the commandment for the Israelites to slaughter the inhabitants of Canaan …

Deuteronomy 20:10–17

When you draw near a city to fight against it, offer terms of peace to it. And if its answer to you is peace and it opens to you, then all the people who are found in it shall do forced labour for you and shall serve you. But if it makes no peace with you, but makes war against you, then you shall besiege it; and when the Lord your God gives it into your hand you shall put all its males to the sword, but the women and the little ones, the cattle, and everything else in the city, all its spoil, you shall take as booty for yourself … Thus you shall do to all the cities which are far from you, which are not cities of the nations here. In the cities of these people that the Lord your God gives you [for] an inheritance, you shall save alive nothing that breathes but you shall utterly destroy them, the Hittites and the Amorites, the Canaanites and the Jebusites, as the Lord your God has commanded.…

The Amorites, the Canaanites, and the Jebusites were peoples who lived in Canaan, the "promised land" of the Bible. The identity of the Hittites is more problematic. The Hittites of Anatolia, part of modern Turkey, were one of the Middle Eastern superpowers of the period. However, some scholars doubt whether the Hittites of the Bible are the same people.

It is interesting to hear the comments of the *Illustrated Bible Dictionary* on the massacre of the Canaanites:

It is enough that Joshua clearly knew this was the will of God, who employs his terrible agencies, famine, pestilence, and war, in the righteous government of the world. The Canaanites had sunk into a state of immorality so foul and degrading that they had to be rooted out of the land with the edge of the sword. "The Israelite's sword, in its bloodiest executions, wrought a work of mercy for all countries of the earth to the very end of the world."

Notice then the actions of Joshua are justified because it was the will of God. Never mind that the Canaanites were considered "immoral" simply because they worshipped other gods (e.g. Numbers 33:52, Deuteronomy 7:4-5).…

The consequences of the "cocktail"

We shall now see how all these three elements (intolerance, inscrutability of God's wisdom and the definition of morality as what is commanded by God) were the underlying causes for many horrible acts perpetrated by Christians throughout history.

Thus Christian intolerance of outsiders and heretical insiders, mixed with the other two elements, had resulted in:

- the persecution of pagans,
- the persecution of heretics,
- the crusades against Islam,
- the inquisition against the Albigenses,
- the Spanish inquisition against closet Jews and Muslims,
- the wars of religion between Catholics and Protestants,
- the anti-semitic persecutions that had plagued Jews since the advent of the Christian myth of their responsibility for the death of Jesus.

That this intolerance leads many times to the killing or massacre of the opposition makes perfect sense for the believers. For wasn't Joshua commanded to kill the Canaanites because they were of other religions?

The second and third elements of the cocktail when mixed together had also resulted in much suffering.

- The perpetuation of slavery in Christendom until fairly recent times was due largely to the fact that the Bible did not condemn slavery. Thus it was never considered immoral to own slaves.
- The subordinate position of women in Christendom was rooted in the Bible and the teachings of the church fathers (who were merely following through on the Bible's teachings on this).
- The medieval witch hunt which resulted in the death of an estimated two million people was the result of a consistent application of the two principles above in interpreting Galatians 5:19 and Exodus 22:8.
- The case of Dr. Simpson and the resistance of the Scottish clergy to the use of anesthesia during childbirth is another example of how Christian morality is not premised on the reduction of human pain and suffering but on what the Bible (hence God) commands.

It is clear … that the atrocities and injustices above were committed, not in spite of Christianity, but because of it.

The Albigenses were a religious sect in southern France in the 12th century. The popularity of the sect spread quickly. In 1233 Pope Gregory IX established the papal Inquisition and sent Dominican friars to France to conduct inquests. Suspected heretics were tried and, if found guilty, were handed over to secular authorities for punishment.

Do you agree with the author's claim that slavery lasted so long in Christian countries because the Bible does not condemn the practice of keeping slaves? What other factors might have been involved?

Sir James Young Simpson (1811–1870) was a Scottish physician who pioneered the use of chloroform during childbirth. He ran into severe opposition on health, moral, and religious grounds, but the use of the anesthetic by Queen Victoria at the birth of Prince Leopold in 1853 led to the practice gaining acceptance.

PM DECRIES MISUSE OF RELIGION BY TERRORISTS
Neena Vyas

Neena Vyas is a journalist. This article appeared on February 10, 2003, in The Hindu, an Indian national daily newspaper.

NO

Misuse of religion by terrorists who use it as a cover for their campaign of hatred was strongly criticised by the Prime Minister, Atal Behari Vajpayee, here today, as he emphasised that "no organisation, whether it claimed to espouse the cause of the majority or the minority community, can be allowed to inflame passions, spread hatred and incite violence".

Democracies and liberal societies were the most vulnerable to terrorist attacks—India was one of the worst-affected—and often the financiers of terrorist organisations were military and totalitarian regimes, Mr. Vajpayee argued. Terrorism attacked democratic societies because it is intolerant and impatient to impose its own social order on peoples. Fighting the menace often meant taking unpopular steps which included some infringement and curtailment of liberties, Mr. Vajpayee said, adding that "human rights of terrorists cannot override those of their victims".

"Jihadi terrorism" is terrorism carried out by Islamic fundamentalist "jihadis" (religious warriors). Jihadi terrorist groups include Hamas and Hezbollah in the Middle East, and Al Qaeda.

No religion preaches intolerance

Inaugurating the International Youth Conference on Terrorism organised by the Bharatiya Janata Yuva Morcha, the youth wing of the BJP, Mr. Vajpayee unwaveringly pointed his finger of suspicion: "Jihadi terrorism has become the principal form of terrorism, not because Islam justifies it … no religion preaches hatred or sanctions killings … but terrorist groups were using religion as a shield, a cover for the campaign of hatred".

A fatwa is an Islamic decree. A burqa is a traditional garment that covers a woman from head to toe. Orthodox Muslims believe that women should wear the burqa as a sign of modesty; opponents see the burqa as a symbol of the oppression of women.

These groups were also trying to impose an intolerant social order on the people, he added, perhaps referring to the "fatwa" on the wearing of the "burqa" by women and "orders" prohibiting women from working outside their homes.

He did not spare the extremists of his own ideological family, the Sangh Parivar, when he obliquely referred to organisations claiming to work for the majority community spreading their campaign of hatred, inciting passions and violence, but stopped short of describing them as terrorists.

Atal Bihari Vajpayee (1926–) was prime minister of India from 1998 until 2004 at the head of the National Democratic Alliance, a coalition that included his Bharatiya Janata Party.

COMMENTARY: Storming the Golden Temple

The Golden Temple in Amritsar was built in its present form during the reign of the Sikh ruler Ranjit Singh (1792–1839). The temple contains the most sacred text of the Sikhs, the Granth Sahib.

Of the one billion people who live in India, Hindus make up the majority (about 81 percent); approximately 12 percent are Muslims, 2.3 percent are Christians, 2.5 percent follow Buddhism, Jainism, and other faiths, while around 1.9 percent are Sikhs.

Guru Nanak (about 1469–1539) founded Sikhism, a monotheistic faith, in the 15th century. When the subcontinent was split into India and Pakistan in 1947 (see Volume 19, *World Politics*, *Religion and partition of India*, page 42), many Sikhs emigrated from Muslim-dominated Pakistan to Punjab state in northwest India. Today 90 percent of India's Sikhs live in Punjab.

Separatist Sikhs

Communal violence has been a recurring problem since the partition of India. It has most often involved Hindus and Muslims, but in the late 1970s a Sikh separatist movement emerged under fundamentalist preacher Jarnail Singh Bhindranwale (1947–1984), and violence broke out in Punjab state between Sikhs and Hindus. As a result, the Indian government brought the state under its direct control in 1983. Bhindranwale and his armed followers had already sought sanctuary in the Golden Temple complex in Amritsar, the holiest shrine of the Sikh religion.

The government was determined to oust Bhindranwale. On the night of June 5, 1984, the Indian Army launched Operation Bluestar, its bid to evict the separatists, and stormed the Golden Temple. According to official figures, Bhindranwale and almost 500 of his followers were killed, as well as more than 80 soldiers; unofficial figures claim that Sikh casualties were actually much higher. Sikhs were outraged by the attack on their sacred site. The following October Prime Minister Indira Gandhi (1917–1984), who had ordered the assault, was murdered by her Sikh bodyguards. The assassination sparked anti-Sikh riots, particularly in the Indian capital, New Delhi, in which 3,000 people died.

Mr. Vajpayee then went on to emphasise that India had lost 60,000 innocent lives to terrorism over two decades but the menace became part of the collective global consciousness only after the September 11 attack on the twin towers of the World Trade Centre in New York 17 months ago. Major terrorist attacks in Moscow, Bali and Mombasa had reinforced the consciousness. Terrorism was a menace from which no country was immune, he warned.

"Dubious logic"

He reiterated that there can be no double standards in dealing with terrorism—terrorist acts cannot be described as terrorism in one country and as "freedom struggle" somewhere else. Such an attitude was counterproductive. It was "dubious logic", he said.

The international community had to remain vigilant to prevent terrorist organisations getting chemical, biological and other weapons of mass destruction. But there was no need to be frightened of terrorism for it was bound to be defeated.

The young people had always been attracted by idealism and they dreamed of a "good future for themselves, their nations and the world," Mr. Vajpayee said.

He was glad that the conference had a positive emphasis. It was not only "against terrorism" but also "for a global dialogue for peace".

On October 12, 2002, two bombs exploded on the Indonesian island of Bali, killing more than 200 people; on October 23, 2002, Chechen terrorists took over a Moscow theater, resulting in more than 150 deaths when the security forces stormed the building; on November 28, 2002, 16 people, including three suicide bombers, died in an attack on a hotel in the Kenyan city of Mombasa.

See Volume 19, World Politics, Topic 5 Is violence a viable way to bring about effective political change?

Summary

The first article is by Paul N. Tobin, an atheist, and comes from his website "A Skeptic's Guide to Christianity." He believes that monotheistic religions are less tolerant than others, basing his argument on a book by sociologist Rodney Stark, *One True God: The Historical Consequences of Monotheism*. In his book Stark contends that the root causes of intolerance in monotheism are its exclusiveness and particularism. Tobin argues that the message of monotheism—that there is one true god, one true message, and one true religion—inevitably leads to conflicts. In polytheistic religions, which are characterized by belief in many nonexclusive deities, he says there is no need for followers to seek to overthrow or suppress other gods. He claims that the intolerance inherent in monotheism, combined with particular Christian theological concepts of God and morality, is responsible for many historical examples of religious intolerance. Tobin concludes that many episodes from history, ranging from the Crusades to slavery, were committed not in spite of Christianity but because of it.

In the second article Neena Vyas reports on the reaction of India's then prime minister, Atal Bihari Vajpayee, to increasing levels of terrorism in the 21st century. Vajpayee argues that "Jihadi terrorism has become the principal form of terrorism, not because Islam justifies it ... no religion preaches hatred or sanctions killings ... but terrorist groups were using religion as a shield, a cover for the campaign of hatred." He is critical of extremists who incite violence while claiming to speak for the majority of people. His comments allude in part to the Hindu nationalist movement, which has been involved in communal disturbances in India for two decades.

FURTHER INFORMATION:

Books:

Kirsch, Jonathan, *God against the Gods: The History of the War between Monotheism and Polytheism*. New York: Viking Compass, 2004.

Stark, Rodney, *One True God: Historical Consequences of Monotheism*. Princeton, NJ: Princeton University Press, 2001.

Useful websites:

http://www.historyforkids.org/learn/religion
History for Kids page covering religious history.
www.polytheism.net
An overview of polytheism from a Christian perspective.
http://www.wf-f.org/JFH-ReligousFreedom%26Tol.html
"Religious Freedom and the Dogma of Tolerance" by James Hitchcock.

The following debates in the Pro/Con series may also be of interest:

In this volume:

Topic 2 Would there be fewer wars if religion did not exist?

Topic 4 Should governments have the right to outlaw religions?

Topic 13 Does Islam condone terrorism?

ARE MONOTHEISTIC RELIGIONS MORE INTOLERANT THAN OTHER RELIGIONS?

YES: Monotheists believe that theirs is the one true religion and that all others are false

YES: Polytheistic systems are respectful of other faiths because they do not hold that there is one absolute truth

PARTICULARISM
Is intolerance inherent in monotheistic religions?

INCLUSIVENESS
Is tolerance inherent in polytheistic religions?

NO: Most monotheists are used to living in multifaith societies and respect even faiths in which they do not believe

NO: Wars waged in the name of polytheistic faiths such as Hinduism show that they can be as intolerant as any other religion

ARE MONOTHEISTIC RELIGIONS MORE INTOLERANT THAN OTHER RELIGIONS?

KEY POINTS

YES: Monotheism encourages an instinctive rejection of all other beliefs, which is a mark of a zealot

YES: Some monotheistic religions encourage their followers to believe that they have a mission to convert and "save" nonbelievers

FANATICISM
Does monotheism encourage religious zealotry?

NO: There are many contemporary examples of cooperation that show that Christians and other monotheists are happy to work with and learn from other faiths

NO: Monotheistic faiths are not alone in aiming to make converts; Buddhism and, more recently, Hinduism also use missionaries to recruit followers

Topic 13
DOES ISLAM CONDONE TERRORISM?

YES

FROM "A CALL TO MUSLIMS OF THE WORLD"
HTTP://WWW.FAITHFREEDOM.ORG/ARTICLES/SINA/CALL_TO_MUSLIMS.HTM
FAITH FREEDOM INTERNATIONAL

NO

"DOES ISLAM PROMOTE VIOLENCE?"
WWW.IVIEWS.COM, AUGUST 20, 2002
JAVEED AKHTER

INTRODUCTION

Since the attacks on the World Trade Center and the Pentagon on September 11, 2001, many leading American political commentators and policymakers have expressed a distrust of the Islamic religion. The attackers were extremist Muslims—followers of Islam—who believed that they were dying in an attack encouraged by Islam against the "evil" of the western world in general and the United States in particular. Other Muslims have also used the same argument to justify violence. They claim that the faith promotes the idea of "jihad," or "holy war," against non-Muslims. Many Americans have come to accept that Islam is an aggressive religion. Others argue that to find support in Islam for acts of violence is to misread its teaching. Like the majority of Muslims, they claim that the 9/11 hijackers and other Islamic extremists use religion to justify violence that in reality has economic or political roots.

Islam, which literally means "submission" and "peace" in Arabic, is a monotheistic religion that arose in the seventh century A.D. Like Judaism and Christianity, it is descended from the religious tradition of the biblical patriarch Abraham: It is classified as an "Abrahamic" religion.

In the 21st century the majority of the world's 1.2 billion Muslims belong to the Sunni branch of Islam, while the rest follow the second-largest branch, Shi'ah Islam, and other smaller denominations. About 85 percent of Islam's followers are non-Arab: South Asia has around 275 million Muslims, the largest number in the world.

The Koran (Qur'an) is Islam's holy book, written as the word of Allah (God) as told to the Prophet Muhammad (about 570–632) via the angel Jibreel (Gabriel). Muslims believe that the Koran contains Allah's final and complete guidance for all humankind. It is in the words of the Koran that some people find support for terrorism. Others, however, find the condemnation of violence. They stress that Islam shares with other religions an emphasis on tolerance and charity, and that it has a past that is no more violent than that of, say, Christianity. Christianity's history includes, among other things, the Inquisition, the Crusades, and terrorism against people defending civil rights, such as abortion. There are many examples of Muslims being more tolerant than Christians: When the Muslim leader Saladin expelled the Crusaders from Jerusalem in the 12th century, he invited back to the city the Jews expelled by the Crusaders. While Catholic and Protestant clergy were accused of playing a part in the 1994 Rwandan genocide of Tutsis by Hutu death squads, some Muslims hid the persecuted. Since then many Rwandans have converted to Islam, and the Muslim population has doubled: It now makes up 14 percent of the country's 8.2 million citizens.

> *"Islam does not promote terrorism or the killing of people."*
> —MUHAMMAD ALI, FORMER BOXING CHAMPION (2001)

Islam also has a tradition of helping the needy. In the Middle East and South Asia, for example, Muslims have helped tackle social ills by banning alcohol and encouraging sexual modesty, they claim. In the United States Malcolm X, a convert to Islam, used a form of Islam to encourage economic and social empowerment among African Americans during the civil rights movement. Many blacks converted to Islam at this time.

But some scholars question why Islam of all the great faiths is particularly linked to terrorism if it is such a good and benevolent religion. At the heart of the question lies the interpretation of Allah's words. The Koran, for example, states that people have the right to defend themselves when attacked but must not take an innocent life, which is a crime. Most Muslims believe that attacking noncombatants, especially women and children, violates the Islamic law of war. Fundamentalists disagree. They believe that Islam is under attack—from the western powers and through the creation of the Jewish state of Israel on formerly Arab land. Since the late 1970s various groups have emerged that use terrorism in what they call a "jihad," a holy war against the West.

Moderate Muslims argue that this is a misinterpretation of the word "jihad." They read it as meaning "struggle in the path of God," and take it as a personal spiritual challenge. Islamic scholar Suzanne Haneef states, "The first and most essential jihad which the Muslim must carry on, is within himself in a never-ceasing effort at self-improvement and self-purification."

Such Muslims argue that extremists like Osama Bin Laden, leader of the Al Qaeda terrorist group, represent a fundamentalist strain of Islam that distorts the true meaning and intention of Islamic law. They claim that the media have helped endorse the idea that Islam promotes terrorism through their negative representation of the religion. The media tend to characterize the killers as Muslims first and terrorists second; most Muslims see it the other way around.

The following extracts examine how or if Islam condones terrorism.

A CALL TO MUSLIMS OF THE WORLD
Faith Freedom International

YES

☑ Dear Friends,

The tragic incident of September 11 has shocked the world. It is unthinkable how anyone could be so full of hate as to commit such a heinous act and kill so many innocent people. We people of Muslim origin are as much shaken as the rest of the world and yet we find ourselves looked upon with suspicion and distrust by our neighbors and fellow citizens. We want to cry out and announce that we are not terrorists, that those who perpetrate such despicable acts are murderers and are not part of us. But, in reality, because of our Muslim origin we just can not erase the stigma of "Islamic Terrorists" from our identity!

Most Muslims believe: "Islam would never support killing innocent people. Allah of the Holy Quran never advocated killings. This is all the work of a few misguided individuals at the fringe of the society. The real Islam is sanctified against violence. We denounce all violence. Islam means peace. Islam means tolerance."

But is it true? Does Islam really preach peace, tolerance and non-violence? Those Muslims who perpetrate crimes in the name of Allah think differently. They believe that what they do is a Jihad (holy war). They say that killing the unbelievers is mandatory for every Muslim. They do not kill because they break the laws of Islam but because they think this is what a true Muslim should do....

Are they completely misguided? Where did they get this distorted idea? How did they come to believe that killing innocent people pleases God? Or is it that we are misguided? Does Islam really preach violence?...

Do you think this is a fair opinion? Should all coreligionists feel responsible for the actions of extremists? What about Christians and Christian extremists?

Asking rhetorical questions helps keep your audience engaged and raises ideas quickly.

What we are told

Quran tells us to: "not to make friendship with Jews and Christians" (Q. 5:51), fight them "until they pay the Jizya (a penalty tax for the non-Muslims living under Islamic rules) with willing submission, and feel themselves subdued" (Q. 9:29), "kill the disbelievers wherever we find them" (Q.2:191), "murder them and treat them harshly" (Q. 9:123), "fight and slay the Pagans, seize them, beleaguer them, and lie in wait for them in every stratagem" (Q. 9:5).

[The] Quran says that all those who disbelieve in Islam [will] go to hell (Q. 5:10), they are najis (filthy, untouchable, impure) (Q. 9:28), and [it] orders us to fight the unbelievers until no other religion except Islam is left (Q.2:193). It prohibits a Muslim to befriend a non-believer even if that non-believer is the father or the brother of that Muslim (Q. 9:23), (Q. 3:28).…

The holy Prophet prescribes fighting for us and tells us that "it is good for us even if we dislike it" (Q.2:216). Then he advises us to "strike off the heads of the disbelievers"; and after making a "wide slaughter among them, carefully tie up the remaining captives" (Q.47:4). Our God has promised to "instill terror into the hearts of the unbelievers" and has ordered us to "smite above their necks and smite all their finger-tips off them" (Q.8:12) and "to strike terror into (the hearts of the enemies" (Q.8:60).

The notion of the holy war

He has made the Jihad mandatory and warns us that "Unless we go forth, (for Jihad) He will punish us with a grievous penalty, and put others in our place" (Q.9:39). Allah speaks to our Holy Prophet and says "O Prophet! strive hard against the unbelievers and the Hypocrites, and be stern against them. Their abode is Hell, an evil refuge indeed" (Q. 9:73).…

Dear fellow Muslim: Is this the Islam you believe in? Is this your Most Merciful, Most Compassionate Allah whom you worship daily? Could God incite us to kill other peoples? Please understand that there is no terrorist gene but there could be a terrorist mindset. That mindset finds its most fertile ground in the tenets of Islam. Denying it and presenting Islam as a religion of peace similar to Buddhism to the lay public is suppression of truth. The history of Islam between 7th and 14th centuries is riddled with violence, fratricide and wars of aggression, starting right from the death of the Prophet and during theso-called "pure" or orthodox caliphate. And Muhammad himself hoisted the standard of killing, looting, massacres and bloodshed. How can we deny the entire history? The behavior of our Holy Prophet as recorded in authentic Islamic sources is quite questionable from a modern viewpoint. The Prophet was a charismatic man but he had few virtues. Imitating him in all aspects of life (following Sunnah) is firstly impossible and secondly dangerous in the 21st century. Why are we so helplessly in denial on this simple issue?…

> Go to the library, and find a copy of the Koran, or look for the Koran online at www.google.com to find these passages. Would you interpret the text in the same way?

> Some critics of the Bible argue that it also has passages in which it sounds intolerant and appears to preach violence. Other people argue that many religions needed to be prepared to defend themselves when they were first established.

> In the American Revolution George Washington and other Patriots were seen as terrorists by the British. What elements of a "terrorist mindset" might they share with modern terrorists?

The hatred has filled the air and the world is bracing itself for its doomsday. Should we not ask ourselves whether we have contributed, unwittingly, to this tragedy and whether we can stop the great disaster from happening?

Unfortunately the answer to the first question is yes. Yes, we have contributed to the rise of fundamentalism by merely claiming Islam is a religion of peace, by simply being a Muslim and by saying our shahada (testimony that Allah is the only God and Muhammad is his messenger). By our shahada we have recognized Muhammad as a true messenger of God and his book as the words of God. But as you saw, those words are anything but from God. They call for killing, they are prescriptions for hate and they foment intolerance. And when the ignorant among us read those hate laden verses, they act on them and the result is the infamous September 11, the result is human bombs in Israel, massacres in East Timor and Bangladesh, kidnappings and killings in Philippines, slavery and genocide in Sudan, honor killings in Pakistan and Jordan, torture in Iran, stoning and maiming in Afghanistan and Iran, violence in Algeria, terrorism in Palestine and misery and death in all Islamic countries. We are responsible because we endorsed Islam and hailed it as a religion of God. And we are as guilty as those who put into practice what Quran preaches and ironically we are the main victims too.

Do you think religions are the main cause of conflict? See Topic 2 Would there be fewer wars if religion did not exist?

A religion of peace?

If we are not terrorists, if we love peace, if we cried with the rest of the world for what happened in NYC, then why are we supporting [the] Quran that preaches killing, that advocates holy war, that calls for murder of non-Muslims? It is not the extremists who have misunderstood Islam. They do literally what Quran asks them to do. It is we who misunderstand Islam. We are the ones who are confused. We are the ones who wrongly assume that Islam is the religion of peace. Islam is not a religion of peace. In its so-called pure form it can very well be interpreted as a doctrine of hate. Terrorists are simply doing that and we the intellectual apologists of Islam are justifying it....

In their purest form can all religions be seen as doctrines of hate? Do they all encourage their own believers to feel superior to and aggressive toward followers of other religions?

Dear friends, there is no time to waste. Let us put an end to this lie. Let us not fool ourselves. Islam is not a religion of peace, of tolerance, of equality or of unity of humankind. Let us read the Quran. Let us face the truth even if it is painful. As long as we keep this lie alive, as long as we hide our head in the sands of Arabia we are feeding terrorism. As long as you and I keep calling Quran the unchangeable book of God, we cannot blame those who follow the teachings therein. As long as we pay our Khums and Zakat our money goes to promote Islamic expansionism and that means terrorism, Jihad and war.

Islam divides the world in two parts: Darul Harb (land of war) and Darul Islam (land of Islam). Darul Harb is the land of the infidels, Muslims are required to infiltrate those lands, proselytize and procreate until their number increase and then start the war and fight and kill the people and impose the religion of Islam on them and convert that land into Darul Islam.

There are around 1.2 billion Muslims in the world, most of whom live peacefully. If the situation was as dire as the authors state, would there be even more terrorism and war?

In all fairness we denounce this betrayal. This is an abuse of trust. How can we make war in the countries that have sheltered us? How can we kill those who have befriended us? Yet willingly or unwillingly we have become pawns in this Islamic Imperialism. If this sounds to you abhorrent, we ask you how can you support a doctrine that is so deceiving, so cunning and so ruthless?…

Conclusion

We know too well that it is not easy to denounce our faith as it means denouncing a part of ourselves. We are a group of freethinkers and humanists with Islamic roots. Discovering the truth and leaving the religion of our fathers and forefathers was a painful experience. But after learning what Islam stands for, we had no choice but to leave it. After becoming familiar with the Quran, the choice became clear: it is either Islam or it is humanity. If Islam is to thrive, humanity has to die. We decided to side with humanity. We are still Muslims culturally but we no more believe in Islam as the true religion of God. We are humanists. We love humanity. We endeavor for the unity of humankind. We work for equality between men and women. We strive for secularization of Islamic countries, for democracy and freedom of thoughts, beliefs and expressions We have decided not to live anymore in self-deception but to embrace humanity, enter into the new millennium hand in hand with people of other cultures and beliefs in amity and in peace.

Is it possible to be both a free thinker and religious? Are the two mutually exclusive? See Topic 3 Does organized religion stifle free thought?

We denounce the violence that is eulogized in Quran as holy war (Jihad). We condemn killing in the name of God. We believe in sacredness of human life, not in the inviolability of beliefs and religions. And we invite you to join us and the rest of the humanity and be part of the family of humankind with love, camaraderie and peace.

DOES ISLAM PROMOTE VIOLENCE?
Javeed Akhter

Javeed Akhter is the executive director of the International Strategy and Policy Institute.

In November 2001 religious broadcaster and leader Pat Robertson (1930–) argued that Muslims wanted to exterminate the Jews. Franklin Graham (1952–), son of the evangelist Billy Graham, is said to have commented on the NBC Nightly News that Islam was an evil and wicked religion that ordered the killing of non-Muslims.

"Exegesis" (plural, exegeses) means the critical interpretation of a text, such as the Koran or the Bible.

Fazlur Rahman is professor of Islamic thought at the University of Chicago, IL. He has written many books on Islam and is a well-respected scholar.

NO

The evangelist Franklin Graham and the conservative Christian commentator Pat Robertson's assertion that Islam exhorts its followers to be violent against non-Muslims, are only two of the most prominent voices that are part of a rising cacophony of vicious criticism of the Qur'an. One can read and hear a whole range of negative opinions about this issue in the media. Few have taken an in depth look at the issue. What does the Qur'an actually say about violence against non-Muslims? Does it say what Robertson and Graham claim it does? Does it say that it is the religious duty of Muslims to kill infidels? But first some basic principles about reading and understanding the Qur'an. After all, studying the Qur'an is not exactly like reading Harry Potter. Like any other scripture there are rules that may be followed for a proper understanding of the text.

Muslim scholars suggest that those who read the Qur'an should keep at a minimum the following principles in mind. First, the reader should have an awareness of the inner coherence in the Qur'an. As the verses are connected to each other, the reader should study at the least, the preceding and following verses for a sense of the immediate context. Also the reader should look at all of the verses that deal with the same subject in the book. These are frequently scattered all over the scripture. The indices provided in many of the exegeses of the Qur'an as well as the books of concordance allow the reader to get this information relatively easily. Often there is information available about the occasion of revelation, the historical context, of a particular verse. This requires at least a cursory knowledge of prophet Muhammad's life.

As Professor Fazlur Rahman of the University of Chicago would frequently point out, the Qur'an, in part at least, may be looked upon as a running commentary on the mission of Prophet Muhammad. Finally Qur'anic scholars advise us to analyze the way Prophet implemented a particular directive in a verse of the Qur'an in his own life and ministry. For all Muslims [the] Prophet Muhammad was the ultimate exemplar of the Qur'an and its living embodiment.

Let us examine the verses in question with these exegetical principles in mind. One of the verses says "put down the polytheists wherever you find them, and capture them and beleaguer them and lie in wait for them at every ambush" (Koran 9:5). The immediate context, as Muhammad Asad (The Message Of The Qur'an) points out, is that of a "war in progress" and not a general directive. It was an attempt to motivate Muslims in self-defense.

> The Koran states that people can defend themselves if attacked. However, this does not, critics argue, justify the use of terrorist action.

Muslims were given permission to defend themselves around the time of Prophet Muhammad's migration from Makkah, where he grew up, to the city of Madinah where he spent the rest of his life. This occurred in the 13th year of his 23-year mission. The danger to Muslims in Makkah at this time was extreme and there was a real possibility of their total eradication. They were permitted to fight back in self-defense against those who violently oppressed them.

> Muhammad is believed to have migrated to Madinah in 633.

"Permission is given (to fight) those who have taken up arms against you wrongfully. And verily God (Allah) is well able to give you succor. To those who have been driven forth from their homes for no reason than this that say 'Our Lord is God." Qur'an goes on to add, "Hath not God repelled some men by others, cloisters and churches and synagogues and mosques, wherein the name of God is ever mentioned, would assuredly have been pulled down." (Qur'an 22: 39-42) On another occasion Qur'an says, "Fight in the cause of God those who fight you, but don't transgress limits; for God loves not the transgressor." ... [And] "And fight them on until there is no more oppression, and there prevail justice and faith in God; but if they cease let there be no hostility except to those who practice oppression." (Qur'an 2: 190-193)

The justification of war

Muslim scholars are of the opinion that war is permitted in self defense, when other nations have attacked an Islamic state, or if another state is oppressing a section of its own people. When Muslims were to fight a war they had to maintain great discipline, avoiding injury to the innocent and use only the minimum force needed. Striking a blow in anger, even in battle, was prohibited. The prisoners of war were to be treated in a humane fashion. However, this is only a part of Jihad that Muslims are allowed to practice. A greater Jihad is struggle against one's own inner self.

> Does this idea conflict with the idea of a holy war?

The word Jihad comes from the root Arabic word "Jahd," which means to struggle or to strive. It is understood by piety minded Muslims as a positive, noble and laudatory term. That is how most apply it in their personal, social, political and

This 19th-century Spanish print depicts a crusader as a Christian hero with a halo. From the 11th to the 13th centuries Christian armies launched seven crusades against the Ottoman Turks in order to reclaim control of the Holy Lands. The brutality and bloodshed were justified by a proclamation in 1095 by Pope Urban II: "Deus lo volt!"—"God wills it!"

military lives. The history of the Muslim rulers, on the other hand, gives us examples of those who attempted to sanctify their wars of personal aggrandizement as wars for a noble cause by applying the label Jihad to them. A few even named their war departments as the departments of Jihad. This kind of behavior may be likened to a politician's attempt to wrap him in the flag. Such exploitation of the term should not be allowed to corrupt the original or the commonly understood meaning of the word, which is to strive for the highest possible goals, struggle against injustice and practice self denial and self control to achieve the moral purity to which all piety minded people aspire.

The "holy war" concept, for which many non-Muslims use the word Jihad, is foreign to Islam. Rather, it comes from a concept first used to justify the Crusades by the Christian Church during the middle Ages. The concept of "holy war" may even go back to the time when the emperor Constantine the Great allegedly saw a vision in the sky with the inscription on the cross, "in hoc signo vinces" (in this sign you will be the victor). The Arabic term, as has been pointed out by scholars, for "the holy war" would be al-harab al-muqaddas, which neither appears in the Qur'an or the sayings of the Prophet Muhammad (Hadith). Prophet Muhammad's wars were defensive wars against groups who sought to eradicate Islam and the Muslims.

It is interesting and useful for social scientists or philologists to study how the meaning and usage of words differ in different communities. Ironically the word "crusade," because of its association with the crusades in the middle ages, should have had a pejorative sense to it and yet the word has acquired an ennobled meaning in the West. This in spite of the fact that the Church itself, along with most historians, acknowledge the injustice of the Crusades and the atrocities done in the name of faith. On the other hand, the word "Jihad" which means for Muslims, striving for the highest possible goal, has acquired the negative connotation of the holy war.

It is clear from even a cursory study of the Qur'an that Islam does not permit, condone or promote violence. Just the opposite, it abhors violence and allows it only in self-defense. A claim to the contrary is no more than bad fiction. The critics of the Qur'an should remember that if the Bible were similarly quoted out of context, it would appear to be an extra ordinarily violent scripture. I will leave Graham and Robertson to defend the violence in the Bible and the history of Christianity.

Many people believe religious conflicts arise from misinterpretations between faiths. Do you agree? What other reasons might there be?

Constantine the Great made his soldiers carry shields with this emblem engraved on them. His military victories convinced him to make Christianity the official religion of the Roman Empire.

This is an important issue to remember if you are quoting text. Do not extract it in such a way as to change the meaning.

Summary

Historically most religions have had extremist followers who have used violence to attain their ends. After the attacks of September 11, 2001, many people—both Muslims and non-Muslims—have wondered whether Islam in particular condones terrorism. These two articles look at the debate in detail.

In the first Faith Freedom International takes an unambiguous stand. The authors strongly reject the notion that Islam is at heart a religion of peace. They argue that the history of the spread of Islam was itself characterized by warfare and great violence. They also identify many passages from the Koran that they claim provide conclusive textual evidence that Islam is in fact a religion of violence. They argue that nonviolent Muslims must come to terms with this aspect of their religion if they are to preserve it from terrorists and other people of violence.

Islamic commentator Javeed Akhter, however, strongly disagrees. "It is clear from even a cursory study of the [Koran]," Akhter concludes, "that Islam does not permit, condone, or promote violence." He selects his own passages from the Koran to show that the ideas behind "jihad," or holy war, are the result of a misreading of the religious text. He concludes that Islam is not the only religion open to misinterpretation: "If the Bible were similarly quoted out of context, it would appear to be an extraordinarily violent scripture."

FURTHER INFORMATION:

Books:

Esposito, John L., *Unholy War: Terror in the Name of Islam*. New York: Oxford University Press, 2003.

Useful websites:

http://www.americancatholic.org/
e-News/FriarJack/fj012804.asp
Article that looks at the Abrahamic faiths, including Islam, and argues that Islam does not promote terrorism.
http://hnn.us/articles/3289.html
Article by Daniel Pipes on the History News Network debating whether it is necessary to read the Koran to understand Islamic terrorism.
http://www.hti.umich.edu/k/koran/browse.html
The full text of the Koran online in English. Includes various search functions and notes.
http://www.washingtonpost.com/ac2/wp-dyn/A46961-2001Sep17?language=printer
2001 *Washington Post* article that examines Osama Bin Laden's interpretation of Islam versus that of most moderate Islamists.

The following debates in the Pro/Con series may also be of interest:

In this volume:

Topic 2 Would there be fewer wars if religion did not exist?

Topic 12 Are monotheistic religions more intolerant than other religions?

Topic 15 Should Christianity be the official religion of the United States?

In *U.S. Foreign Policy*:
September 11, 2001, pages 176–177

DOES ISLAM CONDONE TERRORISM?

YES: There are so many passages in the Koran that encourage violence and hatred

YES: Suicide bombers, for example, believe that self-sacrifice will be rewarded with perpetual paradise after death

KORAN
Does the Koran encourage militantism?

MARTYRDOM
Does Islam encourage terrorists by making them martyrs?

NO: For every passage in the Koran that appears to condone violence, there is another that preaches peace and tolerance

NO: The Koran makes it clear that people may defend themselves only when attacked. It offers no reward for killing innocents or taking one's own life.

DOES ISLAM CONDONE TERRORISM? KEY POINTS

YES: Jihad means "holy war," and Muslims are encouraged to wage war against non-Muslims

YES: The Koran, like any other holy scripture, is not open to interpretation: It is the word of Allah.

JIHAD
Does the concept of jihad encourage violence?

INTERPRETATION
Are critics wrong to accuse fundamentalists of misinterpreting the Koran?

NO: Jihad is first and foremost a spiritual struggle undertaken by every Muslim with themselves

NO: The Koran, like the Bible, is often quoted out of context; in this way it can be made to appear to support almost any point of view

PART 4

RELIGION IN THE UNITED STATES

INTRODUCTION

Religion is highly important in the modern United States, which is predominantly Christian. In a 2003 survey on the religious beliefs of Americans, 69 percent of respondents claimed to believe in Hell, and 84 professed a belief in the existence of miracles. There are other signs of the significance of religion in the nation's life: Presidents pray with their cabinets, TV channels are devoted to spreading Christianity, and Christian novels based on the Rapture—when the "elect" will be taken up to Heaven by God—top the bestseller charts. About 40 percent of Americans class themselves as "born-again" Christians: That broadly means that they have made a conscious decision to embrace a faith. Born-again Christians generally belong to nonconformist Protestant churches such as the Baptists or the Methodists but also include representatives of all branches of Christianity.

Religion played a vital role in the settlement and history of North America. Among the earliest Europeans who came to America were Spanish Christian missionaries seeking to make converts among the native inhabitants of the Southwest. The colonization of the East Coast and the establishment of the 13 original colonies were inspired to a large degree by religion. Many of the immigrants from England, Germany,

Sweden, and elsewhere were followers of minority Protestant religions who faced persecution in their homelands. They included, for example, the Puritans of New England and the Anabaptists and Moravians, who arrived from continental Europe, as well as groups such as the Quakers. In the Massachusetts Bay Colony the Puritans declared their intention to establish a "city upon a hill" as an example to the rest of the world.

Although the establishment of different churches was not always smooth—the Quakers, for instance, were unpopular among other Christians for their refusal to acknowledge any form of political authority—a tradition of multifaith tolerance did emerge. It was enshrined in the United States Constitution, the first amendment to which forbade the establishment of an official state religion.

Great Awakening

Twice in American history great waves of evangelical Christianity have swept the country, in the Great Awakening of the 1740s and the Second Great Awakening of the early 1800s. Many American religions were characterized by their rejection of the bishops and of the elaborate rituals that characterized established European churches. The Presbyterian church, for example, was effectively governed by its own congregations rather than by an episcopal hierarchy.

In frontier communities, where there were few churches or other elements of organized religion, another distinctly American tradition emerged. It was "revivalism," in which fundamentalist evangelical preachers toured the country giving sermons wherever they could gather a congregation. Also during the 19th century Americans created their own purely American religion, the Church of Jesus Christ of Latter-day Saints, or Mormons, a Christian group that followed the

combined total of Protestants. Many Protestant churches are deeply divided, however, into different creeds.

Religion in the United States continues to evolve. In the 20th century, for example, the country absorbed large numbers of Asians, many of whom continued to practice their traditional religions such as Hinduism, Buddhism, or Islam. In 1953 science-fiction writer L. Ron Hubbard (1911–1986) established the Church of Scientology (see pages 58–59), while the closing decades of the century saw the emergence of millenarian movements such as Heaven's Gate,

---

"No person can be punished for entertaining or professing religious beliefs or disbeliefs."
—HUGO BLACK (1886–1971), SUPREME COURT JUSTICE

---

teachings of Joseph Smith (1805–1844). Led by Brigham Young (1801–1877), the Mormons fled persecution in the 1840s to establish their own community at Salt Lake City in Utah.

Continuing religious change

During the late 19th and early 20th centuries growing immigration to the United States from Ireland and southern Europe brought an increasing number of Catholics to the country. The numbers were boosted further by large-scale immigration from the countries of Latin America, the majority of which are Catholic owing to the influence of original European colonists from Spain and Portugal. Today Catholics form the single largest faith in the United States, with more than 62 million followers. But that number is still dwarfed by the

which promoted the idea that Earth would be destroyed and the faithful taken to everlasting life.

The topics in this section take up some of the most interesting questions about the place of religion in American life today. Topic 14 considers whether church and state should remain separate, as specified in the U.S. Constitution. Topic 15 examines a different aspect of this issue by asking whether Christianity should become the official religion of the United States. Both debates refer to the highly visible influence of Christians in U.S. politics. Topic 16 examines this phenomenon from the point of view of the rest of the world. It asks whether the rise of the religious right has isolated the United States from countries that do not share such religious fervor.

Topic 14

IS THE SEPARATION BETWEEN CHURCH AND STATE STILL NECESSARY?

YES

FROM "THE REAL VICTIMS OF A CHURCH–STATE MERGER:
BE CAREFUL WHAT YOU WISH FOR"
FREE INQUIRY, VOL. 20, NO. 4, FALL 2000
ALAN M. DERSHOWITZ

NO

"WHY RELIGION HAS A PLACE IN THE PUBLIC SQUARE"
THE ARIZONA REPUBLIC, AUGUST 17, 2003
ALAN E. SEARS

INTRODUCTION

In 1789 the first 10 Amendments to the Constitution—also known as the Bill of Rights—enshrined in law the individual rights of citizens. The Framers of the Constitution dealt with the issue of religion in the First Amendment in what are now known as the "Establishment clause" and the "Free Exercise clause." The amendment stated, "Congress shall make no law respecting an establishment of religion, or prohibiting the free exercise thereof." The Framers were seeking to ensure that the government could not establish an official religion and that citizens could worship freely.

Historically many people have interpreted this wording to mean that there must be a separation between church and state—that civil authority and religious authority must be kept separate. For over 200 years, however, politicians and religious and legal commentators have disputed whether

such a church–state divide is necessary or, indeed, whether it was what the Framers intended.

Integral to the debate is the extent to which the Framers intended religion to be separated from government. One of their guiding principles was that of religious tolerance. Many early Americans were fleeing religious persecution in their homelands. Some settlers were members of religious minorities, such as the Quakers or Protestant sects; they had come from countries such as England and the states of Germany, which had established religions and where minorities were persecuted. The First Amendment was meant to safeguard citizens against similar discrimination.

Some interpreters have insisted that the Framers intended the First Amendment to create a clear distinction between church and state authority: In 1802 President Thomas Jefferson

(1801–1809) described it as "building a wall of separation between church and state." His successor James Madison (1809–1817) wrote a decade later of the "separation between religion and government in the Constitution." The Supreme Court has on numerous occasions supported this interpretation of the amendment. In 1947, for example, Justice Hugo Black ruled in *Everson v. Board of Education* that "The First Amendment has erected a wall between church and state. That wall must be kept high and impregnable."

> *"A government cannot be premised on the belief that all persons are created equal when it asserts that God prefers some."*
> —JUSTICE HARRY A. BLACKMUN,
> *LEE V. WEISMAN* (1992)

Critics of such a view, however, maintain that the Framers did not intend to exclude religion from public life. They claim that there is a legitimate place for religious expression in the public arena. Such critics believe that the First Amendment should be interpreted only as meaning that government should not make one religion an official religion. Since the amendment does not contain explicit wording to support the "wall" between church and state, there is no reason to stop religious-related activities such as organized prayers in schools or the erection of religious monuments. A USA Today/CNN/Gallup poll conducted in 2003, for example, found that 77 percent of people disagreed with a U.S. District Court decision to remove the Ten Commandments monument from the rotunda of the Alabama Judicial Building on the grounds that its clear Christian inspiration made it unconstitutional.

People who want to see closer links between church and state argue that discrimination is not a problem in countries in which state and church are not separated. In the United Kingdom, for example, the queen is both head of state and head of the Church of England. Nevertheless, Britons are still allowed to practice other religions without fear of persecution. This has led critics to ask why the United States still needs the "wall."

For many of those who support the maintenance of the divide—they include both religious believers and atheists (who do not believe in God)—the answer is very clear. George W. Bush, who became president in 2001, is strongly influenced by his born-again Christian faith. Many Americans were concerned at how much Bush's faith would manifest itself in government policy. His decision in May 2004 to host a National Day of Prayer at the White House—the event was broadcast on evangelical Christian and satellite networks—was criticized for bringing church and state too close together. The existence of the "wall" serves to ensure that even a religiously committed president cannot take steps to empower one religion at the expense of others.

The following articles by legal professor Alan M. Dershowitz and religious commentator Alan E. Sears, examine the debate further.

THE REAL VICTIMS OF A CHURCH–STATE MERGER: BE CAREFUL WHAT YOU WISH FOR
Alan M. Dershowitz

Alan M. Dershowitz is a professor at Harvard Law School, and a writer. This article originally appeared in the Free Inquiry magazine in 2000.

YES

The "wall" has long been a useful and poetic metaphor. It separates neighbors as well as great nations. It protects and defends, but it also rejects and offends. The wall of separation between church and state, a metaphor attributed to Thomas Jefferson, is in danger of crumbling in the nation that first built it. There are multiple ironies in this danger. Unlike the broken wall which separated East and West Germany, the wall between church and state in America is not broken. Originally designed to protect the church against the secularizing intrusions of the state, our wall is working extremely well. Churches, synagogues, and mosques are thriving in this land of separation. Religious attendance is higher than in any Western democracy with an established church. Belief in God is widespread throughout the land. Yet the right to disbelieve or to be skeptical is accepted—at least in theory.

> Do you agree that all Americans have an equal right not to believe in God or to believe in a God other than the Christian one?

A contrast

The successful status of American religion is to be contrasted with the sorry state of religion throughout most of Europe. When my family and I travel to Europe, we love to visit the old churches—not for prayer, but for artistic appreciation. Our favorite time to observe a church is on Sunday morning, when it is being used as intended. In recent years, we have seen fewer and fewer parishioners in churches throughout England, France, Italy, Germany, and Spain—except, of course, on special occasions. It is no coincidence, in my view, that organized religion is thriving in America and dying in much of Europe.

The separation of church and state is good for religion. When church and state merge, the natural antagonism that citizens feel toward their government carries over to the church. Moreover, when the state tries to enforce religious practices, enmity is generated. Witness Israel, a country that I visit frequently. Because the mechanisms of the state

> Why do you think the author claims that is it "natural" for citizens to feel antagonism toward their government?

Oliver Wendell Holmes, Jr., served on the U.S. Supreme Court from 1902 to 1932.

COMMENTARY: Oliver Wendell Holmes, Jr.

Oliver Wendell Holmes, Jr., was born in 1841. The son of a celebrated Boston family, Holmes was a contemporary of Henry Adams and Henry James. He served with distinction in the Civil War and later became a prominent member of the Massachusetts bar. An ambitious man, Holmes was determined to make his mark on society. He wrote extensively on the law and society, and was appointed to the Supreme Court by President Theodore Roosevelt (1901–1909) in 1902. He believed in eugenics—the science of genetic improvement through selective breeding, including using sterilization to discourage the genetically inferior from reproducing. One of Holmes's most famous rulings involved the proposed sterilization of a young woman in the case of *Buck v. Bell* in 1917.

Buck v. Bell

In 1907 Indiana became the first of around 30 states to pass laws permitting involuntary sterilization on eugenic grounds. Most were based on a model outlined by Harry Laughlin of the Eugenics Record Organization (ERO), which called for compulsory sterilization of the "socially inadequate." Religious and civil rights bodies strongly criticized the laws, but by 1930 more than 3,000 people had been sterilized without their consent—the homeless and those with low IQs among them.

In 1924 Carrie Buck, a teenager from Charlottesville, Virginia, was accused of having a child out of wedlock. Buck's mother lived in an asylum for the feeble-minded and epileptic; Carrie was accused of being promiscuous and the possible parent of "socially inadequate offspring." She was chosen to be the first victim of sterilization under the newly passed state eugenics laws. A suit challenging the ruling was filed on Buck's behalf, but Laughlin, who had never met Buck, wrote condemning her and her daughter Vivian. The judge ruled in the state's favor. On appeal the Supreme Court ruled 8–1 to uphold the ruling, and Holmes, by then chief justice, stated famously, "Society can prevent those who are manifestly unfit from continuing their kind.... Three generations of imbeciles are enough."

Buck v. Bell formed the basis for other eugenics-based cases. Forced sterilizations continued until the 1970s in the United States despite opposition from religious groups: Around 60,000 Americans were sterilized.

are employed in support of Orthodox Judaism, a sharp division has developed between the Orthodox community and the vast majority of secular Jews. Many secular Jews feel strongly that their freedoms have been impinged on, not only by Orthodox Judaism, but by the state as well. Today there is more anti-Orthodox feeling in Israel than in any other part of the world.

For these reasons, I believe that, if the wall of separation were to crumble in America, the ultimate losers would be the churches, the synagogues, and the mosques. To be sure, organized religion would benefit initially from the support—financial, political, and ideological—of the state. Many religious leaders who are currently strapped for cash see the wall of separation as a barrier to filling their coffers. But in the long run, organized religion would suffer greatly from state involvement in their affairs. The state, by paying the organist, would call the hymn. This would be a tragedy both for religious and secular Americans. Religion, if it remains independent of the state, can serve as a useful check and balance on the excesses of government. For example, during the 1920s, eugenics became the rage among scientists, academics, and intellectuals. Thirty states enacted forcible sterilization laws that resulted in 50,000 people being surgically sterilized. In 1927, the United States Supreme Court upheld these laws in a decision by the great Justice Oliver Wendell Holmes, who wrote: "It is better for all the world, if instead of waiting to execute offspring for crime or to let them starve for their imbecility, society can prevent those who are manifestly unfit from continuing their kind." The only dissenting opinion came from a religious Catholic. Churches fought hard against sterilization laws. In this instance, religion was right: government and science were wrong.

Various governments have advocated the implementation of eugenics laws. See the box opposite for information on Judge Oliver Wendell Holmes, Jr., and the landmark case Buck v. Bell.

In countries where the state controls religion, it is far more difficult for churches to serve as checks upon the excesses of the state. Were the wall of separation to come crumbling down, disbelievers and skeptics would also suffer greatly—at least at the outset. I doubt we would have crusades, inquisitions, or pogroms—as in centuries past. But there would be discrimination. Indeed, even today, there is discrimination in practice despite its prohibition under the Constitution…. But in the long run, the number of openly skeptical Americans would increase. Church membership would drop.

Do you think religious discrimination would increase if the church–state wall came down? Does religious hatred exist in America? Go to www.cnn.com and find articles on the subject.

Would this be good for America? Would this be good for secular humanists? Since none of us is a prophet, it is impossible to know with certainty what an America, without a wall of separation, would look like. It would almost certainly become a different place than the one we now inhabit, which is still the envy of the world. We are a prudent and cautious people. As such, we should not take the risks of breaking an edifice that has served us so well for so long.

WHY RELIGION HAS A PLACE IN THE PUBLIC SQUARE
Alan E. Sears

Alan E. Sears is president of the Alliance Defense Fund (ADF), which promotes the "legal defense and advocacy of religious freedom, the sanctity of human life, and traditional family values."

There have been concerted efforts to remove monuments of the Ten Commandments from public places in America, including one situated on state land in Phoenix, Arizona. Similarly, bronze plaques citing verses from the Bible were removed from Grand Canyon National Park. See http://www.sfgate.com/cgi-bin/article.cgi?f=/news/archive/2003/07/24/state1008EDT7438.DTL for further information. Do you think the removal of religious monuments is right?

NO

America was founded on the pursuit of religious liberty, including the liberty to acknowledge God and to pray in the public square.

This liberty originates in higher law, or "the laws of nature and of nature's God," as the Declaration of Independence puts it. In the words of Rabbi Daniel Lapin, the founders [Framers] modeled themselves "upon God's ancient people" and "wrote what they considered to be a modern-day interpretation of the basic biblical principles of government."

Making the First Amendment something it isn't?

Those principles demand a place for religious expression in the public square. Unfortunately, radical advocates have long been trying to re-write the Constitution by making the First Amendment say something it doesn't. The First Amendment plainly forbids the creation of a national denomination, because that would be an "establishment of religion." It says nothing about the so-called "separation of church and state."

Even those who agitate to remove the Ten Commandments monument at the Arizona capitol and the now-famous Grand Canyon plaques with Hebrew Scriptures will admit—when pressed—that the so-called "separation of church and state" is not in the Constitution.

What did the founders [Framers] do and say to make us think religion has a place in the public square?

Let us consider General George Washington. When Washington received a copy of the Declaration of Independence from the Continental Congress, he immediately issued orders that "The Colonels or commanding officers of each regiment are directed to procure Chaplains accordingly; persons of good Characters and exemplary lives."

The Declaration which motivated Washington's appointment of chaplains contains four references to God: God as the Creator and the source of liberty ("all men are endowed by their Creator with unalienable rights"), God the law giver ("law of nature and of nature's God"), God the

George Washington (1732–1799) was the first president of the United States. See page 186 for more information on Washington and the church–state relationship.

George Washington was a Framer of the Constitution and was America's first president from 1789 to 1797. Go to http://www.whitehouse.gov/history/presidents/gw1.html to find out more about him.

ultimate judge ("the Supreme Judge of the World"), and God as the king above all earthly rulers, as the Sovereign ("Divine Providence").

After he led the army to victory, Washington presided over the Constitutional Convention, and was then elected our first president under the Constitution.

At Washington's first inauguration in New York City, Washington took the oath of office on a Bible opened to Genesis 49 and 50, and added the words repeated by every president since, "So help me God." He told his audience at Federal Hall that, "It would be peculiarly improper to omit, in this first official act, my fervent supplications to that Almighty Being who rules over the universe, who presides in the councils of nations."

Washington then went very publicly to pray at St. Paul's Chapel before he attended inaugural festivities. Eight years later, in his farewell address, Washington said "Of all the dispositions and habits which lead to political prosperity, Religion and morality are indispensable supports."

Washington, as perhaps the leading founding father, demonstrated repeatedly that religion has a legitimate place in the public square. The hue and cry over the Ten Commandments monument and the plaques would seem ludicrous to him and to all who served with him.

In light of that history, why would anyone object to posting "Sing to God, sing praises to his name; lift up a song to him who rides upon the clouds his name is the Lord, exult before him," at the Grand Canyon?

Washington lived in a predominantly Christian country. Is it really possible to judge what he might have thought about such a situation in the modern, multiethnic United States?

Fairness

If religion in general is the thing that keeps radicals up worrying late at night, then why haven't they also demanded that the Hindu names for canyon locations—Brahma Temple, Vishnu Temple, Siva Temple—be changed? Maybe for the same reason they want to banish the Ten Commandments from the capitol grounds—they hate orthodox religious expressions in the public square.

Remember, the monument is one of 20 similar monuments that celebrate Arizona's history, culture, and diversity. Surely, the Ten Commandments monument adds diversity. And what about the Arizona state motto, "Ditat Deus," or "God Enriches." No doubt the demand to change the motto will come soon.

Why would any irreligious person care about the monument on Wesley–Bolin Plaza? Perhaps they should follow the advice so freely doled out by the radicals like the

The Wesley–Bolin Plaza in Phoenix, Arizona, had a monument of the Ten Commandments and one dedicated to missionary, church founder, and teacher Father Albert Braun. Braun's statue was permitted to stay.

ACLU, who want child pornography protected as free speech, to "just change the channel" and turn away from the monument.

The ACLU and other civil liberty groups believe that the protection of free speech is essential. Go to www.aclu.org, and read the ACLU's opinion on this subject.

Perhaps we need a little more accurate history about the so-called "separation of church and state." In the early 1800s, many of the original states had churches sanctioned by state governments. These were "established churches," and because they were a state matter they were not forbidden in the U.S. Constitution.

A free and just society recognizes that freedom of speech and religion applies to public religious expression as well as to private. Our founding fathers knew this, as did most previous generations. Forgetting the hard-won lessons of the past is, in our time, freedom's greatest threat.

We will lose our liberties if we don't fight. We'll lose when we give in to all the ACLU's demands. We'll lose when we quit singing God Bless America, or when we take In God We Trust off our currency. We'll lose when we return to morally and legally repugnant practice of issuing governmental licenses to clergymen and their printers, as the English did here in the 1700s and as totalitarian regimes still do.

Do you think it would be fair to pass a law stating that all public monuments have to be nonreligious in subject matter?

Religion should be booted from the public square only if we prefer tyranny to liberty.

Summary

Whether the separation between church and state is still necessary is a key question in the debate about the position of religion in the United States in the 21st century. Alan M. Dershowitz believes that the "wall of separation between church and state" works well in the United States, where religious bodies are thriving—unlike in some other parts of the world where the state is involved in religious matters. Citing the example of the forced sterilization laws enacted in the 1930s, he observes that the separation means that religious bodies can act as a useful check on government, but he argues that this can only happen if churches retain their independence. He concludes by cautioning against change: "[W]e should not take the risks of breaking an edifice that has served us so well for so long."

Alan E. Sears takes a completely different view. He argues that "the United States was founded on ... the liberty to acknowledge God and to pray in the public square." He believes strongly that the Framers were guided by religious principles and showed by their actions that they thought there was a place for public religion. Sears goes on to question what he sees as a lack of consistency in the position of radical bodies such as the American Civil Liberties Union and condemns Justice Hugo Black's judgment in *Everson v. Board of Education* (1947). He concludes: "Religion should be booted from the public square only if we prefer tyranny to liberty."

FURTHER INFORMATION:

Books:

Dwyer, James G. *Religious Schools vs. Children's Rights*. Ithaca, NY: Cornell University Press, 1998.

Noonan, John T., Jr., *The Lustre of Our Country: The American Experience of Religious Freedom*. Berkeley, CA: University of California Press, 2000.

Useful websites:

www.aclu.org/students/slrelig.html
American Civil Liberties Union Freedom Network site. Users can ask Sybil Liberty religious liberty questions.
www.au.org
Religious liberty organization Americans United for the Separation of Church and State site.
http://www.infidels.org/library/modern/church-state/index.shtml
Site with links to various articles on the subject.
http://www.religioustolerance.org/const_am.htm
Separation of state and church issues page on Religious Tolerance site.

The following debates in the Pro/Con series may also be of interest:

In this volume:
Topic 15 Should Christianity be the official religion of the United States?

In *Individual and Society*:
Topic 9 Should there be a right to violate laws for religious reasons?

In *The Constitution*:
Topic 9 Does the Constitution protect religious freedom?

IS THE SEPARATION BETWEEN CHURCH AND STATE STILL NECESSARY?

YES: Church attendance in the United States is far healthier than in many European countries, for example, where there is an official state religion

YES: The arrangement means that churches are free to challenge government actions that threaten civil or human rights

BENEFIT

Has religion benefited from the continuation of the "wall" between church and state?

HEADING

Does the separation of church and state act as a check on government excesses?

NO: Religions would benefit financially if they could be funded by federal and state bodies

IS THE SEPARATION BETWEEN CHURCH AND STATE STILL NECESSARY?

KEY POINTS

NO: The influence of President George W. Bush's Christian beliefs suggests that in some cases religion still inspires rather than checks government policy

YES: They were conscious of the religious persecution many of their forebears and contemporaries had suffered and wished to make such persecution impossible in the United States

YES: The "wall" continues to allow church leaders to take a lead in condemnation of government policy, as in the civil rights movement of the 1960s

INTENTIONS

Did the Framers intend church and state to be completely separate?

CIVIL LIBERTIES

Is the separation of church and state still necessary to protect the civil liberties of the U.S. citizens?

NO: They wanted to avoid the establishment of a single state religion, not to restrict the influence of religion on government

NO: The separation did little, for example, to protect the right of Muslim citizens after the 9/11/2001 terrorist attacks

189

Topic 15

SHOULD CHRISTIANITY BE THE OFFICIAL RELIGION OF THE UNITED STATES?

YES

"A CHRISTIAN NATION?"
PCANEWS.COM, MONTHLY DEBATE, AUGUST 2003
CRAIG S. BULKELEY

NO

FROM "IS AMERICA A 'CHRISTIAN NATION'? RELIGION, GOVERNMENT, AND INDIVIDUAL FREEDOM"
HTTP://WWW.AU.ORG/RESOURCES/BROCHURES/CHRISTIANNATION.HTM
AMERICANS UNITED FOR SEPARATION OF CHURCH AND STATE

INTRODUCTION

According to a Pew Research Center report published in 2002, 82 percent of Americans consider themselves to be Christian. Of all respondents 67 percent regard the United States as a "Christian nation." Such surveys suggest to some people that Christianity should be recognized as the official, or established, religion of the United States. Others point out that this would violate the Establishment clause of the First Amendment, which states that "Congress shall make no law respecting an establishment of religion."

An estimated 1,500 to 2,000 religions are practiced in the United States, while about 14 percent of Americans have no religion. This variety of beliefs, critics insist, makes it all the more important to underline religious liberty by not making Christianity the state religion.

Many early settlers were Christians who came to America to escape persecution in their homelands.

However, they often sought religious freedom only for their own churches, not for all denominations. Most colonies introduced official churches and levied taxes for their support. For example, the Church of England became the legally established religion throughout the Southern colonies. In the South, except in Maryland, all residents were required to become church members.

In 1786 the Virginia Assembly passed Thomas Jefferson's (1743–1826) Statute for Religious Freedom, which forbade the punishment of religious belief. It was the model for the First Amendment of the Constitution, in which the Framers enshrined the principles of religious liberty and the separation of church and state.

Although the Constitution contains no mention of Christianity, some people maintain that the Framers founded the United States as a Christian nation. As proof they cite the Declaration of

Independence, which contains several references to God. More evidence comes from quotes by, for example, George Washington (1732–1799), who said in 1796, "It is impossible to rightly govern the world without God and the Bible." In a Supreme Court decision of 1892 (*Holy Trinity v. United States*) Justice David Brewer cited a total of 87 precedents to conclude that "this is a Christian nation."

"There can be no religious freedom without the freedom to dissent."

—ANNE GAYLOR, FREEDOM FROM RELIGION FOUNDATION

Until the 20th century, some people argue, Christianity was the dominant social and cultural force in the United States. In the last hundred years, they say, through a succession of Supreme Court rulings enforcing the separation of church and state and, to a certain extent, the influence of greater numbers of non-Christian immigrants, the nation has gradually removed religion from American life. Critics claim this has resulted in a decline in moral standards that can only be halted if society adheres to Christian values. A way to achieve this, they argue, is through such activities as school prayer and Bible study classes. The Supreme Court has ruled that such activities violate the Establishment clause.

People opposed to an official religion argue that the reintroduction of Bible study into public schools would be offensive to non-Christian students.

They also express concern about other ways in which the state gives the impression of favoring Christianity over other religions—for example, the inclusion of the words "under God" in the Pledge of Allegiance and "In God We Trust" on currency, and the public display of Christian symbols. In 2003 Alabama Chief Justice Roy Moore defied a federal order to remove a monument of the Ten Commandments from the state courthouse. He argued that the monument was a statement of the Christian roots of America's law. His critics countered that if the monument remained, followers of different faiths would be entitled to wonder if they could find justice in Alabama's courts.

Numerous commentators wonder what would happen to other faiths if Christianity ever became the official religion of the United States. Their fear is that Christian fundamentalists would impose a moral code on everyone else. They might, for example, restrict women's and gay rights or freedom for religious minorities or nonbelievers. Pat Robertson (1930–), founder of the evangelical lobby organization Christian Coalition, has said, for example, that he believes only Christians should be allowed to hold political office. If the government were to go further and enforce uniformity of religion, critics claim this would contradict the values of equality and freedom on which the United States was founded.

Advocates point out, however, that an established religion does not necessarily encourage intolerance of other faiths: The United Kingdom has two official religions—the Church of England and the Church of Scotland—but freedom of religion is generally respected there.

The following articles offer opposing views in this debate.

A CHRISTIAN NATION?
Craig S. Bulkeley

Craig S. Bulkeley
is an attorney
and pastor of
Friendship
Presbyterian
Church in Black
Mountain, North
Carolina. He wrote
this piece
in August 2003
as part of a debate
on "Is America a
Christian Nation?"
for PCANews.com,
an online magazine
for the
Presbyterian
Church.

YES

Critics of the Chief Justice of the Alabama Supreme Court, Roy Moore, ought to hold on a minute and reconsider their position. You remember. He's the one who has posted the Ten Commandments in the courthouse. A United States Federal District Court judge thinks he's wrong and ordered them removed. But America has been a Christian nation since its founding and that fact ought to be proclaimed, praised, preserved and promoted.

"This is a Christian nation"

Until not so long ago, we could find everywhere a clear recognition of this truth. Among other matters note the following: The form of oath universally prevailing, concluding with an appeal to the Almighty; the custom of opening sessions of all deliberative bodies and most conventions with prayer; the prefatory words of all wills, "In the name of God, amen;" with the general cessation of all secular business, and the closing of courts, Legislatures, and other similar public assemblies on that day; the churches and church organizations which abound in every city, town and hamlet; the multitude of charitable organizations existing everywhere under Christian auspices; the gigantic missionary associations, with general support, and aiming to establish Christian missions in every quarter of the globe. These, and many other matters which might be noticed, add a volume of unofficial declarations to the mass of organic utterances that this is a Christian nation.

Now you may say "Enough! Who is this loony-tune? How ignorant! Has he no understanding of our United States Constitution and the separation of church and state? Doesn't he understand American history and what America is all about? Silence him! How can you print this nonsense?"

Now take a deep breath. Almost all the words in the second paragraph above (all of them from "a clear recognition" to the end) are not mine. They were written by the United States Supreme Court itself in the case of *The Church of the Holy Trinity v. United States* in 1892 (you can find it at 143 U.S. 226). Now that Federal court understood the Constitution (even laws regarding the observance of the

Does the author
present enough
evidence to
persuade you
that "this is a
Christian nation"?

Go to
http://members.
tripod.com/~candst/
case17.htm for an
explanation of and
two different
perspectives on
this case.

A crucifix rests on the American flag. In view of the fact that more than 80 percent of Americans are Christians, some people argue that Christianity should be the official religion.

Sabbath). It understood America as it had been since its founding and for more than a hundred years (and the Court cites documents that prove it). Even the Framers of the Constitution itself concluded it with the words "done … in the Year our Lord …"

We've come a long way (mostly in just the last 50 years or so). Even the Supreme Court of the United States of America was once unashamed of Jesus Christ.

The failure of the courts (and the press) to acknowledge this truth now comes either from ignorance of history or simple dishonesty and censorship. Better in charity to impugn education (even intelligence) than integrity. But as the debate continues, let those who engage do so with knowledge of the facts and let them contend with the facts. In fairness, those who want the Ten Commandments out of public life have no basis to claim the "high ground" of the Constitution or historic Constitutional interpretation. They (and not the Judge Moore types) are the "Johnny-come-latelys" trying to overturn the established order and institute a different one.

De Tocqueville's thoughts

The French jurist and historian Alexis de Tocqueville traveled about America in the mid-1800's. He wrote about it in his *Democracy in America*. "… There is no country in the world," he said, "where the Christian religion retains a greater influence over the souls of men than in America; and there can be no greater proof of its utility and conformity to human nature than that its influence is powerfully felt over the most enlightened and free nation of the earth." He said, "Religion in America takes no direct part in the government of society, but it must be regarded as the first of political institutions. … I do not know whether all Americans have a sincere faith in their religion … but I am certain that they hold it to be indispensable to the maintenance of republican institutions. This opinion is not peculiar to a class of citizens or a party, but it belongs to the whole nation and to every rank of society." The Frenchman was merely observing the fruits of the ex-pat Puritan Brits who came to America 200 years earlier.

Sadly, most folks these days have forgotten Christ and prefer the order of ancient Rome. Rome had its Pantheon, affirming the equal legitimacy of all gods, as long as each bowed ultimately to the state. In our fallen nature, one who can exert power (at whatever level) usually prefers something other than the Ten Commandments and the

Does the fact that Christianity is not the official religion suggest that the United States is "ashamed" of Jesus Christ? What other reasons might there be not to have an official religion?

Alexis de Tocqueville (1805–1859) is best known for Democracy in America, published between 1835 and 1840. Widely regarded as one of the most influential books of 19th-century social science, it is still read as a great study of the nature and institutions of American democracy.

A pantheon, from the Greek words pan, meaning "all," and theos, meaning "god," is a temple or shrine dedicated to all the gods. The Pantheon that stands today in Rome was rebuilt by the Emperor Hadrian between A.D. 118 and 128.

"Golden Rule." Why limit yourself to "an eye for an eye" when you can really make your point and further consolidate your power by exacting a head for an eye? Mix power with pride, greed, vainglory and selfish ambition, and who wants "just weights and measures," much less a cross?

The "Golden Rule" refers to a value common to most religions. In Christianity it is embodied in the biblical verse: "Do to others as you would have them do to you" (Matthew 6:31). See http://patriot.net/~bmcgin/golden.html for more information.

Christians have sinned, but then so has everyone. We could all use more repentance and right doing. And a "Christian America" has not always done right. But we'd be better off with it than with what we've been getting. There was a day when our government didn't need to put metal detectors in our schools. Out with the Bibles, in with the knives and guns. There was a day when our government didn't take the good metal out of our money. By the time Rome collapsed, the silver content in its coins was less than 5%. We've debased ours to less than that in about 50 years. As we've debased our national faith, so we've debased the measure of our labor. (If someone offers you a bag of quarters minted in 1963 for ones minted in 2004, take it quick.) And even the Romans did not go for homosexual "marriage." There's obviously a litany of other ails—abortion, drugs, pornography and the like —which one could compose. All scar the heart and leave the soul empty.

What is the author implying by adding quotation marks around the word "marriage"?

Our need for grace and truth

The Ten Commandments isn't really the issue. Without repentance and love from the heart, the law written on stone will help little. But it is the representation of it. What we all need is the grace of God and the truth about justice and mercy. Grace and truth are found chiefly in Jesus Christ through whom one can find forgiveness of sins and peace with God. It is also found in the Bible, God's Word. Why should we forsake the revealed will of God which has shown itself to be true and of such great value to our nation since its founding? The Ten Commandments bear testimony to that God of grace and truth, and to the blessings of "a Christian nation."

Thank you, United States Supreme Court—1892. (Maybe it'll come through again.) Thank you, Judge Moore.

In November 2003 the Alabama Supreme Court stripped Roy Moore of his position as chief justice for defying a federal order to remove the Ten Commandments monument from the state courthouse. Moore's appeal was rejected in April 2004.

IS AMERICA A "CHRISTIAN NATION"? RELIGION, GOVERNMENT, AND INDIVIDUAL FREEDOM
Americans United for Separation of Church and State

Americans United for Separation of Church and State is a religious liberty watchdog group based in Washington, D.C. This extract is taken from a brochure available on the organization's website (www.au.org).

NO

Religious Right groups and their allies insist that the United States was designed to be officially Christian and that our laws should enforce the doctrines of (their version of) Christianity. Is this viewpoint accurate? Is there anything in the Constitution that gives special treatment or preference to Christianity? Did the founders of our government believe this or intend to create a government that gave special recognition to Christianity?

The answer to all of these questions is no. The U.S. Constitution is a wholly secular document. It contains no mention of Christianity or Jesus Christ. In fact, the Constitution refers to religion only twice—in the First Amendment, which bars laws "respecting an establishment of religion or prohibiting the free exercise thereof," and in Article VI, which prohibits "religious tests" for public office. Both of these provisions are evidence that the country was not founded as officially Christian.

Commentators point out that some of the Framers did not hold traditional Christian views— several were Deists or Unitarians. See http://www.ffrf.org/ fttoday/janfeb04/ ?ft=bolton.txt for an overview of these beliefs.

Dangers of a church–state union

The Founding Fathers did not create a secular government because they disliked religion. Many were believers themselves. Yet they were well aware of the dangers of church–state union. They had studied and even seen first-hand the difficulties that church–state partnerships spawned in Europe. During the American colonial period, alliances between religion and government produced oppression and tyranny on our own shores.

Trinitarian Protestants are Christians who support the doctrine of the Trinity—that is, that God is one God existing in three distinct persons, the Father, the Son, and the Holy Spirit.

Many colonies … had provisions limiting public office to "Trinitarian Protestants" and other types of laws designed to prop up the religious sentiments of the politically powerful. Some colonies had officially established churches and taxed all citizens to support them, whether they were members or not. Dissenters faced imprisonment, torture and even death.

These arrangements led to bitterness and sectarian division. Many people began agitating for an end to "religious tests" for public office, tax subsidies for churches and other forms of state endorsement of religion. Those who led this charge were not anti-religion. Indeed, many were members of the clergy and people of deep piety. They argued that true faith did not need or want the support of government.

Respect for religious pluralism gradually became the norm. When Thomas Jefferson wrote the Declaration of Independence, for example, he spoke of "unalienable rights endowed by our Creator." He used generic religious language that all religious groups of the day would respond to, not narrowly Christian language traditionally employed by nations with state churches....

Others do not agree with this interpretation of the language used in the Declaration of Independence. For example, go to http://www.christian parents.com/ declarid.htm for a summary of its "godly thoughts."

Religious freedom for all

Jefferson, James Madison and their allies among the state's religious groups ended Virginia's established church and helped pass the Virginia Statute for Religious Liberty, a 1786 law guaranteeing religious freedom to all.

Jefferson and Madison's viewpoint also carried the day when the Constitution, and later, the Bill of Rights, were written. Had an officially Christian nation been the goal of the founders, that concept would appear in the Constitution. It does not. Instead, our nation's governing document ensures religious freedom for everyone.... Article VI, which allows persons of all religious viewpoints to hold public office, was adopted by a unanimous vote. Through ratification of the First Amendment, observed Jefferson, the American people built a "wall of separation between church and state."...

Given that American society has changed so much in the last 200 years, do you think it still matters whether or not the Framers intended the United States officially to be a Christian nation?

Early national leaders understood that separation of church and state would be good for all faiths—including Christianity. Jefferson rejoiced that Virginia had passed his religious freedom law, noting that it would ensure religious freedom for "the Jew and the Gentile, the Christian and Mahometan, the Hindoo, the infidel of every denomination."

Other early U.S. leaders echoed that view. President George Washington, in a famous 1790 letter to a Jewish congregation in Newport, R.I., celebrated the fact that Jews had full freedom of worship in America. Noted Washington, "All possess alike liberty of conscience and immunities of citizenship."

Go to http://www. us-israel.org/jsource/ US-Israel/bigotry. html for information on George Washington's (1732–1799) letter to the Newport Jewish community.

Washington's administration even negotiated a treaty with the Muslim rulers of north Africa that stated explicitly that the United States was not founded on Christianity. The pact, known as the Treaty with Tripoli, was approved unanimously by the Senate in 1797, under the administration of John Adams. Article 11 of the treaty states, "[T]he government of the United States is not, in any sense, founded on the Christian religion...."

Admittedly, the U.S. government has not always lived up to its constitutional principles. In the late 19th century especially, officials often promoted a *de facto* form of Protestantism. Even the U.S. Supreme Court fell victim to this mentality in 1892, with Justice David Brewer declaring in *Holy Trinity v. United States* that America is "a Christian nation."

The Holy Trinity decision is the same one that provides the basis of much of Craig S. Bulkeley's "Yes" article.

It should be noted, however, that the *Holy Trinity* decision is a legal anomaly. It has rarely been cited by other courts, and the "Christian nation" declaration appeared *in dicta*—a legal term meaning writing that reflects a judge's personal opinion, not a mandate of the law. Also, it is unclear exactly what Brewer meant. In a book he wrote in 1905, Brewer pointed out that the United States is Christian in a cultural sense, not a legal one.

A more accurate judicial view of the relationship between religion and government is described by Justice John Paul Stevens in his 1985 *Wallace v. Jaffree* ruling. Commenting on the constitutional right of all Americans to choose their own religious belief, Stevens wrote, "At one time it was thought that this right merely proscribed the preference of one Christian sect over another, but would not require equal respect for the conscience of the infidel, the atheist, or the adherent of a non-Christian faith such as Mohammedism or Judaism. But when the underlying principle has been examined in the crucible of litigation, the Court has unambiguously concluded that the individual freedom of conscience protected by the First Amendment embraces the right to select any religious faith or none at all."...

An "infidel" is someone who is not a Christian, or who disbelieves a specified religion; an "atheist" is someone who denies the existence of God.

Attempts to amend the Constitution

In the mid 19th century, several efforts were made to add specific references to Christianity to the Constitution. One group, the National Reform Association (NRA), pushed a "Christian nation" amendment in Congress in 1864. NRA members believed that the Civil War was divine punishment for failing to mention God in the Constitution and saw the amendment as a way to atone for that omission.

The National Reform Association still exists today. Its website (www. natreformassn.org) states its mission to be to "promote in our national life the Christian principles of civil government, which include ... Jesus Christ is Lord in all aspects of life, including civil government ... and should be explicitly confessed as such in any constitutional documents."

The NRA amendment called for "humbly acknowledging Almighty God as the source of all authority and power in civil government, the Lord Jesus Christ as the Ruler among the nations, [and] His revealed will as the supreme law of the land, in order to constitute a Christian government." Ten years later, the House Judiciary Committee voted against its adoption. The committee noted "the dangers which the union between church and state had imposed upon so many nations of the Old World" and said in light of that it was felt "inexpedient to put anything into the Constitution which might be construed to be a reference to any religious creed or doctrine."

Similar theocratic proposals resurfaced in Congress sporadically over the years....

Religious pluralism

Today, America's religious demographics are changing, and diversity has greatly expanded since our nation's founding.... In addition, many Americans say they have no religious faith or identify themselves as atheists, agnostics or Humanists. According to some scholars, over 2,000 distinct religious groups and denominations exist in the United States.

In her book A New Religious America, *published in 2001, Diana Eck points out that today there are more American Muslims than there are American Episcopalians, Jews, or Presbyterians.*

An "agnostic" is someone who believes that nothing is or can be known about the existence of God.

Also, even though most Americans identify as Christian, this does not mean they would back official government recognition of the Christian faith. Christian denominations disagree on points of doctrine, church structure and stands on social issues. Many Christians take a moderate or liberal perspective on church–state relations and oppose efforts to impose religion by government action.

Americans should be proud that we live in a democracy that welcomes persons of many faiths and none. Around the globe, millions of people still dwell under oppressive regimes where religion and government are harshly commingled.... Many residents of those countries look to the United States as a beacon of hope and a model for what their own nations might someday become.

Only the principle of church–state separation can protect America's incredible degree of religious freedom. The individual rights and diversity we enjoy cannot be maintained if the government promotes Christianity or if our government takes on the trappings of a "faith-based" state.

Use the Internet to research the Faith-Based Initiatives promoted by the government of George W. Bush. Some people have criticized this program for eroding the division between church and state. Do you agree?

The United States, in short, was not founded to be an officially Christian nation or to espouse any official religion. Our government is neutral on religious matters, leaving such decisions to individuals. This democratic and pluralistic system has allowed a broad array of religious groups to grow and flourish and guarantees every individual American the right to determine his or her own spiritual path—or to reject religion entirely. As a result of this policy, Americans enjoy more religious freedom than any people in world history....

Summary

In the first article Craig S. Bulkeley asserts that the United States has been a Christian nation since its founding. He quotes Justice Brewer's words in an 1892 Supreme Court decision:"this is a Christian nation." For Bulkeley this phrase represents a correct interpretation of the Constitution and supports the position of Roy Moore in a 2003 controversy over a Ten Commandments monument in the Alabama state courthouse. Bulkeley accuses the courts of failing to acknowledge the Christian heritage of the United States and claims that Americans have debased their national faith. He urges them not to forsake the will of God, which, he claims, has served the nation well.

The article from Americans United for Separation of Church and State focuses on the historical background to the debate. The writer explains that, although many of the Framers were religious themselves, they were also conscious of the dangers of not separating church and state, and therefore rejected attempts to recognize Christianity in the Constitution. The author considers various Supreme Court decisions and attempts to add references to Christianity to the Constitution before concluding that there is no basis for the argument that the United Sates was founded as a Christian nation.

FURTHER INFORMATION:

Books:

Eck, Diana L., *A New Religious America: How a "Christian Country" Has Become the World's Most Religiously Diverse Nation*. San Francisco, CA: HarperSanFrancisco, 2001.

Eidsmore, John, *Christianity and the Constitution: The Faith of Our Founding Fathers*. Grand Rapids, MI: Baker Book House, 1987.

Marshall, Paul, *God and the Constitution: Christianity and American Politics*. Lanham, MD: Rowman & Littlefield, 2002.

Useful websites:

http://www.aclu.org/ReligiousLiberty/ReligiousLibertyMain.cfm
Site of the American Civil Liberties Union, with news and opinion on religious freedom in the United States.
www.firstthings.com
The Journal of the Institute of Religion and Public Life.
http://people-press.org/reports/display.php3?ReportID=150
Report on the Pew Research Center's 2002 survey, "Americans Struggle with Religion's Role at Home and Abroad."

The following debates in the Pro/Con series may also be of interest:

In this volume:
Topic 14 Is the separation between church and state still necessary?

Topic 16 Has the religious right isolated the United States from the rest of the world?

In *The Constitution*:
Topic 9 Does the Constitution protect religious freedom?

In *Education*:
Topic 3 Is swearing allegiance to the flag in schools unconstitutional?

SHOULD CHRISTIANITY BE THE OFFICIAL RELIGION OF THE UNITED STATES?

YES: More than 80 percent of Americans are Christians. This fact should be officially recognized and celebrated.

YES: Religious liberty exists in other countries with established religions, such as the United Kingdom

CHRISTIAN NATION
Is the United States a "Christian nation"?

RESPECT
Are established religions respectful of other faiths?

NO: The United States is the most religiously diverse nation in the world. An established religion would alienate many people of many different faiths.

NO: During the American colonial period official religions exercised oppression and tyranny over other faiths

SHOULD CHRISTIANITY BE THE OFFICIAL RELIGION OF THE UNITED STATES?

KEY POINTS

YES: There are many quotes from individual Framers such as George Washington that appear to endorse Christianity

YES: The Declaration of Independence contains several references to God

FRAMERS
Did the Framers found the United States as a Christian nation?

NO: Some of the Framers themselves rejected orthodox Christianity, including Thomas Jefferson, who wrote the Virginia Statute for Religious Freedom

NO: The Constitution contains no reference to God or to Christianity, and the First Amendment specifically prohibits the establishment of religion

Topic 16

HAS THE RELIGIOUS RIGHT ISOLATED THE UNITED STATES FROM THE REST OF THE WORLD?

YES

FROM "GOD HELP AMERICA"
THE GUARDIAN, AUGUST 25, 2003
GARY YOUNGE

NO

"GOD AND AMERICAN DIPLOMACY"
THE ECONOMIST, FEBRUARY 6, 2003
THE ECONOMIST

INTRODUCTION

Shortly after the terrorist attacks of September 11, 2001, Jerry Falwell, a leader of the religious right, appeared on the TV show of fellow Christian fundamentalist M.G. "Pat" Robertson. Falwell told his host, "… the pagans, and the abortionists, and the feminists, and the gays and lesbians who are actively trying to make that an alternative lifestyle … to all of them who have tried to secularize America, I … say, 'You helped this happen.'"

Conservative Christians like Falwell believe that God withdraws protection from nations that violate his will, and that the United States is such a country. Their avowed aim is to make America Christian; since more than 80 percent of Americans belong to the Judeo-Christian tradition, they potentially have a huge constituency.

In 1992 the Christian Coalition, a conservative advocacy group founded by Pat Robertson, helped win the Republican Party majorities in both Houses of Congress for the first time in 40 years. Since then, some critics argue, the influence of the religious right on politics has grown. It was confirmed with the election as president of George W. Bush in 2001. Bush is a born-again Methodist who is known to canvas the opinions of evangelists such as Pat Robertson. Although it is not unusual for a president to be a Christian, Bush's sympathy with the religious right has alarmed observers within the United States and abroad.

Developments in the United States have always affected people in other countries. In part this reflects the United States' powerful economy and the widespread influence of its culture, particularly through TV, movies, and popular music. But people also look to the United States for other reasons;

particularly in the West the United States has long been viewed as the protector of liberal democracy. Its intervention in both world wars helped preserve democracy in Europe and elsewhere. During the Cold War—the long standoff with the communist Soviet Union and its allies—the United States again appeared as the protector of values such as individual freedom.

> *"The battle to regain the soul of America won't be pleasant ... but we will win it."*
> —PAT ROBERTSON,
> CHRISTIAN COALITION (1992)

Most allies of the United States— mainly the western European nations— are, however, relatively secular. In many church attendance is declining, and the role of religion in politics is limited. To some of their citizens the views of the religious right in America seem alien and old-fashioned. They are alarmed by its hostility toward, for example, abortion and homosexuals; they also condemn its support of the death penalty, although supporters of legal execution are by no means all fundamentalist Christians.

One of the main reasons for world concern about the role of the religious right is its influence on U.S. foreign policy. The United States is the world's greatest military power, and many of its critics fear that it may use that power irresponsibly. Following the September 11, 2001, terrorist attacks in the eastern United States, the majority of the world supported George W. Bush's call for a

"War on Terrorism." Despite their sympathy for the Americans, however, many people overseas were uneasy when Bush described the campaign as a "crusade." The word had negative allusions to the religious wars launched from the 11th to the 13th centuries by European Christians against the Islamic Turks who occupied the Holy Land. The White House acknowledged the error, and the president did not repeat the phrase. However, many of his public utterances still have religious echoes, such as his identification of Iran, Iraq, and North Korea as an "axis of evil."

Such rhetoric alarms some observers overseas because it suggests that U.S. foreign policy has a theological basis. To them the War on Terrorism seems to be conceived largely as a struggle between Christianity and Judaism on one hand and Islam on the other. Such a view is confirmed in many eyes by the United States' continued support for the state of Israel. The existence of Israel still angers many Arabic and Islamic people: The country was established under international law in 1948 on land previously occupied by Palestinian Arabs, most of whom were Muslims.

The U.S. decision to invade Iraq in 2003 without the support of the full international community also aroused suspicion of the motives of Bush and his advisers. Few people believed that Iraq was connected with the 9/11 attacks. Even Islamic nations that had fought on the side of the United States in the Persian Gulf War against Iraq in 1991, and that had condemned the 9/11 atrocities, now argued that the United States was attacking Islam. Comments from some members of the religious right did little to allay their fears.

The following articles examine the debate in more depth.

GOD HELP AMERICA
Gary Younge

Gary Younge is a columnist for the British daily newspaper The Guardian. *He wrote this article in 2003.*

YES

☑ Montgomery, Alabama, is no stranger to stand-offs. The gold star embedded into the marble at the front of the state capitol marks the spot where Jefferson Davis stamped his foot and declared an independent Confederacy and where former governor George Wallace promised "segregation now, segregation tomorrow, segregation forever". From that very point you can make out the bus stop where Rosa Parks took her seat and the church where Martin Luther King made his stand, launching the bus boycott that sparked a decade of civil rights protest.

Stand on the star today and you can witness the city's latest confrontation as the Alabama supreme court house plays host to prayer circles and television trucks in a showdown between the state's most senior judge and the country's highest court.

Violating the church-state separation

This particular dispute is cast in stone. Two-and-a-half tonnes of granite, displaying the 10 commandments, which was placed in the rotunda of the courthouse two years ago by Alabama's chief justice, Roy Moore. The US supreme court told him to remove the monument, which violates the separation of church and state. Moore refused, saying that Christianity forms the bedrock of the American constitution and his conscience.

Some Christian commentators argue that the Framers of the Constitution never intended the United States not to be a Christian nation despite the separation of church and state.

Since the deadline passed at midnight on Wednesday, Christian activists have descended on the town from all over the country, keeping a 24-hour watch to make sure the monument is not moved and establishing phone trees to rally the faithful if it is. Many have T-shirts with slogans every bit as intolerant as the south's reputation. "Homosexuality is a sin, Islam is a lie, abortion is murder," says one. (It is difficult to imagine how many more people you could offend on one piece of summerwear.)

Do such slogans as these have any place in religious debate? Or is it important for everyone to declare what they truly believe no matter how it might appear to other people?

They appear as dotty as they do devout and determined. "What you're watching is that the socialist, communist elements are attempting to push out God from the public domain," Gene Chapman, a minister from Dallas, told the Montgomery Advertiser. Those subversive elements include

The roots of the First Amendment to the Constitution, which separates church from state, can be traced to Thomas Jefferson (1743–1826), third president of the United States.

The Christian Coalition is a conservative Christian political interest group. Go to www.cc.org to find out more about them.

the national rightwing Christian coalition and the seven southern, Republican judges.

On Thursday afternoon, Moore vowed his undying opposition to the removal of the commandments; by Friday he had been suspended and his lawyers announced he was prepared to relent. Yesterday, the monument was still there and the crowds of believers kept coming, determined to martyr themselves before a lost cause.

It would be easy to deride the defenders of the monument or to dismiss the whole charade as the latest illustration of the scale of degradation in America's political culture. However, Britons would do well to remove the mote in their own eye before resorting to ridicule. The only reason America can have these disputes is that it has a constitution that separates church and state (which we don't).

Respect for the Bible and the Constitution

Do you agree that the United States is "aggressively religious"? If so, how does this manifest itself?

For, while the spectacle is certainly ridiculous, its symbolism is significant. The US is at one and the same time one of the most fiercely secular and aggressively religious countries in the western world. The nation's two most sacred texts are the Constitution and the Bible. And when those who interpret them disagree, the consequent confusion resonates way beyond Montgomery.

This is a country where 11 states, including Alabama, refuse to give government money to students who major in theology because it would violate the Constitution, and where nativity plays are not allowed in primary schools. It is also a country where, a Harris poll showed, 94% of adults believe in God, 86% believe in miracles, 89% believe in heaven, and 73% believe in the devil and hell.

Younge feels that the two attitudes he outlines in this paragraph show a contradiction in U.S. attitudes. Do you agree?

These two competing tendencies produce some striking contradictions. The supreme court and both houses of Congress all invoke God's blessing before they start work. But children are not allowed to say the words "under God" when they pledge allegiance to the flag at the start of school.

For a debate on this subject see Volume 16, Education, Topic 3 Is swearing allegiance to the flag in schools unconstitutional?

So while there is a constitutional, albeit contested, barrier between church and state, there is almost no distinction between church and politics. Indeed, when it comes to elections, religion is the primary galvanising force and the church the central mobilising vehicle.

This is one of the few truths that transcends both race and class. White evangelicals and black Protestants are the two groups most likely to say that their religion shapes their votes at least occasionally, according to a survey by the non-partisan Pew research centre. Since these two constituencies form the cornerstone of both major parties, it would be impossible for either to win an election without them and inconceivable that they could do so without the support of the church.

But the influence of religion goes beyond domestic politics or social issues such as abortion and gay rights to crucial areas of foreign policy. Another Pew poll revealed that 48% of Americans think the US has had special protection from God for most of its history. Moreover, 44% believe that God gave the land that is now Israel to the Jewish people, while 36% think that "the state of Israel is a fulfilment of the biblical prophecy about the second coming of Jesus".

International implications

At this point America's internal contradictions become an issue on the world stage: the nation that poses as the guardian of global secularity is itself dominated by strong fundamentalist instincts. There are two problems with this. The first is that, as became clear in Montgomery last week, there is no arguing with faith. Fundamentalists deal with absolutes. Their eternal certainties make them formidable campaigners and awful negotiators—it is difficult to cut a bargain with divine truth. The second is that America's religiosity is not something it shares with even its few western allies, let alone the many countries that oppose its current path. Yet another poll shows that among countries where people believe religion to be very important, America's views are closer to Pakistan's and Nigeria's than to France's or Germany's.

These differences ... explain much of the reason why the tone, style, language and content of America's foreign policy has been so out of kilter with the rest of the developed world, particularly since September 11. For these fundamentalist tendencies in US diplomacy have rarely been stronger in the White House than they are today. Since George Bush gave up Jack Daniels for Jesus Christ, he has counted Jesus as his favourite philosopher. The first thing he reads in the morning is ... a book of evangelical mini-sermons. When it came to casting the morality play for the war on terror he went straight to the Bible and came out with evil. "He reached right into the psalms for that word," said his former speech writer, David Frum.

Bush speaks in the name of the [Framers] but believes he is doing the work of the holy father. He cannot do both and condemn fundamentalism. But if he feels he must try, he might start with the commandment: "Thou shalt not kill."

The author is referring to the belief among some Christians that the return of the Jews to the Holy Land, through the establishment of Israel in 1948, is in line with biblical prophecy and is necessary for the return of Jesus to reign on Earth. This phenomenon, known as "Christian Zionism," is distinguished from the political belief that the Jews have the right to a homeland in Israel.

Do you think that America's foreign policy has been "out of kilter" with the rest of the world? If so, in what ways could it be brought more in line?

President George W. Bush gave up drinking alcohol on the day after his 40th birthday in 1986. His career up until 1992 was not that successful, and he had pleaded guilty to drunken driving in 1976.

GOD AND AMERICAN DIPLOMACY
The Economist

NO

Only one thing unsettles George Bush's critics more than the possibility that his foreign policy is secretly driven by greed. That is the possibility that it is secretly driven by God. War for oil would merely be bad. War for God would be catastrophic: the beginning of a "clash of civilisations" that would pit Christians and Jews against Muslims.

Outlining the opposing argument before you state your own can be an effective debating technique.

Waging war for God?

Is there anything to this? The war-for-God crowd can certainly point to bits of evidence. The current White House is the most religious since Jimmy Carter's days. In his memoirs of his time as a presidential speechwriter, David Frum says that the first words he heard in the Bush White House were "Missed you at Bible Study". Mr Bush, a born-again Christian who turned to God after many years of hard drinking, starts each day kneeling in prayer. Michael Gerson, his main speechwriter, is a master at clothing public policy in religious language.

"Born again" refers to the practice of Christians renewing their commitment of faith, often after a difficult period in life. President George W. Bush was "born again" in 1986.

The second piece of evidence is that America, despite a decline in churchgoing, is a much more religious place than Europe, supporting more than 200 Christian television channels and 1,500 Christian radio stations. Religion is particularly important to Mr Bush's party. Republican voters attend church more frequently than Democrats do. Evangelical southerners constitute the praetorian guard of the Republican Party.

The praetors were the imperial bodyguards of the Roman Empire.

The third piece of evidence is the scariest: some right-wing Christians seem to be spoiling for a clash of civilisations. Jerry Falwell has called the Prophet Muhammad a "terrorist". He has since apologised, but Pat Robertson, who called him a "wild-eyed fanatic", a "robber" and a "brigand", has not. Franklin Graham, son of Billy, has branded Islam "evil". Many American evangelicals believe that the complete restoration of the nation of Israel is a prerequisite for the Second Coming. Thwarting [Israeli prime minister] Ariel Sharon is thus tantamount to thwarting God's master-plan.

Billy Graham (1918–) has been a prominent Christian evangelist since the 1940s. He has been called the Pope of Protestant America. His son Franklin (1952–) heads the Billy Graham Evangelistic Association.

A born-again president; a highly religious country; a bunch of extremist Republican stormtroopers: doesn't this all add up to a clash of civilisations? The surprising answer is no. John Maynard Keynes once described one of Friedrich von Hayek's books as "an extraordinary example of how, starting with a mistake, a remorseless logician can end up in Bedlam". The war-for-God crowd start with not one mistake but three.

The real role of religion

The first mistake is to equate the role of religion in America with its role in theocratic societies. Americans often argue about where the line between church and state should be drawn—about whether "faith-based charities" are permissible under the Constitution, for example—but nobody really doubts there should be a line. Islam is one of the fastest-growing religions in America. Mr Bush has been careful to visit mosques and invite Muslim leaders to the White House. He has also been careful to make his public speeches as ecumenical as possible, couched in the language of faith in general rather than Christianity in particular. Yes, he once uttered the world "crusade", but that slip of the tongue has not been repeated. Yes, he has chosen to cast America's enemies as "the axis of evil", but some of the sternest proponents of regime change in the Middle East are secular liberals who want to bring the benefits of the Enlightenment to an area repressed by religious orthodoxy.

The second mistake is to assume that all religious Americans think alike about foreign policy. In fact, no anti-war protest is complete without a large contingent of religious leaders. The Catholic church, America's biggest, is particularly iffy on this subject (and, incidentally, also on Israel). Even the evangelical community is divided. A bishop in Mr Bush's own denomination, the United Methodist Church, appears in a television commercial arguing that going to war against Iraq "violates God's law and the teachings of Jesus Christ".

The third mistake is to equate influence on the margins with influence over essentials. Evangelical Christians have certainly put their stamp on some areas of foreign policy, most notably population control in the developing world. But their influence has been constrained by questions of realpolitik and economic sense. The evangelicals failed dismally in their campaign against granting China its most-favoured-nation trading status.

Down-to-earth imperatives

Since September 11th America's foreign policy has primarily been driven not by religious passions but by an all-too-earthly fear of three things: terrorist networks, rogue states and

The prominent economists Keynes (1883–1946) and Hayek (1899–1992) were rivals. "Bedlam," the popular name of an old British asylum, refers here to a state of confusion.

A theocracy is a religious state governed by divine guidance.

Do you think Bush's use of "crusade" can be seen as a slip of the tongue? The use of such rhetoric is at the core of the opposing argument.

The "axis of evil" refers to Iran, Iraq, and North Korea. Go to http:// news.bbc.co.uk/ 1/hi/world/americas/ 1796034.stm for an article about Bush's use of this term.

"Realpolitik" means politics based on practical rather than moral or ideological concerns.

President George W. Bush is felt by some people to be closely allied to the religious right; critics are concerned that fundamentalist principles are too influential on his policies.

highly destructive weapons. The people who steer foreign policy on a day-to-day basis, people like [Defense Secretary] Donald Rumsfeld and [National Security Advisor] Condoleezza Rice, are hard-headed realists: Hobbesians rather than holy rollers. The "visionaries" who have been warning about rogue states for years are not evangelical Christians but sophisticated, secular conservative intellectuals who hang out in Washington think-tanks and write for highbrow magazines.

"Hobbesians" favor the thinking of English philosopher Thomas Hobbes (1588–1679). Go to Volume 19, World Politics, page 17, for more information on Hobbes.

What about Israel? Isn't this one area of foreign policy where America is sacrificing its national interest to the combined might of evangelical Christians and the Israel lobby? The answer here can only be wait and see. In the past, the Republicans have never had any trouble standing up to the Israel lobby when national interest demanded it: remember Ronald Reagan's decision to sell radar systems to Saudi Arabia. The alliance between the evangelicals and supporters of Israel has certainly deepened. But the main reason why most Americans, including Mr Bush, have backed Mr Sharon is surely because the Palestinians made the catastrophic mistake of continuing with suicide bombings in the months after September 11th.

President Reagan (1981–1989) wanted Saudi Arabia to increase oil production and so lower the price. To achieve this, Reagan gave the Saudis the airborne radar protection system they wanted, mainly to protect themselves from Iran. Israel objected strongly to the decision.

So Mr Bush is not on a crusade. Yet the fact that he has frightened non-Americans in this way is not helpful to his cause. Religious rhetoric may stir the nation, but Mr Bush's words carry much further. America's squabble is with terrorism rather than Islam. He should keep saying that as often as possible.

Ending on a succinct, forceful statement can add power to your argument.

Summary

In the first article British journalist Gary Younge focuses on the standoff between the Supreme Court and the Alabama state authorities caused by the installation in the courthouse at Montgomery of a tablet bearing the Ten Commandments, a possible violation of the First Amendment. Younge believes that the dispute is symptomatic of the growing influence of the religious right in the United States. The problem, he argues, is that Christian fundamentalism has led many Americans to believe that they have "special protection from God." That certainty has affected President George W. Bush, a devout born-again Christian, and his foreign policy. Younge concludes that the perception of the United States as a nation of religious fundamentalists has placed it at odds with friends and foes alike, particularly over relations with Israel, a nation whose creation more than one-third of Americans believe is connected with the fulfillment of a biblical prophecy.

The author of the *Economist* article recognizes that the Bush administration is associated with the religious right, some of whose views—especially on Islam—are extremist. However, the author argues that the link between the White House and evangelical Christianity is more imagined than real. Freedom of worship is guaranteed in the United States, and one of the nation's fastest-growing faiths is Islam, the religion most commonly denigrated by right-wing Christians. The author points out that there is no political consensus even within a single church: Bush led the war on terrorism while other members of his church denounced military intervention in Iraq. The author concludes that the president is a politician first and a born-again Christian second.

FURTHER INFORMATION:

Books:

Boston, Robert, *Close Encounters with the Religious Right*. Amherst, NY: Prometheus Books, 2000. Olasky, Marvin, *Compassionate Conservatism: What It Is, What It Does, and How It Can Transform America*. New York: Free Press/Simon & Schuster, 2000.

Useful websites:

www.au.org
Site of Americans United for Separation of Church and State.
www.patrobertson.org
Site of M.G. "Pat" Robertson of the religious right.
www.theocracywatch.org
Project on "The Rise of the Religious Right in the Republican Party" by a nonsectarian educational organization at Cornell University.

The following debates in the Pro/Con series may also be of interest:

In this volume:
Topic 14 Is the separation between church and state still necessary?

Topic 15 Should Christianity be the official religion of the United States?

In *Constitution*:
Topic 9 Does the Constitution protect religious freedom?

HAS THE RELIGIOUS RIGHT ISOLATED THE UNITED STATES FROM THE REST OF THE WORLD?

YES: George W. Bush's use of words like "crusade" and "axis of evil" clearly show that he sees the war as a holy war; some of his Christian right colleagues are more explicit about this

YES: The rhetoric of some influential Christian speakers in the United States makes people in other, more secular states suspicious of U.S. motives

RELIGIOUS WAR
Is the War on Terrorism really a holy war on Islam?

INTOLERANCE
Has the United States' religious fervor alienated it from its allies?

NO: The war is against all terrorists, not against all Muslims. Terrorists are enemies of the United States because of their crimes, not because they follow Islam.

NO: Most U.S. allies recognize that rhetoric is only rhetoric, and that U.S. foreign policy is really guided by pragmatism, not dogma

HAS THE RELIGIOUS RIGHT ISOLATED THE UNITED STATES FROM THE REST OF THE WORLD?
KEY POINTS

YES: Key figures on the religious right have the ear of President George W. Bush and thus have great influence on the policies of his government

YES: The influence of vocal lobby groups such as the Christian Coalition show that although church and state might be separated, church and government definitely are not

INFLUENCE
Does the religious right have too much influence on government policy?

NO: Although issues such as gay rights and the right to abortion are anathema to the religious right, they remain enshrined in law, which shows that their opponents have only limited influence

NO: Although President George W. Bush consults with a range of spiritual advisers, he is also surrounded by hard-headed pragmatists who make sure government decisions reflect political priorities

GLOSSARY

abortion the premature termination of a pregnancy, usually by artificial methods.

Abramic a term describing religions that recognize Abraham as a patriarch; they include Judaism, Christianity, Islam, and the Bahá'í World Faith.

agnostic someone who believes that humans cannot know whether or not a God exists.

Anglicanism the beliefs and organization of the Church of England and the national churches of the Anglican Communion (including the American Episcopal Church).

anti-Semitism a hatred or hostility toward Jews. *See also* Judaism.

Bahá'í a faith founded in 1844 by Baha'u'llah (Glory of God) in Iran. Based on Islam, it promotes democracy and equal rights.

baptism in Christianity a ceremony usually performed by a member of the clergy to welcome an individual into the church. Denominations disagree about the exact form baptism should take. *See also* Christian.

Baptists a group of Christian denominations that do not baptize infants but wait until people can personally profess their faith.

Bhagavad-Gita The "Song of the Lord," a holy text in Hinduism. *See also* Hinduism.

Bible Christian holy text comprising Hebrew Scripture (the Old Testament) and Christian Scripture (the New Testament). *See also* Abramic, Christian.

blasphemy actions or expressions that are disrespectful to a god.

Brahma One of the trinity of Hindu deities along with Shiva and Vishnu, Brahma is the creator. *See also* Hinduism.

Branch Davidians a doomsday cult whose leader, David Koresh, died with many other members during a 1993 FBI raid in Waco, Texas. *See also* cult.

Buddha Prince Siddhartha (560–480 B.C.) after his enlightenment. Buddhism is the world religion based on his beliefs.

bull, papal a letter from the pope to the Catholic Church. The name is derived from Latin *bulla* ("seal"). *See also* pope.

civil society a community of citizens that shares religious or moral values.

caliph Muslim term for community leader.

Canon law used in the Roman Catholic church, this is a body of church laws.

Catholicism name given to one of the three oldest branches of Christianity, and to the beliefs and practices of the Catholic Church. *See also* Abramic.

Christ from the Greek word "christos" meaning "annointed" or "chosen one." It is the biblical name of Jesus in his role as Messiah. *See also* Jesus.

Christian a person who believes that Jesus is the Christ and who follows Christianity.

Christian Science a Christian denomination founded in 1879 by Mary Baker Eddy.

constitution a written codification of the basic principles and laws of a state.

contraception the prevention of conception by destroying sperm before they reach the egg, stopping a fertilized egg from growing in a woman's uterus (womb), or stopping egg or sperm production.

cult a small religious group that exists in a state of tension with the main faith.

devil the Christian synonym for Satan.

Enlightenment in Buddhism the state of having escaped the cycle of birth, death, and rebirth. *See also* Nirvana.

evangelical normally the conservative wing of Protestant Christianity.

exorcism driving evil spirits from the body.

fatwa an Islamic term meaning "an answer to a question," usually by a Muslim scholar.

First Amendment part of the Constitution and the Bill of Rights, it both protects individual freedom of worship and bars the establishment of a religion.

free will the liberty of humans to make choices unconstrained by outside agencies.

fundamentalist any of the most conservative groups in Christianity, Islam, or Judaism.

guru in eastern religions a spiritual teacher who guides students to enlightenment.

Heaven in Christianity and Islam the abode of God, where the souls of the blessed go after death. *See also* Hell.

Hell one of two destinations for an individual after death in Christianity, Islam, and some other religions. Hell is generally believed to be a place of eternal punishment and torment. *See also* Heaven.

heresy literally "wrong belief," ideas that are forbidden by the ruling body of a group.

Hinduism the world's third largest religion, after Christianity and Islam. It has neither a theological system nor central organization and consists of thousands of groups that have evolved in India since 1500 B.C.

Holocaust the systematic killing of millions of Jews and others by the Nazis (1933–1945).

Holy Spirit (Holy Ghost) part of the Christian Trinity, along with God the Father and God the Son (Jesus Christ).

humanism nontheistic philosophy that regards humans as the sole determiners of their own morality.

imam Muslim term for a national leader or the leader of worship in a mosque.

Islam the second-largest religion in the world after Christianity. *See also* Koran.

Jehovah's Witnesses a Protestant denomination founded in the United States in 1884 by Charles Taze Russell.

Jesus a teacher and prophet born in Bethlehem and active in Nazareth; his life and sermons form the basis of Christianity. *See also* Christ, Christian.

jihad in Arabic literally "struggle in the path of Allah," although adopted by fundamentalists to refer to a Holy War waged by Islam against other faiths.

Judaism the original Abramic religion, the Jewish faith was the earliest monotheist religion. *See also* Abramic, anti-Semitism.

Koran (Qur'an) the holy text of Islam.

monotheism a belief in a single deity.

morality a value system that differentiates between right and wrong.

moral relativism the philosophy that moral standards are not absolute but develop from social traditions.

Muhammad the final and greatest prophet and founder of Islam. *See also* Islam.

Nirvana in Buddhism release from the cycle of birth, death, and rebirth.

pedophilia a perversion in which adults are sexually attracted to children.

polytheism a belief in many gods.

pope the religious head of the Roman Catholic Church.

Protestantism a branch of Christianity that arose from people protesting certain practices or abuses within the Catholic Church in the 16th century. *See also* Reformation.

Reformation a Christian movement that began in the 16th century as an attempt to reform Roman Catholicism but led to a split in the Catholic Church and the emergence of Protestantism.

Satan a fallen angel or devil mentioned in Hebrew and Christian Scriptures.

Second Coming Jesus's return to earth as described in the biblical book Revelations.

Taliban an Islamic fundamentalist political and religious group that emerged in Afghanistan in the 1990s.

Ten Commandments Old Testament instructions given by God to Moses, a descendant of Abraham. *See also* Abramic.

theocracy a government in which the church and state are unified.

Torah first five books of the Hebrew Scriptures (Old Testament): Genesis, Exodus, Leviticus, Numbers, and Deuteronomy.

Yahweh a word favored by most theologians for the name of God ("JHWH") found throughout the Hebrew Scriptures (Old Testament). Alternatively "Jehovah."

Acknowledgments

Topic 1 Does Evil Exist?

Yes: From"Why Does Evil Exist?" by Bill Bradford, *The Good News magazine*, January/February 2002. Reprinted by permission of *The Good News magazine*.
No: "Does Evil Exist?" by John R. Mabry (www.apocryphile.net/jrm/articles.html). Reprinted by permission of the author.

Topic 2 Would There Be Fewer Wars If Religion Did Not Exist?

Yes: "Murder in the Name of Religion" by James A. Haught, *Free Inquiry*, Summer 1990. Copyright © 1990 by Free Inquiry. Reprinted by permission.
No: "If There Were No Such Thing as Religion There Would Be No Wars" by Simon Cohen, www.adamandeveit.net. Used by permission.

Topic 3 Does Organized Religion Stifle Free Thought?

Yes: "Religion Stops a Thinking Mind" by Eric Harrington. Used by permission.
No: "Living The Question: Evangelical Christianity and Critical Thought" by Robert Wuthnow, *Cross Currents*, Vol. 40, Issue 2, Summer 1990. Used by permission.

Topic 4 Should Governments Have the Right to Outlaw Religions?

Yes: "Ban Islam!" by Dick O'Connor, *The Senior Conservative*, Copyright © 2001 by WebToday. Used by permission.
No: "The Wrong Churches in China" by Kevin Platt. Reproduced with permission from the December 21, 1999 issue of *The Christian Science Monitor*. Copyright © 1999 The *Christian Science Monitor* (www.csmonitor.com). All rights reserved.

Topic 5 Is Morality Possible without a Religious Basis?

Yes: "Morality Requires God ... Or Does It?" by Theodore Schick, Jr., *Free Inquiry*, Volume 17, Number 3, Summer 1997. Reprinted by permission.
No: "Morality Without God: A House Built on Sand" by Garry K. Brantley, *Reason & Revelation*, November 1995, 15[11]:86. Used by permission of Apologetics Press, 230 Landmark Drive, Montgomery, Alabama 36117-2752, USA.

Topic 6 Is Abortion a Religious Issue?

Yes: "Pope Canonizes Mother Who Refused Abortion" by Sophie Arie, *The Guardian*, May 17, 2004. Copyright © 2004 by Sophie Arie. Reprinted by permission.
No: From "Beyond Apocalypse and Apology: A Moral Defense of Abortion" by Caitlin Borgmann and Catherine Weiss, American Civil Liberties Union, Reproductive Freedom Project, New York (http://www.aclu.org/reproductiverights/reproductiverights/cfm?ID=11626&c=143). Reprinted by permission

Topic 7 Is the Use of Contraception Wrong?

Yes: "The Harms of Contraception" by One More Soul (www.omsoul.com). Used by permission.
No: From "The Civilizing Force of Birth Control," by Margaret Sanger. Used by permission of Alexander C. Sanger, International Planned Parenthood Federation.

Topic 8 Should Adultery Be a Criminal Offense?

Yes: "Unconstitutional Adultery" by Abdalla F. Hassan, *Cairo Times*, July 25–31, 2002, Volume 6, Issue 21. Reprinted by permission.
No: "Shari'ah Law, Adultery and Rape" by the International Society for Human Rights (www.ishr.org). Reprinted by permission.

Topic 9 Is Divorce Ever Acceptable?

Yes: From "Is Divorce Ever Right?" by Dave Hatcher. Used by permission.
No: "The Unhealed Wound: The Damage of Divorce to Children" by John Omicinski, *CRISIS Magazine*, April 7, 2003. Reprinted with permission from *CRISIS Magazine*.

Topic 10 Should the Bible Be Interpreted Literally?

Yes: "Is the Bible Literal?" by James H. Boyd. Copyright © 1999 by James H. Boyd. Used by permission.
No: From "Some Reasons Why Humanists Reject the Bible" by Joseph C. Sommer (www.humanismbyjoe.com). Reprinted by permission.

Topic 11 Has the Catholic Church Dealt Properly with Sexual Abuse Allegations against Priests?

Yes: "A Time for Redemption" by David Reinhard, *Sunday Oregonian*, March 31, 2002. Used by permission.
No: "Sin City: Harboring Sinners and Criminals" by John O'Sullivan, *National Review* online, January 31, 2002. Copyright © 2002 by John O'Sullivan. Used by permission.

Topic 12 Are Monotheistic Religions More Intolerant than Other Religions?

Yes: "The Root Causes of Religious Atrocities" by Paul N. Tobin, *The Rejection of Pascal's Wager: A Skeptics View of Christianity,* 2002. Used by permission.
No: "PM Decries Misuse of Religion by Terrorist" by Neema Vyas, *The Hindu*, February 10,2003. Used by permission.

Topic 13 Does Islam Condone Terrorism?

Yes: "A Call to Muslims of the World" by Faith Freedom International (www.faithfreedom.org). Used by permission.
No: "Does Islam Promote Violence?" by Javeed Akhter, International Strategy and Policy Institute, August 20, 2002 (www.iviews.com). Used by permission of Javeed Akhter and IslamiCity.

Topic 14 Is the Separation between Church and State Still Necessary?

Yes: From "The Real Victims of a Church–State Merger: Be Careful What You Wish For" by Alan M. Dershowitz,

Free Inquiry, Vol. 20, No. 4, fall 2000. Used by permission. Alan M. Dershowitz is a professor of law at Harvard Law School and author of The Case for Israel.
No: "Why Religion Has a Place in the Public Square" by Alan E. Sears, *The Arizona Republic*, August 17, 2003. Used with permission. Permission does not imply endorsement.

Topic 15 Should Christianity Be the Official Religion in the United States?

Yes: "A Christian Nation?" by Craig S. Bulkeley, PCANews.com, monthly debate, August 2003. Copyright © Craig S. Bulkeley. Used by permission.
No: "Is America a 'Christian Nation'? Religion, Government and Individual Freedom" by Americans United for Separation of Church and State. Reprinted with permission.

16. Has the Religious Right Isolated the United States from the Rest of the World?

Yes: "God Help America" by Gary Younge, *The Guardian*, August 25, 2003. Copyright © 2003 by *The Guardian*. Reprinted by permission.
No: "God and American Diplomacy" *The Economist*, February 6, 2003. Copyright © 2003 by *The Economist*. Reprinted by permission.

The Brown Reference Group plc has made every effort to contact and acknowledge the creators and copyright holders of all extracts reproduced in this volume. We apologize for any omissions. Any person who wishes to be credited in further volumes should contact The Brown Reference Group plc in writing: The Brown Reference Group plc, 8 Chapel Place, Rivington Street, London EC2A 3DQ, U.K.

Picture credits

Cover: Corbis: John and Lisa Merrill
Bridgeman Art Library: 129; **Corbis:** 181, Grzegorz Galazka 145, 150/151, Douglas Kirkland 37, Brooks Kraft 210, Alessia Pierdomenico/Reuters 77, Bill Ross 6/7; **Library of Congress:** 185, 205; **Mary Evans Picture Library:** 17, 25, 70, 172; **Photos.com:** 86/87, 193; Rex Features: 49, Fotos International 58/59, Sipa Press 103, 159; **Topham Picturepoint:** Eastcott/Momatiuk/The Image Works 160, Monika Graff/The Image Works 53.